D1674150

How to Write the History of a Bank

How to Write the History of a Bank

Edited by

MARTIN M.G. FASE,
GERALD D. FELDMAN AND
MANFRED POHL

SCOLAR PRESS

Published by
SCOLAR PRESS
Gower House
Croft Road
Aldershot
Hants GU11 3HR
England

Ashgate Publishing Company
Old Post Road
Brookfield
Vermont 05036
USA

British Library Cataloguing-in-Publication Data

How to Write the History of a Bank
    I. Fase, M.M.G.
    332.10722

    ISBN 1–85928–227–X

Library of Congress Cataloguing-in-Publication Data

How to write the history of a bank/edited by Martin M.G. Fase,
    Gerald D. Feldman, and Manfred Pohl.
        p.   cm.
    English and French.
    'First Academic Colloquium, 16th–17th September, 1992, De Nederlandsche Bank, Amsterdam.'
    'Published in association with the European Association for Banking History.'
    ISBN 1–85928–227–X (hardback —: alk. paper)
    1. Banks and banking—Europe—History—Congresses. I. Fase, Martin M.G. II. Feldman, Gerald D. III. Pohl, Manfred, 1944–IV. Nederlandsche Bank (Amsterdam, Netherlands) V. European Association for Banking History.
    HG2976.H69   1995
    332.1'094—dc20   95–18629
                                                                       CIP
    ISBN 1 85928 227 X

Typeset in Sabon by Raven Typesetters, Chester and printed in Great Britain by The University Press, Cambridge

Contents

List of tables and figures

Preface

This volume contains the papers and comments, some expanded for publication, given at the First Academic Colloquium of the European Association for Banking History. The Colloquium, which appropriately bore the title 'How to Write the History of a Bank', took place at the headquarters of De Nederlandsche Bank in Amsterdam on 16 and 17 September 1992. It was attended by more than 50 historians and bank representatives.

The editors wish to express their gratitude to De Nederlandsche Bank for its kind invitation to hold the Colloquium at its headquarters and for its hospitality. They would especially like to thank Dr Wim F. Duisenberg, President of the Bank, for his willingness to deliver the opening speech at a moment of great unrest in the European Monetary System, and all of those members of staff who took part in organizing the Colloquium; in particular Dr V.F.V. Vanthoor, deputy manager of the Econometric and Special Studies Department and head of the historical section.

The Colloquium proved to be a lively and informative forum for discussion, and we are grateful to the organizers and the participants for making this volume possible.

Martin M.G. Fase
Gerald D. Feldman
Manfred Pohl

CHAPTER ONE

From Latin Monetary Union to European Monetary Union

W. F. Duisenberg[1]

'How to write banking history' seems a most worthy topic and I feel that you will be given a unique opportunity to exchange views over these two days on how to set about writing the history of a bank. The mere fact that experts on banking and monetary history from practically all over Europe have come together here gives this gathering a special flavour, particularly now that the monetary unification of Europe has come on today's political agenda.

As to the European unification, I have not been able to resist the temptation to tell you something of one of its historical predecessors. This choice is inspired not merely by its topicality and the fact that, as President of the Dutch central bank, I am closely involved in its progress. It must also be remembered that the history of individual banks cannot as a rule be abstracted from the wider institutional framework of the financial world in which banks operate both nationally and internationally.

Latin Monetary Union from the nineteenth century

The drive for monetary union in Europe is not without precedent. There were similar endeavours notably in the past century. In various states monetary unification was part of political unification, while countries already united in political entities attempted to alleviate their monetary problems by concluding monetary treaties. Characteristic of the monetary systems of the mid-nineteenth century was the bimetallic standard whereby both gold and silver could be used without restriction for minting, the price relationship between the two metals being enforced by law. Problems arose whenever the value of one of the two fell below the official price and Gresham's well-known Law, which tells us that bad money drives out good money, became applicable.

It was these circumstances which led to the establishment of the Latin Monetary Union, a treaty that had been concluded in Paris on 23 December 1865 between France, Italy, Belgium and Switzerland; Greece joined some years later. France had been the driving force behind this pact, keen as it was for the bimetallic standard – gold and silver – to be applied all over the world so that the disadvantages of the system would be minimized. The greater the area, so the French argued, the lesser the chances of driving out good money, while the advantage over the single standard remained in that the value of the currency would not be dependent on either of the two metals. Moreover, the French Emperor Napoleon III knew very well that a monetary union encompassing a large number of countries led by France would be an excellent instrument of political and economic power.

The Latin Monetary Union may have been envisaged as a global monetary system, but its participants never grew in number. Although several other countries came to adopt the French franc system after 1865, they never joined the Union. Needless to say the French desire for greater applicability of the bimetallic standard was hardly compatible with the international quest for a different monetary system. So much became clear at the international monetary conference of Paris in 1867, where more than 20 countries reached an agreement about a monetary system based exclusively on gold. Even though the French gold five-franc coin was to form the basis for the new system, the plan eventually came to nought because France continued to oppose the exclusive use of gold.

The Latin Monetary Union was really doomed when Germany, after achieving political unification in 1871, attained its own monetary union, adopting the single (gold) standard, setting an example which was soon followed by other countries; a case in point is the Scandinavian Monetary Union of 1872. Consequently Gresham's Law continued to apply on occasion in the countries taking part in the Latin Monetary Union; silver, being the inferior metal, continued to drive out gold, and the currencies of the member states depreciated against the currencies of countries which had adopted the single standard. External causes apart, such as a steady increase in the output of silver, the depreciation was equally attributable to the malfunctioning of the system itself. Italy, for example, failed to maintain the value of Italian banknotes in the free market, while in Greece, too, inferior paper money with an enforced exchange rate continued to circulate. As a result, two kinds of money, with different values, circulated in these countries. This situation proved to be an ideal breeding ground for speculative capital movements, which soon sprung up on an extensive scale and could be contained neither through national measures nor by means of a treaty revision.

At the end of 1926 the Union was disbanded tacitly, following the withdrawal of Belgium which had meanwhile formed a monetary union with Luxemburg. That the Latin Monetary Union nevertheless existed for more than 60 years was due first to its ability to change with the circumstances. In 1878, for example, silver ceased to be used for minting, which meant that although the Union did not officially adopt the limping standard, it did do so to all intents and purposes; gold became the standard metal, though silver coins continued to be valid. The system also adjusted to events in the First World War. Belgium came off the gold standard in 1914, adopting an ametallistic monetary system. Another example was Switzerland which was flooded with silver when the monetary system in the other member states of the Union collapsed completely. A new treaty was consequently signed in 1921, whereby the countries involved committed themselves to repurchasing part of the stocks of silver coins which had accumulated in Switzerland. As a result, that country remained linked to the Union only through its gold coins. After the First World War, the Union lay more or less dormant. When Belgium withdrew at the end of 1926, the Government of Switzerland announced that it considered the Union to have been dissolved. As the other member states did not protest, the Latin Monetary Union officially ceased to exist. This paved the way for a general introduction of the gold standard, though for various countries outside the Union it simply meant a return to the monetary system they had adopted before the war.

EMU in the twentieth century

It would be beyond the scope of my address to discuss the history of the Latin Monetary Union at great length here. I would rather draw a parallel with the present, in the form of the European Economic and Monetary Union (EMU) which the Maastricht Treaty, negotiated in December 1991, sees as an essential part of the European Union meant to take shape before the turn of the century.[2] In this context, there is an important conclusion to be drawn from the history of the Latin Monetary Union. It is that monetary unification of countries with different monetary systems is not easily attained; a treaty aimed at unification is ultimately doomed to failure if it is more or less imposed by a political and economic power on the other signatories to the Treaty, who are prepared for financial reasons to submit to its provisions without observing the necessary monetary discipline. The Latin Monetary Union glossed over the fact that exchange rate relationships were determined not by statutory stipulations but by economic factors.

It is this element which eventually shaped the history of the monetary agreement in the Treaty of Maastricht. The Second World War had only just ended when the first proposals were tabled for monetary union within Europe, where the hurdle presented by the variety of monetary systems had meanwhile been taken. Monetary unification preoccupied not only the government leaders of the day. One of my predecessors, Dr M.W. Holtrop, who was the first president of the Nederlandsche Bank after the War, was told when taking office in April 1946 by his former employer – de Koninklijke Nederlandsche Hoogovens en Staalfabrieken – to provide for a sound silver guilder and I quote: 'which will in time become part of a single European currency'. It was to be 45 years before that prediction would become a political reality founded on a Treaty, but that was not, however, because European policymakers twiddled their thumbs for 45 years.

The first form of monetary cooperation was the European Payments Union which was set up in 1950 to smooth the path to a recovery of external convertibility, induced as it was by the economic chaos after the Second World War. A firm basis was created by the establishment of the European Economic Community in 1957, which provided the institutional framework for a democratically approved economic integration of European countries with equivalent political and economic systems, although the Treaty of Rome gave an indication of the monetary goals and direction rather than setting out the concrete measures to be taken. A more definitive plan of action was contained in the Barre Plan published in 1969, providing the basis for the first blueprint of the various stages towards economic and monetary union designed by a committee of monetary experts led by the Prime Minister of Luxemburg, Mr Werner, which was intended to be realized by 31 December 1990.

An article in *The Times* of 6 March 1970 drew a parallel with the monetary conference of Paris of 1867 which I mentioned earlier. Considering that the implications of the two agreements were exactly the same, *The Times* wondered why monetary union would be a viable option now, as nothing had come of it in 1867. The somewhat peevish explanation was that the current monetary union was based on the US dollar forming a link between all other currencies. After all, 'as any European hotel porter or shopkeeper will tell you, the dollar passes current in all other States'. More to the point was the remark that:

> the 1867 attempt never got off the ground because the other states were not in practice prepared to accept the sort of political coordination with French policy, required to keep inflation sufficiently in line to operate a permanently fixed exchange rate. The realists in Europe today are under no illusion that only such a commitment can make a reality of the monetary integration.

Before long, however, these expectations were overtaken by other realities. In 1971 the Bretton Woods system came to an end. Moreover in mid-1973 the European Commission had to admit that, owing to a lack of political will on the part of the European ministers, the first stage of monetary union, though it had meanwhile commenced, had not really come off the ground. The second stage, which should have begun on 1 January 1974, was consequently replaced by 'a' second stage, envisaged as a kind of three-year speed-up manoeuvre, during which the governments were to contemplate measures that would ensure closer cooperation within the near future. At the same time the then Belgian Prime Minister, Mr Tindemans, was commissioned to study the conditions on which the Community, which had come to encompass nine countries, could be transformed into a political union. The report, when it materialized, was inconclusive owing to internal discord. European cooperation consequently flagged in the mid-1970s, seemingly suffering from the same ills which once assailed the Latin Monetary Union, the one difference being that France's dominating role had been taken over by Germany.

Introduction of the EMS

A totally new situation, also in comparison to the Latin Monetary Union, arose in early 1978 when France and Germany reached agreement about a plan to revive monetary cooperation in Europe. As you know, this plan led to the establishment of the European Monetary System (EMS) designed to create 'a zone of monetary stability' in Europe entailing the introduction of a European currency by the name of the ECU and a mechanism aimed at stabilizing exchange rate relationships. The EMS became operative on 13 March 1979. It heralded the onset of a new stage in the drive for monetary union in Europe, even though several hurdles had to be cleared before the system was to bear fruit.

One main obstacle was the political dilemma confronting France in the early 1980s. On the one hand, the French were keen, in the interests of their fight against inflation, to adhere to the external discipline imposed by the EMS, which was largely dictated by the high priority assigned by Germany to a policy of internal stability. On the other hand, the French authorities wished to make the system domestically acceptable by ensuring that it did not gain the character of a Deutsche Mark bloc. France was not the only member state to take exception to the anchor role played by Germany within the new system, but from the outset the Netherlands' standpoint was that the German anti-inflation policy should be thwarted as little as possible. This view was sustained by the conviction that such a line of action would only benefit the stability of the other member states and that German participation in the system might otherwise not be guaranteed. Another problem threatening the exchange rate stability within the EMS was posed by increasing capital mobility consequent on the partial abolition of exchange controls in various European countries. This was encouraged by the European Commission striving for general liberalization of capital transactions as part of the proposal made in 1987 for the completion of the single internal European market in 1992.

That the EMS was not immune to tensions is evidenced by the seven realignments which were effected between March 1979 and March 1983. Relative calm was restored to the exchange markets when in early 1983 a new realignment made France change course to a consistent anti-inflation policy aimed at a stabilization of the exchange rate between the French franc and the Deutsche Mark. Moreover, in September 1987 a code of conduct was adopted by the EMS participants at Nyborg, Denmark, providing for adjustment of monetary policy in the event of exchange rate tensions. Pursuant to this code of conduct, exchange rate tensions would have to be countered in good time by establishing appropriate interest rate differentials so as to deter speculators.

The Delors Report – three stages to EMU

The EMS has exerted an important disciplinary effect on national economic policies. The progress made manifested itself in a growing convergence of domestic price movements towards a low German level. In 1988 this prompted European policymakers to embark upon a renewed quest for economic and monetary unification, resuming the threads of 1970. From then on the European cooperation gained added momentum. The spring of 1989 saw the publication of the Delors Report setting out the implications of the irrevocable locking of the European currencies, which is still one of the cornerstones of monetary union.

According to the Delors Report, one of these implications was the need for a single monetary policy aimed at price stability, which would be conducted by an independent European System of Central Banks (ESCB) which would be composed of the new European Central Bank (ECB) and the existing national control banks of the member states. On this point the plan clearly differed from the EMS. The Report also stressed the importance of parallel progress of economic and monetary integration, an aspect which the Netherlands never failed to emphasize as being essential to European unification. The Report distinguished three stages on the road to EMU, without specifying their duration. The intention was that during stage one, policy coordination would be boosted within the existing institutional framework and the preparations made for amendment of the Treaty of Rome. During stage two, the European System of Central Banks would be set up but would not, for the time being, be vested with statutory powers, while the third and final stage would see the transfer of monetary powers and the institution of binding rules for public sector budgets.

In line with the Delors Report, the European Council decided that stage one of EMU would commence on 1 July 1990, the date on which the Directive providing for general liberalization of capital movements in Europe was to take effect. At a meeting held in Rome in October 1990, the European Council mentioned 1 January 1994 as a possible starting date for stage two, on the condition that the internal market had been completed and the member states had ratified the amendment of the Treaty of Rome. The end of 1990 also saw the start of an intergovernmental conference with adopted the draft statute of the ESCB drawn up in the meantime by the Committee of Governors of the central banks of the member states of the European Community. The conference also laid down the criteria for economic convergence which were to form the basis for the decision to grant member states access to the final stage of EMU.

Although all this happened very quickly, there had long been differences of opinion notably as to the institutional shape of stage two. Some member states were in favour of setting up the ECB at the very start of stage two, while others came up with plans for the creation of a totally new institution during that stage, whose duty it would be to supervise the development of a new common currency. Under the Presidency of the Netherlands, the European Council eventually decided on the establishment at the beginning of stage two of a European Monetary Institute (EMI), whose task it would be to pave the way for the ECB by stimulating the coordination of monetary policies and setting about the technical preparations for the final stage. The motivation underlying the Netherlands' stance, which I still fully endorse, was that establishment of an ECB would be senseless as long as the monetary policies pursued by the member states continued to be the responsibility of national authorities. Under those circumstances the ECB would be almost inevitably doomed to remain in the shade, incapable of acquiring the status needed at the start of stage three.

The Maastricht Treaty

I have given you a broad outline of the history which led up to the Maastricht Treaty on European Union. As you have all been able to read in the press, the European Council really took the bull by the horns at Maastricht. One of the items agreed was that the European Monetary Institute should start its operations on 1 January 1994. Another entailed that a decision be taken before the end of 1996 as to whether the majority of the member states meet the criteria for access to the final stage. If they do, the date for the start of stage three can be fixed. If they do not, the final stage will have to commence on 1 January 1999 at the latest for those countries which, in the eyes of the European Council, meet the criteria set. The Treaty was signed by the governments of all member states in February 1992; for the United Kingdom and Denmark a reservation was included with regard to participation in stage three of EMU.

The question whether EMU will be realized in accordance with the provisions of the Maastricht Treaty will ultimately be answered by the national parliaments, which have to decide on ratification before the year is out. Constitutionally, some member states are allowed to hold a referendum and two of them did so in the first half of 1992. The disappointing result achieved in Denmark is offset by the positive outcome recorded in Ireland. Whether a majority of the French will say 'oui' to the Treaty is still uncertain at the present time. Symptomatic of this uncertainty is the unrest which has arisen in the exchange markets in recent weeks. Despite the substantial interest rate increases to which some European central banks resorted, a realignment within the EMS has proved unavoidable. The devaluation of the Italian lira and the subsequent cuts in interest rates show that much still needs to be done by the twelve EC member states.[3] However, I might perhaps recall in this context that history shows that the achievement of monetary unions has always been a strained and difficult process. Yet it is essential that we continue to have confidence in the final outcome of today's monetary unification, all the more so because I believe that both the Economic and Monetary Union as well as the European Political Union, as envisaged in the Maastricht Treaty, could form pillars of stability in a continent which will be characterized by political and economic unrest on its Eastern flank for some time to come.

If I may take you back to the beginning of my address, it is fair to say that the monetary unification about to commence in Europe at the end of this century differs markedly from the Latin Monetary Union of 1865, which I presented more or less as its precursor. It is true that the quest for European unification pursued since the Second World War has not been straightforward, and that the result has been achieved by trial and error. From time to time it has been plagued by insufficient political will and a lack of coordination of the member states' economic and monetary policies. But it is also true that at crucial stages the deadlock was broken by the untiring efforts of inventive government leaders, Heads of State and central bank governors. The existing Community institutions never had a chance to fall into the state of dormancy in which the Latin Monetary Union eventually found itself. But there is another difference which is no less important. I told you earlier that the protracted existence of the Latin Monetary Union was due notably to the adjustments made by its members to the changing situation. In a sense that also goes for the postwar drive for unification, although the adjustments made after 1945 ultimately resulted in a strengthening of monetary integration, in contrast to the Latin Monetary Union, where the adoption of a limping standard and the legitimation of the lack of coordination in the form of incessant treaty amendments were symptoms of an adjustment which only helped to undermine integration further.

Some member states view the present pace of European integration with trepidation. They fear a further strengthening of the 'Eurocracy' at Brussels and of the dominant role played by Germany in the process of monetary integration, the monetary agreements of Maastricht sometimes being regarded as a 'Europeanization' of the Deutsche Mark.

I must say I do not share these fears. I see the Europe of tomorrow primarily as a conglomerate of identities, each with a culture of its own, which will transfer powers to Brussels only in respect of those issues which absolutely need to be dealt with at a central level. I also feel that the role played by Germany is not as threatening as it may seem to some, at least not so long as that country's monetary policy continues to give the highest priority to price stability. Moreover, even a united Germany will have to relinquish sovereignty in the EMU as it is presently envisaged, which means that it would have to give up its leading position with regard to European monetary policy. I believe Germany will be prepared to do so, not just out of political motives, but also because it would, if isolated, be unable to continue its pursuit of stability in an inflationary environment. But it is expressly because Germany is required to make concessions that it is able to lay down conditions; and it is in the interest of us all that those conditions be specified as concretely as possible and that the policies of the individual member states be attuned to such an extent that the 'zone of monetary stability' envisaged in 1979 can really flourish in the future EMU.

Conclusion

These reflections on our present and future monetary environment conclude my address. I realize only too well that history is always bound to the past and that it is – as the well-known Dutch historian Geyl pointed out – a discussion without end. However, that does not mean that we can afford to ignore other eras. Usually it is the present which gives us good reason to look at the past, at the same time forming tomorrow's history. With this in mind, I return to the theme of the present symposium. Those who are concerned with banking history cannot be blind to the fact that banks everywhere invariably operate in a specific environment. The fact that that environment is subject to shocks and changes gives an extra dimension in historiography. Where Europe is concerned, there can in my mind be no doubt that the monetary agreement of the Maastricht Treaty, once ratified, will have a profound impact on the institutional environment in which banks undertake their activities. National central banks will change in character, if only because, once supranational authority has been established, they no longer have at their disposal any monetary policy instruments of their own. It goes without saying that all this will not fail to affect the policies conducted by commercial banks as well. They in turn will have to adjust their organization and tasks to new, and probably larger, areas of operation. It is these institutional and functional factors which – in combination with the attending consequences in terms of financial and human resources – will have an important impact on banking behaviour, an aspect for which we will have to make serious allowance in the future when we are considering 'How to write banking history'.

Notes

1. This lecture was held in the midst of the international turmoil on Wednesday, 16 September 1992, some hours before Great Britain and Italy decided to abandon the exchange rate mechanism of the EMS and the Spanish peseta was to be devalued by 5 per cent *vis-à-vis* the other EMS currencies. President Duisenberg ended his lecture by telling the audience that De Nederlandsche Bank was going to write history: that day the Dutch and Belgian central banks reduced their interest rates as part of an effort to keep the British pound within the EMS currency system.
2. The Treaty of Maastricht contains the agreements reached on economic and monetary union as well as on political union. Together they form the European Union.
3. The Treaty of Maastricht took effect on 1 November 1993, after the internal market had virtually been completed on 1 January of that year. Meanwhile, 1 January 1994 marked the start of stage two of EMU, which is regarded as a period of increasing convergence, notably with regard to price stability and sound public finances. On the same date, the Frankfurt-based European Monetary Institute, the forerunner of the ESCB, started its operations.

CHAPTER TWO

Opening Statement

Herman van der Wee

The European Association for Banking History, which is supported and financed by a large and growing number of European banks, wants to promote the history of banking. It does so for several reasons: first, European banking has a rich history of many centuries, which goes back to Greek and Roman times, as Professor Raymond Bogaert of the University of Ghent explained so brilliantly in his many publications on the subject, including his recent contribution to *The History of European Banking*. In the same volume I tried to prove that accelerations in the development of financial and banking techniques occurred again in the course of the Middle Ages and in Early Modern Times in Italy during the twelfth and thirteenth centuries, in the Low Countries during the sixteenth and seventeenth centuries and in England from the late seventeenth until the early eighteenth centuries. In the same publication, Professor Ginette Kurgan-van Hentenryk of the University of Brussels presented an excellent overview of the spectacular growth of the European bank sector in the course of the nineteenth and twentieth centuries. Within the context of such a long and rich history systematic scientific research could generate a better knowledge of the banking system and could help in improving the long-term strategies of the bank sector.

The Association has a second reason for promoting historical research on banking. The history of banks implies the personal story of its shareholders, its managers, and its employees. It is therefore also the history of people, the history of those involved in financial activities, and generates an insight into their 'expérience vécue' as individuals or as a social group. This kind of history is not only a source of pleasure for the readers, it enriches them also from a humanistic point of view, it increases their personal wisdom, and deepens their view on life and society.

Last but not least the Association wants to promote research on banking history because it can contribute substantially to a more global scientific approach to the past and the present. Recent development has shown that historians are increasingly tempted to specialize, to imprison themselves more and more in subdisciplines, thus neglecting the complex character of reality and the synchronic and diachronic aspects of its structural coherence. Historical research in the field of finance with its many interlocking effects on the other components of social, economic and political life, can help in encouraging researchers to maintain an open positive attitude towards a more global historical approach.

In order to enable bank historians to achieve the goals set by the European Association for Banking History, high literary and scientific standards have to be met. Hence the idea put forward by the Board of Management and by the Academic Advisory Council to study in its first scientific colloquium the problem of 'How to write the history of a bank', so that it will not only be of high scientific quality, but will also be a book with attractive literary merits, accessible to and appreciated by a large public in and outside the bank sector.

Before opening the first session let me be the spokesman of the Association and of all of you in expressing our warmest thanks to those who made this colloquium possible. We are very grateful to the Nederlandsche Bank, and in particular to its President, Dr Duisenberg, to Professor Dr Martin Fase, to his staff and to all other collaborators of the bank, for having organized the colloquium in a most efficient and gracious way; with such a perfect hosting it can take place under optimal conditions. We are also very grateful to Professor Manfred Pohl, to Mrs Brigitte Hatke-Beck and to the whole secretariat at Frankfurt for having been so helpful too in the organization. Last but not least, my thanks to all of you who prepared reports, comments and interventions, thus guaranteeing a very successful meeting.

CHAPTER THREE

The Wreszynski Case and the Limits to Tolerance – 'Not intended for publication'

Johan de Vries

The subject and its dilemma

Although modern Netherlands banking history is rooted in the second half of the nineteenth century, most banks conducted a policy that was anything but modern until well into the twentieth century. One of these banks was R. Mees & Zoonen, established in 1720 in Rotterdam, a bank with very old-fashioned working methods, as became evident in the 1920s. Before the Second World War, this flourishing bank had been able to ignore the cost factor. In fact, money was not important as it was amply available. This was translated into a surplus of staff members, who were treated in a friendly but haughty way by the partners in the firm. In Rotterdam, a position with Mees & Zoonen was regarded as a life insurance and was considered better than being a public servant. In this patriarchal structure, retired authorized signatories would still discuss their personal problems with their former managers, even when this involved a walk to the Crooswijk Graveyard to seek the advice of Henri Mees, who had died 40 years before.[1]

At the time, Mees & Zoonen constituted the heart of banking in the Netherlands. Banks of all forms and sizes were established throughout the country, Amsterdam being the centre and Rotterdam, The Hague and 's-Hertogenbosch being the subcentres. Particularly in the 1920s, banking concentration started to play an important role. The agricultural credit banks had seen a favourable development and, notably after 1918, Amsterdam held an important position in the field of international trade financing, partly owing to the establishment of a number of German banks, such as Mendelssohn & Co., Berlin. Mees & Zoonen was also the heart of Netherlands banking as it managed to survive the hard times of the early 1920s. After the end of the First World War, the Netherlands economy experienced a short boom which was ended by the economic crisis of 1920. This crisis made itself felt in banking, but its magnitude was also due to the general lack of banking skills and experience, particularly in the provincial banking system. This is reflected in the large number of fraud cases which resulted from this crisis.[2]

The banks for small and medium-sized enterprises and the provincial banks were hit hardest. Owing to the excessive credits granted to vegetable drying-plants (a temporary war industry) and an engineering works, Marx & Co.'s Bank, a large Rotterdam-based universal bank, went bankrupt, causing the Nederlandsche Bank to lose Fl 26.9 million. The most spectacular events concerned another large universal bank, the Rotterdamsche Bankvereeniging. This bank had extended large loans to the business sector before the 1920s, granting credits to, among others, Wm H. Müller & Co., Rotterdam. In May 1924, the Rotterdamsche Bankvereeniging published net profits of Fl 10.4 million only to resort to the Nederlandsche Bank for support not more than six weeks later, facing potential losses of Fl 42 million. This turnaround aroused suspicion of fraud and a complaint was filed with the public prosecutor. However, in the public interest, the matter was not taken to court: the entire business community would suffer great losses if the bank went bankrupt.

A support guarantee granted by the government subsequently enabled the Nederlandsche Bank to carry out a rescue operation which succeeded completely. On the whole, the effects of the banking crisis of the 1920s were positive: banking concentration gained momentum, the scale of operation was increased and the need for internal control by auditors was stimulated. However, a disadvantage was the banking system's reluctance to grant credits to manufacturing industry. This shock reaction did, on the other hand, reduce the banking system's vulnerability during the depression of the 1930s.

For the banking system, the short-term effects of the crisis were favourable. However, from the point of view of banking historiography, it meant that bank archives closed like oysters. This did not only apply to the Rotterdamsche Bankvereeniging, where the most obscure events had taken place and whose managing director stated in 1963 that some events were too recent to be published.[3] Within the banking system, this grew to be a new attitude, not only towards the persons directly involved, but also towards the next generation so as to ensure discretion with respect to the actions of the previous generation. The only exceptions were the historiography of the central bank and the agricultural credit banks.

The Wreszynski case

The 1930s would see some events, two in particular, which did not stimulate any opening-up. Both were of an international nature. The first related to Mendelssohn & Co., mentioned earlier. This institution had taken excessive risks with respect to its international transactions. When its Managing Director, F. Mannheimer, suddenly passed away in 1939, the bank found itself in great difficulties which resulted in its winding-up. Not only was the Nederlandsche Handel-Maatschappij involved with a large loan, but the Nederlandsche Bank, acknowledging that it had been too naive, was also affected as its supervision of the credit system turned out to have failed.[4]

The second event concerned the Wreszynski case. There is no better example to demonstrate the experiences and standards with respect to writing a banking history in the Netherlands. It also indicates its weakness, which is not relevant here, although it is remarkable that this case was so quickly forgotten. As will become evident, the Amsterdamsche Bank was the financial victim of the Wreszynski case. In the volume on the history of this bank, the case is not even mentioned.[5] It had, however, not really been kept a secret; it had been widely discussed in the papers. I only discovered the case at a late stage of my examination, when more or less by chance I met a former staff member of the Nederlandsche Bank, B.W. Kranenburg (born in 1912).

In 1938 he entered the employment of the Nederlandsche Bank and at the beginning of the German occupation of the Netherlands, the board of directors put him in a small room at the entrance of the Bank, where he was to throw out all suspicious looking people with some story or other. One day Wreszynski entered with a story about a German general who had contacts with England. By that time, Wreszynski enjoyed such a bad reputation that he was immediately shown the door. Shortly before the war, this gentleman had cheated the Amsterdamsche Bank out of Fl 16 million (present value Fl 300 million). Incomprehensible, in retrospect, Kranenburg stated, but as he added it is in 'haute' finance where absurdity thrives.[6] Once on the track, I found some data in the archives with respect to the Bank's supervision of the credit system. They were filed under the name of a Mr Norris.

The case must be viewed against the background of the international payments system's deadlock in the 1930s, particularly with respect to the German situation and its Stillhalte-Abkommen. Francis Norris, a former member of the British House of Commons, specialized in the thawing of frozen credits, assisted by Polish-born Siegfried Wreszynski. How they managed to do this in Nazi Germany has never become quite clear. Apparently they had relations with the Nazis, who turned a blind eye in return for their share. During the thirties Norris and Wreszynski visited the Reichsbank in Berlin, where suspicion arose as to these gentlemen and their transactions. Hj. Schacht therefore sent a warning to all central banks in the world. Some research of the Reichsbank by Karl Friedrich Wilhelm, a director since 1939, made clear that there had been a relation between Norris–Wreszynski and the Röhm-Group, who intended to use their cooperation for financing a putsch. After the collapse of the Röhm-Group in June 1934 Norris and Wreszynski stood alone. In 1934, Norris got into trouble when a transaction for Unilever (worth FFr 12 million) was not performed satisfactorily.[7]

The relationship between the Amsterdamsche Bank and these two gentlemen dates back to 1933, when they received Fl 16 million worth of Deutsche Mark claims for collection. This would take some time and meanwhile Wreszynski was badly in need of money, causing him to resort to the Amsterdamsche Bank for a loan of £4,500. There would be no reason to go into this case were it not for the fact that the collateral for the loan was an early self-portrait by Rembrandt, which had been granted a certificate of authenticity by Dr C. Hofstede de Groot in 1928. As Wreszynski failed to repay the loan, the Amsterdamsche Bank sold the painting through an art dealer for Fl 35,000 (late 1936) after which Wreszynski remained indebted for another £631, which he probably never repaid. Nowadays, paintings by Rembrandt are no longer accepted as genuine just like that and, as was to be expected, the painting was found to be one of two famous replicas of a lost self-portrait by the Dutch master.[8]

Like the painting, the Deutsche Mark claims disappeared from sight. In 1938, Wreszynski again contacted the Amsterdamsche Bank, claiming that he knew a way to cash the claims. The Amsterdamsche Bank promised him £120,000 if payment was effected within one month. Norris and Wreszynski subsequently sold the claims of the Amsterdamsche Bank in New York for half their value. The earnings were credited to Wreszynski's account. However, Wreszynski was not charged for this fraud. Instead he was accused in April 1939 before the Amsterdam court of conning Jewish refugees from Vienna, whom he had promised to provide with Argentine visas, naturally against payment. The court blamed Wreszynski for cheating his own people. In addition, Wreszynski was charged with marriage fraud.[9]

As was common in those days, the Wreszynski case was covered extensively by the press. The Amsterdamsche Bank became involved as Wreszynski had tried to gain confidence by publishing the letter in which the bank promised him the £120,000 mentioned above. One of the managing directors of the bank, H.A. van Nierop, was subsequently summonsed. The judge reprimanded him for not having reported the swindle and for putting too much trust in Wreszynski. However, Van Nierop could show the recommendations received from, among others, Sir Basil Blackett, a managing director of the Bank of England. And even though the chance of retrieving some of the frozen credits was small, the bank had to make an attempt. Nevertheless the impression remained that van Nierop had been too tolerant. In the end Wreszynski was convicted, released from prison during the German occupation and transported to the concentration camp Westerbork, where he was set free again. Once more he deluded fellow Jews with false hopes of a visa, against payment. After 1945 he was sentenced to four months' imprisonment for fraud. He died in 1955.[10]

The Amsterdamsche Bank felt the aftermath for years. In 1939 some articles were published accusing the bank of inadequate disclosure. The loss suffered was invisibly deducted from the secret reserves and, inevitably, the question arose why it was not claimed as a Stillhalte loss. In this connection the Nederlandsche Bank will have the final say. In 1939 the bank had written an internal aide mémoire with respect to the case, stating that it had not been informed in advance of the transaction and was of the opinion that this had not been necessary. The Bank was, however, informed when problems arose. Nevertheless it saw no need for intervention as the Amsterdamsche Bank was fully capable of bearing the loss. Only its shareholders lost profits, but protecting their interests was not considered to be one of the tasks of the supervisory institution. The central bank also approved of the fact that the Amsterdamsche Bank did not publish its losses so as to prevent a run on its cashier's offices and those of other banks. The loss suffered had meanwhile become a public secret, which it remained. As I said before, the case was not mentioned in the history of the Amsterdamsche Bank which was published in 1946. According to the Nederlandsche Bank, the only unanswered question was whether the managing director involved had to face the consequences of his actions. However, this was considered a matter to be decided on by the supervisory board of the Amsterdamsche Bank.[11]

Some figures were derived from the archives of the Nederlandsche Bank, as a note was attached to the aide mémoire mentioned above, which indicated how the loss was written off by the Amsterdamsche Bank: in the period 1932–38 a total of Fl 19.5 million was written off against income. (This figure includes Wreszynski's Fl 16 million.) The annual reports of the Amsterdamsche Bank do not mention the case. Exactly the same figures are also found in the journal De Maasbode of 16 April 1939. The article also states that the Amsterdamsche Bank's earning capacity is reflected in its ability to pay dividends ranging between 4 and 5 per cent in the period mentioned above. It is understandable that shareholders wrote angry letters requesting the bank to speak in clear terms. However, the bank refrained from doing so. The question remains whether the reason really was that it wanted to prevent a run on its cashier's offices.

Lesson learned

The foregoing is a successful example of a well-known story, with several unknown details. That was in the 1930s; today we are given more information. Within the supervisory board of the Amsterdamsche Bank a feeling of unease had arisen. The result was that the regulation introduced in 1876 with respect to lending was sharpened. In 1934 the well-known banker A.J. Hengel resigned because he refused to sign the accounts. Van Nierop was requested to resign as general manager and was appointed a member of the supervisory board. He was forced to resign in 1940 and emigrated to the United States just in time.[12]

This story has a happy ending, which is also true from a historical viewpoint; historians do not always succeed in obtaining the more detailed minutes of meetings of the board of management or the supervisory board. It should be kept in mind that this need not be a question of evil intent; usually data are simply not available. However, it is characteristic of the banking system, for it is responsible for hiding these data from research in the first place. This is a trauma for banking historians: I would not like to research the question whether this also applies to other parts of the history of the Netherlands. As far as problems within the banking system are concerned it is evident that the information recorded in the archives of the institutions involved is insufficient or that the historian is often told that it is 'not intended for publication'.

In case of problems, there are always people involved and the protection of private individuals in the Netherlands, justified or not, is extensive. Our country is characterized by a general tendency which was described by H. van Riel when he discussed the learning process of perceiving where actual power lies. He described it as learning to see the way in which cases were being dealt with in the Netherlands; the fact that, curiously, the society's upper class speaks innuendo and never makes unambiguous statements. He went on to say that making ambiguous statements has been developed into an art form in the Netherlands.[13] In my opinion, three more traumas can be distinguished that led to much covering-up.

Traumas of the Netherlands banking system

These traumas concern the Jews, the Catholics and the House of Orange, the reigning dynasty. They are a consequence of the nature of the banking system and partly determine the margins and difficulties of banking historiography. It should be taken into account that most of the banking system in our country was in the hands of Dutch Reformed and liberal managers. For example, until well into the nineteenth century, it was said that the Nederlandsche Bank required that its leading positions were held by Mennonites.[14] As Protestantism was to be the signature of the banking system two other groups involved in banking were rejected: first the Jews and secondly the Catholics. Not rejected, but superior to all other groups, was the House of Orange. For researchers, however, the effect is the same. They face sensitivities of an increasing order towards three different groups.

This sensitivity is slightest towards the Jews in the banking system. This may seem strange as the recent past has shown that the wartime experiences of the Jewish part of the population are still a touchy subject. On the other hand the significance of the Jewish population for the banking system had always been small. There were only two important Jewish bankers in the nineteenth century: A.C. Wertheim and F.S. van Nierop. Naturally there were other Jewish bankers as well as numerous Jewish stockbrokers. The latter group operated on the Amsterdam stock exchange but there too they constituted a minority.[15] Until 1940 the Nederlandsche Bank had hardly any Jewish staff members. Other institutions employed more Jews, albeit in subordinate positions. In the Netherlands the Jews were subject to a latent anti-Semitism. There is one example of an old liberal-Protestant bank which refused to do business with Jews – but also with Catholics. It is striking that in the 1930s the President of the Nederlandsche Bank, L.J.A. Trip, a Catholic, was accused of being pro-Jewish on account of his appointing a Jew, Paul May, as a member of the bank's supervisory board.[16] Consequently the members of the board were no longer able to conclude their meetings by having lunch in De Groote Club, a fashionable Amsterdam club which did not admit Jews. Instead they went to the restaurant Dorrins. In short it can be stated that with respect to the Jews there was rejection or, better perhaps, discouragement, which was not very difficult to achieve as the basis for Jews to enter the system was so weak.

The situation of Catholics within the banking system was totally different. They had been in a subordinate economic position since the seventeenth century; in the late nineteenth century their political and cultural emancipation was also attended by economic emancipation. However, their position in the banking system was not strong. The only important Catholic bank was F. van Lanschot en Zoonen in 's-Hertogenbosch. Since the end of the nineteenth century, a true Catholic banking bastion was built in the form of the agricultural credit banks. There was a typically Dutch schism: a Catholic centre of agricultural credit banks was established in Eindhoven, a liberal-Protestant centre in Utrecht. These centres would not merge until 1970.[17]

The relationship between the government and the Nederlandsche

Bank (1814) caused the top of the banking system to have a governmental and, consequently, conservative character, rejecting Jews and Catholics. The Catholics were feared most as they had the reputation, not unjustifiably, of striving to obtain the absolute majority in terms of size of the population. Shortly after 1945 I experienced what a spectre this was. Until that time, anti-papism and the defensive attitude among Catholics, as reflected in anti-Protestantism and anti-liberalism, had been virulent. In this connection, the fact that Mr Trip was appointed president of the Nederlandsche Bank in 1931 is not significant as he was an unimpeachable liberal who had established a reputation as a man who kept business and religion strictly separate. The influential shipowner and banker, E. Heldring, characterized Trip as Catholic but reliable.[18]

The fact that opposition to Catholics was fiercer than to Jews in Netherlands banking history was underlain by fears that if one Catholic gained a foothold in banking, more would follow. It was all the more a precarious subject as the banking powers of the Catholics had increased to a marked extent.

The House of Orange is considered the most sensitive group. From the early nineteenth century Dutch kings had been actively involved in the economy. King William I, for example, was major shareholder of the Nederlandsche Bank and Nederlandsche Handel-Maatschappij, both key positions of economic power. However, this was not the problem; the real trauma is much less obvious. In this context we should bear in mind Van Riel's description mentioned earlier with respect to ambiguous statements. In addition to its official social hierarchy, the Netherlands had an unofficial social hierarchy, leading straight up to the court. The closer to the court, the higher the standing. There were bankers in high positions, sometimes even in the position of chamberlain extraordinary to the queen. The trauma lies in the fact that the banking historian is confronted with a society of bankers which imitated the court, in that it closed its ranks notably with respect to discretion. Here the phenomenon of rejection also existed. A banker, baronet and chamberlain once told me that in prewar Amsterdam business society a baronet was accepted, but a baron was not.[19]

Netherlands banking historiography: how?

The Netherlands banking historian faces all these traumas. In our country, the question of how to write about the history of banks is first of all translated into the question of whether it is possible to write banking history at all. Until recently it was impossible, at least according to modern scientific standards. There was only a handful of old theses of a limited scope and some publications based on annual reports. A positive exception was the history of the agricultural credit banks and the central bank. Their publications were admittedly written in-house, but at least they were underlain by studies of original sources.[20] In general economic and historical literature the banking system only filled a limited number of pages. Relevant questions with respect to, for instance, the importance of the banking system for our economic growth, could only be answered tentatively. Answers were more or less indirect, to the effect that if it was not evident, it was presumed non-existent.[21]

This meant that, when starting out, the banking historian found only few landmarks on his way. Fortunately, none other than Professor A.M. de Jong had written a history of the first century of the Nederlandsche Bank, the Dutch central bank. His work is of a scientific simplicity, underlain by the assumption that banking history is no different from history in general, i.e. a chronological representation of events in time, on the basis of questions posed which we may call a theme. De Jong focused on the tasks of the central bank and their legal framework, the central banking technique related to the currency standard and the economic background, which naturally also comprised the broad outlines of interaction between the central bank and the banking system. For the years 1814–1914 a well-wrought picture arises which is exhaustively and respectably supported by figures from the quantitative material available. De Jong originally was a lawyer. His career progressed within the bank and he was finally appointed a member of its board of management. With an interest in political history, he rather reminds us of a cliometrist *avant la lettre* if we look at his fascination for figures.[22]

Partly, the way had been paved for later authors wanting to write banking history, with respect to the question of how it should be done. De Jong defined its size and scale as broad, so I did not feel this as a restriction. Furthermore, the tone and approach did not need to be too different. Like De Jong, I restricted myself to presenting outlines of the Nederlandsche Bank against the background of the development of the banking system in general and the Netherlands economic development in particular. There are some differences, however. I undoubtedly and deliberately departed from De Jong's method in two respects: the figures and the persons. In contrast to De Jong, I do not use an abundance of figures.

As far as figures are concerned, I adhere to Charles Wilson's opinion as quoted in Peter Mathias's impressive tribute to this colleague. Wilson's ideas have provided useful guidelines. This applies to his publication on Unilever, in particular, in which the author remarks that history should not be written on the basis of laundry lists.[23] This is also true for central banking history for which no standard recipe exists either. Ingredients of such a recipe might be the statutory functions of the central bank, the relationship between the central bank and the general economic and, mostly also, political situation, the relationship between the central bank, the government and parliament, the significance of the function of the central bank as a banker's bank for the banking system as a whole, the supervision of the credit system and, finally, the aspect of the financial and economic power relations.

Differences in focus remain, however. This also applies to our respective approaches towards persons, for which there are evident reasons. De Jong had described the history of the Nederlandsche Bank until 1914. From that year the historiography of banking is characterized by more personal accents, not only as a result of the authors' own preferences but also because the period required such focus. During the First World War, and subsequently as from September 1936, the Netherlands had a managed currency. Before that period my predecessor had a tendency to keep persons in the background. Naturally his publication does feature some persons, such as the presidents of the Nederlandsche Bank and the Ministers of Finance in office, but they are subordinate to the bank or, in other words, the gold standard. Since 1914, however, this was possible to a lesser degree, an understandable fact as it is important to know who actually managed this paper standard. Not only can our focus on persons not be seen independently of modern ideas on historiography, it also serves a purpose. In order to organize the national economy in times of war, the government and the business sector – including the Nederlandsche Bank – closely cooperated from 1914–18. The question consequently arises, who were the actors? We cannot ignore the persons involved, and that also applies to the period of monetary unrest after 1918, a time in which American and European central banks were striving for cooperation. What story would that be without Montagu Norman, Hjalmar Schacht and Gerard Vissering? And on a national level, how would the obstinate maintenance of the gold standard be expressed without mentioning Prime Minister H. Colijn and the president of the Nederlandsche Bank, L.J.A. Trip? The Second World War would fade if we were to leave out Nazi president M.M. Rost van Tonningen, but also the resistance within the bank, to which names are connected. The history of the bank thus comes into line with general Dutch history with respect to its opinion on right and wrong, which finally comes down to the assessment of individual persons. Attention to these persons is naturally included as an external aspect. I sometimes preferred to concentrate on the structure of personnel, organization and accounting, for I was not only concerned with external aspects.[24]

It is evident, however, that these external aspects are the most important. Focus on them is intrinsic to the tasks of a central bank. In that, the writer has no choice. His only option is to lay different stresses. I was fascinated by the fact that the Nederlandsche Bank increased its supervision of the banking system during the interwar period, and not only on account of Mannheimer and Wreszynski. With hindsight, one realizes that A.M. de Jong paid less attention to supervision in the period described by him and that, had he given the subject more prominence, he would only have done so to prepare the reader for later developments. Sometimes it is hard to distinguish whether some aspects are highlighted because the writer so wishes or whether they constitute an inevitable theme. A case in point is the description of the economic power of the banking system, which is reflected in, among other things, the interweaving of the banking system and the business sector through supervisory directorships.

After the writer has done his research, the moment of writing arrives. Usually this is not discussed when it comes to 'how to write'. I can only refer to the leading examples in the field of historiography and to simple rules with respect to composition, size, scale and periodization. In this field too, there are limits to tolerance but now they relate to the author *vis-à-vis* his work and vice versa. By this time, the author has long forgotten about the Wreszynski case, although it might be useful for him to remember it every now and then, so it may serve as a beacon in the sea, for orientation and more importantly, defence.

Notes

1. Interview with Mr H. van Riel by Joop van Tijn (1970), pp. 25–31. Van Riel was a well-known liberal politician in the Netherlands. Before the Second World War he was a staff member of Mees & Zoonen.
2. De Vries, J. (1992), *Het Nederlandse financiële imperium* (The Netherlands financial empire), an outline of the history of Dutch banking. *Een geschiedenis en bronnenoverzicht* (A history and list of sources), NEHA (Netherlands Economic History Archives), p. 37 ff. Detailed information in de Vries, J. (1989), *Geschiedenis van de Nederlandsche Bank* (History of the Nederlandsche Bank), volume 5. *De Nederlandsche Bank van 1914 tot 1948* (The Nederlandsche Bank from 1914 to 1948). *Visserings tijdvak 1914–1931* (Vissering's era 1914–1931), p. 203 ff.
3. Introduction by De directie Rotterdamsche Bank (The Board of Management of the Rotterdamsche Bank), in Brugmans, I.J. (1963), *Begin van twee banken 1863* (Beginning of two banks 1863), p. v.
4. Cf. de Vries, J., *Geschiedenis van de Nederlandsche Bank* (History of the Nederlandsche Bank) as in 2. *The Trip era – interrupted by World War II 1931–1948* (1994).
5. Brouwer, S., *De Amsterdamsche Bank* 1871–1946, p. 292 (on the years after 1936).

6. Interview with Mr B.W. Kranenburg, 11 July 1990. Letter by Kranenburg to J. de Vries, 22 July 1990, p.2.
7. *De Telegraaf*, 12, 29 and 30 May 1934. *Amsterdamsch Effectenblad*, 7 June 1934. Nothing to be found in Wilson, Charles (1954), *Geschiedenis van Unilever* (History of Unilever), volume 2. It is evident that Mr Norris bought either Sperrmarken or German bonds at a discount (or was being offered to sell Sperrmarken or German bonds by customers), but it is unclear how he cashed these at a higher price in Germany. The only source giving more information on the technique used is Frankfurther, A. (1961), *In klinkende munt* (In hard cash), *Memoirs of a banker*, p. 85 ff. The basis was barter trade. As to Karl Friedrich Wilhelm, I must thank Dr Dieter Lindenlaub from the Deutsche Bundesbank who after the colloquium in Amsterdam, sent me some passages from the memoirs of Wilhelm written in 1954, that helped to complete the picture in relation to the Röhm-Group.
8. Letters by S. Wreszynski to H.A. van Nierop, 28 August, 2 and 3 September 1935 (characterized by Van Nierop as 'dunning letters' in a memorandum written in 1935; Van Nierop's colleagues were willing to grant an advance on the painting; Van Nierop disagrees with this plan), 16 and 20 September 1935. Wreszynski to the Amsterdamsche Bank, 16 November 1935 and the Amsterdamsche Bank to Wreszynski, 1 December 1936 (on the sale of the painting). The art dealer involved was D. Katz in Dieren, who sold the painting to an unknown private person. Cf. Katz to the Amsterdamsche Bank, 30 June and 30 October 1936 and 18 November 1936 (sale settled). Note by the Amsterdamsche Bank, no year indicated, accompanied by a picture of the painting by Rembrandt (self-portrait) and a certificate of authenticity granted by C. Hofstede de Groot, 1928. All data from the archives of the Amsterdamsche Bank (now ABN AMRO). My colleague Mr J. Bruyn was friendly enough to point out the origin of the painting. Cf. Bruyn, J., Haak, B., Levie, S.H., van Thiel, P.J.J., and van de Wetering, E. (1982), *A Corpus of Rembrandt Paintings*, pp. 638–44.
9. Note on fraud case Wreszynski/Amsterdamsche Bank 1933/1939, in the archives of the Amsterdamsche Bank. The promise of £120,000 in a letter from the Amsterdamsche Bank to Wreszynski, 5 October 1938 in *Algemeen Handelsblad*, 13 April 1939.
10. *Daily Express*, 29 December 1938 (front page). *De Telegraaf*, 13 April 1939 (extensive information on Van Nierop and the Amsterdamsche Bank) and 14 April 1939. *Algemeen Handelsblad*, 14 April 1939 (mentions Sir Basil Blacket). In an appeal to the Amsterdam court of justice, Wreszynski was sentenced to four years' imprisonment in February 1940. The Germans released him from prison. Cf. *Algemeen Handelsblad*, 3 January 1946. Wreszyski obituary (1893–1955) in *Het Parool*, 4 January 1955.
11. *De Maasbode*, 16 April 1939 (subtitle: *Het doel waarvoor geheime reserves niet dienen* – The purpose secret reserves do not serve). *Amsterdamsch Effectenblad*, 18 April 1939 (in contrast with *De Telegraaf*, the *Amsterdamsch Effectenblad* does not speak of a breach of confidence in the entire Netherlands financial system). Issue on banks of *Algemeen Handelsblad*, January 1940, p. 13 ff. (banking and credit system in 1939). The journal links the Wreszynski case with the Amsterdamsche Bank's intention to merge with the Rotterdamsche Bankvereeniging in 1939 (on

account of the war, this merger did not take place). *Aide mémoire Nederlandsche Bank*, 4 May 1939.

12. Note to Professor de Jong. Reference: Amsterdamsche Bank N.V., enclosed with the aide mémoire, 4 May 1939, mentioned under 11. For reasons of credit system supervision, banks were under an obligation to submit monthly returns. Cf. same figures in *De Maasbode*, 16 April 1939 under the heading: *Het doel waarvoor geheime reserves niet dienen* (The purpose secret reserves do not serve). Protests by shareholders in: A.J. Torley Duvel in Haarlem to the Amsterdamsche Bank, 17 April 1939, P.G. van Drunen, major-general ret., in Amsterdam to ditto, 20 April 1939, and E. van der Vlugt, attorney in Paris to ditto, 15 April 1939 in the archives of the Amsterdamsche Bank. Minutes of the supervisory board of the Amsterdamsche Bank, 31 May, 31 October 1934; 27 March and 1 May 1935 and 20 April and 28 June 1939, all in the archives of ABN AMRO bank. For this examination, I would like to thank Dr D.C.J. van der Werf in Opijnen. Retirement of A.J. van Hengel: statements by his son, C. van Hengel in Amsterdam.

13. Van Riel, as in note 1 above.

14. Cf. Quack, H.P.G. (1913), *Herinneringen uit de levensjaren van Mr H.P.G. Quack 1834–1913* (Memoirs from the life of Mr H.P.G. Quack, 1834–1913), p. 91 ff. and p. 340 ff. With respect to the Mennonites Quack wrote: 'they mean everything they say but they don't say everything they mean'.

15. Cf. Rijxman, A.S. (1961), *A.C. Wertheim, 1823–1897. A contribution to the history of his life*, with a chapter on Jewish Amsterdam in the second half of the nineteenth century (p. 73 ff.). Ditto Rijxman (1967), 'Frederik Salomon van Nierop 1844–1924', in *Bedrijf en samenleving* (Business and society). Economic and historical studies presented to Prof. I.J. Brugmans, 1967, p. 137 ff. de Vries, J. (1976), *Een eeuw vol effecten* (A century of securities). Historical sketch of the Vereeniging voor de Effectenhandel (Committee of the Amsterdam Stock Exchange) and the Amsterdam Stock Exchange 1876–1976, p. 189 ff.

16. Rijxman mentions (Wertheim, p. 236) that in the second half of the nineteenth century, anti-Semitism in the Netherlands was much stronger than generally assumed. On the twentieth century cf. Daalder, H. (1990), 'Joden in een verzuilend Nederland' (Jews in sectarianist's Netherlands), in *Politiek en historie* (Politics and history), p. 96 ff. On Trip and the appointment of May cf. de Vries, J. as in note 4. For that matter, May was not the first Jewish member of the supervisory board of the Nederlandsche Bank; three succeeded him, among them A.C. Wertheim.

17. de Vries, J. (1973), *De Coöperatieve Raiffeisen-en Boerenleenbanken in Nederland 1948–1973* (Cooperative banks and agricultural credit banks in the Netherlands). *Van exponent tot component* (From exponent to component), p. 224 ff.

18. Stated by F.J.E. van Lennep of Amsterdam in the 1960s.

19. Ibid.

20. Cf. overview of literature used in J. de Vries, *Het Nederlandsche financiële imperium* (The Netherlands financial empire) as in note 2, p. 51 ff. This also lists the publications from 1980 which show a positive turnaround. It is no coincidence that W.M. Zappey published a study on bank secrecy. Some remarks on Netherlands banking history in *Bedrijf en samenleving* (Business and Society) as in note 15 (1967), p. 299 ff.

21. Cf. Brugmans, I.J. (1961), *Paardenkracht en mensenmacht. Sociaal-economische geschiedenis van Nederland 1795–1940* (Horsepower and human power. Social and economic history of the Netherlands 1795–1940), and van Zanden, J.L., and Griffiths, R.T. (1989), *Economische geschiedenis van Nederland in de 20e eeuw* (Economic history of the Netherlands in the twentieth century).
22. De Jong, A.M. (1967), *Geschiedenis van de Nederlandsche Bank* (History of the Nederlandsche Bank). Volume 1: *De Nederlandsche Bank van 1814 to 1864* (History of the Nederlandsche Bank from 1814 to 1864), (originally published in 1930). Volumes 2, 3 and 4: *The Nederlandsche Bank from 1864 to 1914*.
23. Peter Mathias (1992), 'Ricordo di Charles Wilson (1914–1991)' in *Il Datini*, 9, p. 13 ff; Wilson, Charles (1954), *Geschiedenis van Unilever* (History of Unilever), p. x. The remark refers to H.A.L. Fischer.
24. Cf. de Vries, J. as in note 4.

CHAPTER FOUR

Comments on Johan de Vries's Presentation

John S. Fforde

First let me say that I agree with Professor de Vries when he says there is no standard recipe for writing the history of a central bank. I agree also with his list of possible ingredients and with his insistence that proper weight must be given to personalities, especially in any history relating to the epoch of managed currencies.

Next, I am glad to be described in the programme as a former executive director of the Bank of England rather than as its official historian (a post I held from 1984–91). For the latter might have given the impression that I am a professional historian, which I am not. I am an amateur historian and was a central banker by profession. Interested in history since my schooldays, I have always been a keen reader of it. But I have no professional knowledge of historical method. Words like 'historiography' have little meaning for me.

Accordingly, my book *The Bank of England and Public Policy, 1941–58* tended to write itself, helped by painstaking research into a multitude of official documents; to write itself according to a subjective assessment of what was interesting and important, always bearing in mind that an official history has to be as thorough as is feasible or tolerable, so that it can be regarded as the definitive book on the period. The subjective assessment was not difficult in practice. The protracted and often intractable external and domestic monetary problems of the UK during my period were already well known. My task was to examine and assess the bank's contribution to the formation of policy and its implementation, within the constitutional framework that was given statutory form by the Bank of England Act 1946, my primary source being the documents and records in the bank's archive, records hitherto largely uninspected. This documentary evidence was supplemented by 'background' made available in interviews with survivors from the period. It was not my job to seek verification of theoretical propositions by the examination of monetary statistics.

This kind of work can be likened to biography. As De Vries says in the Dutch context: 'outlines of the Netherlands Bank against the background of the development of the banking system in general and the Netherlands' economic development in particular'; and he goes on to stress, as a biographer certainly would, the vital importance of personalities.

What is the purpose of this activity? In attempting to answer this question, it is useful to look at the market for the product. It is a very small market, but a potentially influential one. In my case, only some 3,000 copies were printed. One thousand of these were offered for retail sale at £75 a copy. At that price one may presume the buyers would in the main be libraries, acquiring works of reference for reading by professors and students specializing in the monetary side of economic history. The remaining 2,000 copies were bought by the bank, who paid for the book to be written in the first place. Many complimentary copies have been distributed to other central banks, to senior Treasury officials past and present, to both retired and practising politicians, to a variety of commercial bankers and the like, to senior financial journalists, and the book is of course available within the bank itself. All these latter groups, who have access to the book free of charge, constitute the more important readership (if, that is, they read it, or any significant part of it), on the assumption that the purpose of central bank history is not only to entertain or to fill academic gaps but to suggest lessons from the past as a help in guiding the conduct of the present.

It is arguable, for instance, that central bankers, finance ministries, and their advisers have become over-influenced by the kind of economics that pays massive attention to disputable theory and to econometric modelling derived therefrom, but rather little to that old-fashioned and pre-scientific activity known as 'history'. Central bankers and finance ministries, not to mention other interested parties, might perform better if they were more interested in their own history. The present international monetary situation, or confusion,[1] would scarcely have been imaginable to someone writing in, say, the early 1960s when almost the entire world outside the then communist bloc belonged to the Bretton Woods system that had been constructed precisely in order to avoid the damaging confusion of the interwar years. Yet that kind of confusion, almost of anarchy, has recurred; and it is interesting that some of the most effective comment in the UK at the present time has come not from officialdom but from those journalists who have bothered to revisit the history of the years 1925–33.

So I dare to hold that the recent history of central banks can have the important positive or normative purpose of enticing central bankers and their advisers into examining their own past. I did not set out with that view; but current experience has brought me round to it.

This has implications both for the 'how' to write it and for the 'who' to write it. As to 'who', I suspect there is a very large gap, at least in the UK, between the academic historian and the practising central banker. The latter belongs to an esoteric and rather lonely profession. There is only one central bank in each country. Its technicalities are often daunting for the outsider. Few of the public understand them. The story to be told by the historian (amateur or professional) is often difficult to tell. Personalities and politics frequently become interwoven with highly technical narrative and highly subjective judgements about complex market situations. Who is better suited to write it, an enthusiastic amateur from 'inside' or an experienced professional from 'outside'? The question is difficult to answer. It has to depend in part upon the talent available, which is not likely to be very abundant in so specialized a field, the more so when the work required will absorb much time and energy over a considerable period. But perhaps there is some presumption in favour of the amateur. Though he will have the 'déformation professionnelle' of his trade, he will also have the insider's grasp of motivation and personal feeling, so necessary in a field of specialized biography. There are, however, a few obvious provisos, mostly about the 'how':

1. The amateur must on no account be a hagiographer, and must be an even-handed critic.
2. He or she, just like the academic, must have free and unrestricted access to all the material; and there must be no interference with what is written.
3. The amateur must have the ability to become a very careful and thorough researcher. In my experience it is easy to get a story wrong by going through files too fast or by failing to follow up scents leading to other files. A professional would be less likely to fall into this error.
4. He or she must be able to tell a good story, with full 'human' interest.

The last of these provisos appears to be as important as any. One cannot interest people in a book that not only seems uninteresting at first sight (because of the subject) but actually is dull. One of our foremost comedians was once asked in a TV interview why he had dropped a particular act. He replied that it had been going well and had had a reasonable response from his audience, but it was not good enough and he didn't feel funny when performing it. Likewise, in writing central banking history one has to feel interesting, in the hope that others will find you interesting. They can make their own judgements about the validity of your account and your assessments, but first they have to be interested enough to read beyond the opening pages.

Such comments as I have received on my own book have stressed its readability (to the exclusion of much else). For me, that is sufficient reward.

Note

1. These comments were delivered on 'Black Wednesday', 16 September 1992, when sterling and the Italian lira fell out of the ERM of the EMS.

CHAPTER FIVE

Comment

Dieter Lindenlaub

Since the question of how to write the history of a bank has been put in a general way, that is without asking for the situation in any given country, my answer will be of a general nature, too. I shall not restrict myself to a specific country, such as Germany, even at the risk of being very abstract and of stating nothing but self-evident facts (in particular in comparison with the detailed writings on central bank history of my fellow speakers). Let me single out three issues, the first and most comprehensive of which seems to me also to be the most important.

Which objective should be pursued in writing the history of a central bank?

As in the general science of history, different answers are conceivable. My suggestion is to gear both the general writing of history and the writing of central bank history mainly to the purpose of imparting to others the lessons we can learn from it – lessons which may help us to solve current problems as well as future ones, even if those lessons must often be of a very general nature.

In all likelihood, the objective of 'learning from history' will meet with general approval today. However, this does not apply to the condition to which the attainment of this objective is attached – a condition which can be formulated as follows: you can learn only from theories, never from specific cases. It is only with the aid of theories, i.e. of if–then statements, that explanations or predictions can be made or that measures for attaining specific practical goals can be found. The task of history would be to help to formulate such theoretical hypotheses, to confirm, refute and improve them. The writing of central bank history could fulfil this task by helping to verify and improve the more or less elaborate theoretical concepts which are meant to explain monetary policy decisions (e.g. the economic theory governing politics and bureaucracy), the effects of monetary stimuli on the level of prices, employment or economic growth, as well as the transmission mechanism of such stimuli.

As a rule, historians on the academic level (present company excepted) are unfamiliar with the idea of drawing theoretical conclusions or, what is more, conclusions which are related to concrete practical cases, from their studies. However, whether such studies are suitable for finding solutions to future problems – and, moreover, whether they are original – must remain an open question; the most difficult task is assigned to the reader. As opposed to the academic level, historians who are employed with institutions such as a central bank are in a less convenient position. Unless they are required to provide nothing but adornments for some statements, as sometimes happens, they will find a market for their historical observations only if the latter are suitable to be applied in practice. In my opinion the historian is also able to provide interesting contributions to solutions to current and future problems. For instance, the debate on a European central bank might well profit from the historian's general observations, based on historical experience, on the great importance not only of detailed institutional regulations (governing areas such as the independence of the central bank or political unity), but also of informal factors (such as convictions concerning monetary policy) for the durability and the success in terms of stability of a currency union.

Even those historians who prefer a narrative manner of writing and who leave the drawing of conclusions to others should derive their questions concerning central bank history from theoretical considerations. This would force them to verify their explanatory hypotheses more carefully, e.g. by comparing them with other similar cases. They would also be forced to describe the explanatory facts, as well as the facts which still require explanation, not only in passing but in a precise and systematic manner. And they would be forced always to describe the economic and political environment, as Professor de Vries has pointed out, in the context of cogent explanations of central bank policy, instead of sketching loose explanatory frameworks.

Only such a systematic treatment of the institutional and informal conditions, objectives, intermediate objectives, instruments and functioning of monetary policy decisions can enable others to formulate theoretical conclusions or conclusions which are related to concrete cases of application.

What should be the object of the history of a central bank?

No one can tell historians which subject of central bank history to take an interest in (as a point of departure for a study), and no one can prescribe how thoroughly they are to explain this subject. In this respect, I agree with Professor de Vries when he says there is no fixed canon of subjects for research into central bank history. Points of departure for such studies may be the factors the decisions taken by the central bank are based on, the effects of central bank policy, as well as any part of such factors or effects. Whether the persons involved in the decision-making process should be talked about in detail depends not only on the room for manoeuvre they have but also on the question of the depth in which central bank policy, for example, should be explained, or of the extent to which practical knowledge is to be gained by the study.

As soon as the point of departure and the depth of explanation have been determined, the state of the art in historical research also requires a series of other subjects to be discussed when carrying out the research programme. For example, any study of the influence of a central bank requires a detailed discussion of monetary policy; an explanation of the monetary policy decisions to be taken by certain persons requires, among other things, a discussion of the latter's concepts of monetary policy (not only of their political past). To a certain extent, the explanatory programme as sketched above is binding on the historian. Moreover, in this sense I am of the opinion that there is indeed something like an obligatory canon of subjects for research into central bank history.

Should unpleasant facts be concealed?

Professor de Vries thoroughly described the 'traumas' which so far have prevented the banks of the Netherlands from gaining access to their archives and writing about the history. However, he explicitly excepted the Central Bank of the Netherlands from this 'cordoning-off' practice. Does that mean that the problem of covering up certain unpleasant facts does not apply to central bank history at all? I don't think so. Even a central bank may be tempted to conceal its history. For history has shown that occasionally central banks have 'failed' too. It has shown, also, that sometimes what central bankers tell the public is not what they are thinking; in order to maintain confidence in the currency of their country they in some cases depict the monetary situation as being more stable than they really think it is.

Does the description of such processes undermine confidence in the central bank and in the currency, and is it therefore detrimental to the public interest? Scholars cannot raise the question in this way; if it makes research conditional on the effects this might have, it abandons the very principles it is based on. But as far as I can see, the central banks do not, and rightly so, make such fears the guidelines of their archive policy, quite independently of the fact that in some countries the legislation governing archives exerts a certain pressure to disclose information openly – a pressure which seems to me quite beneficial. To be well informed is better than to trust blindly. Unbiased central bank history makes the public watchful. This also helps the central bank itself. In the long run, central banks fare the better the more the public is aware of the difficulties, but also of the opportunities, of monetary policy. As a consequence of such openness the public would probably be more willing to support central bank activities. And the information policy central banks conduct towards the public need no longer be a subject for discussion.

CHAPTER SIX

Comment

Herman van der Wee

In his report Professor de Vries has emphasized in a very elegant and illuminating way the difficulties and pitfalls connected with the problem of writing the history of a central bank. On the basis of the interesting Wreszynski case, he has shown how delicate it can be to analyse in a book on the history of a bank some bad or unsuccessful experiences the bank went through during its existence.

I would like to make two different kinds of remark: first some more general ones on the problems and difficulties connected with the writing of the history of a central bank and of banks in general as I experienced them when writing the history of the National Bank of Belgium in the interwar period, and when writing with my wife the history of the Middenkredietkas and the Flemish Kredietbank, 1885–1985; secondly, some specific remarks on Professor de Vries's paper.

General comments on writing the history of a central bank

With respect to the problem of heuristics I want to join Professor de Vries in his remark that the official source material on central banks – and I would rather say the official source material of banks in general – is very disappointing. Annual general reports in most cases are only a vague mirror of the bank's overall strategy. The minutes of the meetings of the board of directors or of the supervisory board members do not meet the expectations of the historian either; they indicate the decisions made at the meeting, but only in exceptional cases do they give more precise information on the discussions preceding the decisions and on the identity of the supervisory board members who presented the different arguments.

Information on deposits is in many cases sufficiently available if the archives of the bank have been well preserved. Detailed information on borrowing, on the contrary, is generally very limited or non-existent because of the personal and confidential character of the transactions involved. Finally, balance sheets almost never tell the whole story of the bank's performance during the preceding year. A good illustration of the incomplete character of the balance sheets is given by the custom prevailing in several European countries, and accepted by the authorities, that banks build up secret reserves, which can be used in times of crisis for writing off their losses secretly in order to maintain the confidence of the depositors in the banks under pressure. The technique of the hidden reserves not only obscures the story of a bank's investment strategy *sensu stricto*, but it also falsifies the information on the bank's capital and reserves and the information on the bank's return on both items. The hidden reserves indeed are invested, but no information is available in the official documents about the result of the investments made with these reserves.

For the bank historian the lack of information in the example given is disastrous: he does not obtain a correct view of the global lending policy of the bank under scrutiny, he remains ignorant about the size and the character of the investment failures of the bank in question and he has no complete idea of the real losses involved in them. Furthermore, in the case of hidden reserves the bank historian is unable to assess the financial health of the bank which he studies, nor is he able to evaluate correctly the financial performance of that bank.

How to solve these problems? A complete solution is not available, but some shortcomings can be eliminated, in my view, when trying to look for supplementary information outside the archives of the banks *sensu stricto*. Private papers of top bankers and of public figures often contain useful information which enables the bank historian to fill some gaps. For example, private correspondence or notes of telephone conversations sometimes give interesting detailed information on control strategies of shareholders, on mergers, on capital supply, on long-term or even short-term management decisions. Private papers of industrial entrepreneurs or of other businessmen who need credit from the banks can be helpful in the same way. Interviews can be an excellent source of information too, but they are delicate to handle and often give disappointing results. When the historian interviews bankers who were the decision makers of the bank during the period under study, and when he interviews them at the beginning of his research, he will in most cases receive a biased picture of the bank's policy, i.e. an outspokenly egocentric picture. To be sure, interviews can be very instructive, they can fill important gaps in the information of the written sources, but they should take place at the end of the research effort and they should be organized in such a way that they help to verify some crucial hypotheses of the author. If the author already knows the story of the bank quite well, and already knows the details of important events or decisions, he can test the validity of some hypotheses he made on the basis of well prepared interviews.

Finally, indirect information can also be very helpful. Alfred D. Chandler's studies on the managerial revolution for example (in particular his books *Strategy and Structure: Chapters in the History of the Industrial Enterprise* and *The Visible Hand: The Managerial Revolution in American Business*) show that firms have to adjust their management structure in order to maintain a growth strategy, in other words the organization chart of a firm reflects the successful long-term strategy of its decision-making body or the lack of such a strategy. Following Chandler's method a bank historian can study the shifts over time in the organization chart of the bank under survey in view of acquiring an indirect insight into the changing long-term strategies of the shareholders and managers.

Specific comments on Professor de Vries's paper

Professor de Vries referred to the hard times of the early 1920s which were considered a direct result of the short boom of the Dutch economy immediately after the First World War. There is no doubt that the boom was crucial in provoking the crisis of 1921–22, but in my view the long expansion of the Dutch economy, which had started before the war and became more sustained during the war because of the neutrality of the Netherlands, was an equally important causal factor: the long expansion period must have made it possible for many weak firms to start business or to stay in business artificially; when the downturn came in the early twenties the blow must have been the more heavy.

Concerning the references to Professor de Jong's book on the history of the Nederlandsche Bank 1814–1914, Professor de Vries holds the view that De Jong integrated too many statistics in his book, which made the study too technical for a large public. De Vries wants to avoid this and prefers to give more attention to the literary aspect of the book: a wise decision which I underwrite entirely. First the use of statistics can be very instrumental during the preparatory stage of the book. Quantitative analysis can give interesting insights into the structure of a bank, into its structural development over time and into the short-run fluctuations of its activity. If statistics are not used in the book itself, they should remain a part of the preparatory research. I am sure that this is also De Vries's point of view. Second, if statistics are not integrated into the text of the book in order to avoid a too technical language, there is always the scope for publishing the most important ones in an appendix or in a separate volume in order to give the specialists the opportunity to consult them.

Professor de Vries also deplores De Jong's too exclusive attention to the institutional aspects of the bank's history at the expense of the persons involved in the decision-making process of the bank. De Vries explains De Jong's bias by emphasizing the crucial role of the institution at the initial stage of the bank's development, but he prefers for his own twentieth-century story of the bank to pay more attention to its leading personalities, a decision which I welcome very much. In analytical history persons do indeed matter, as reality is only partially determined by structure and hazard, and influenced substantially by the freedom of men. I have only one comment to add here: if personalities do matter in the history of institutions, we should not forget that the development of institutions has to do with structures too and that the long-term growth of institutions in general has an important structural component. In order to write a balanced history of a bank one should not neglect this structural aspect. I am sure that such a neglect was not Professor de Vries's intention.

CHAPTER SEVEN

The Historiography of Commercial Banking – Britain and Scandinavia

Forrest Capie

Commercial bank historiography may well be amongst the most difficult of all exercises in economic history. This chapter outlines briefly the main problems and presents some thoughts on different approaches. Finally it considers some examples.

Writing bank history should in principle be much like writing any other business history. But there are differences which make the writing of good bank history a difficult task. Banks are different in at least two respects. One is that they deal with money and are therefore inclined naturally to be secretive and protective. Another is that their output is not easily defined, and yet it is of crucial importance in the macroeconomy. The banking firm does not simply make and sell a product and provide after-sales service. Banks create money and are therefore responsible to the monetary authorities and are likely to be subject to a variety of pressures from them.

Some questions (not always raised, let alone answered) can be useful. What is the purpose of the history and who is it written for? How does the history come to be written? Firstly, who is the history being written for? The answer to that is likely to be that the audience is diverse. All manner of historians will be interested in at least some aspects of a bank history. Economists too will have questions to address to the history. Bankers should be interested in the evolving policy and changing behaviour under different circumstances, as should other members of the financial community. Corporate and other customers are more likely to be curious about the story of 'their own' bank. To some extent they should all be satisfied, though there will undoubtedly be tensions between those preferring the glossy and superficial account and those looking for a more serious work.

More precisely, what is it that these respective consumers will be looking for? Monetary historians will have their own set of questions on the management of the bank's portfolio, its lending policies and so on. Political historians may have an interest in matters such as the role played by the bank in some episode with political significance. Economists are more likely to want to know, for example, about the extent of competition and how that affected profitability, in other words to test, or at least throw light on, some proposition from economic theory. This will contrast most sharply with the interests of customers and employees of the bank (the latter will probably receive a copy on their retirement) whose interests are more likely to lie in previous employees (and not just chairmen and directors) and in premises and working conditions. The bank itself will also have some view but above all it will wish to appear in a good light, both in relation to its customers and the sector it operates within. Nor does this list by any means exhaust the possibilities. Banks have often built or acquired fine buildings and many readers will be interested in the architectural history. There is therefore a considerable array of topics that may be covered.

The next issue is how to tell such a story. Whether to adopt a chronological or thematic framework is a common problem in writing history. History is by definition chronological, but such a form is not always appropriate nor is it easy to achieve, particularly when a long time period is tackled. But the problems of a thematic approach may be greater. Treating a theme over a long period runs into the problem of having to explain the changing economic, institutional, or other context. One solution is to break the period up into sub-periods and then treat it thematically. Some subjects are specific to some sub-periods; indeed the sub-periods may be defined in this way.

Table 7.1 presents one possible list of contents. Some sub-divisions by time period would invariably be necessary. Such a structure covers the essential elements and allows the placing of the particular case history in the context of the whole sector. Also, although this table is thematic, some chronological arrangement can be superimposed.

Table 7.1   History of the Very Safe and Sound Bank Ltd by A.Vetted-Historian

---

List of Contents
Introduction
1.   Macroeconomic Background
2.   The Banking Sector
3.   Relationship with Monetary Authorities
4.   Performance of the Bank
5.   Relations with Industry
6.   Personnel
7.   Management Structure and Style
8.   Another Topic
Conclusion

In a typical British example some sub-periods could be introduced, say:

1868 (founding date)–1896 (date of merger); 1897–1919; 1920–45; 1945–71; 1971–84; 1984–92 (epilogue). These dates are decided by a mixture of micro and macro factors. There are other possibilities. Within these sub-periods the subjects outlined in Table 7.1 could all be treated, probably with a different emphasis in different periods. There are many other themes which may be more suited to particular banks: some could be 'balance-sheet driven'; deposits/depositors; other liabilities; loans and advances; investments; bills; other assets. Whatever the structure there will in all probability be a unifying theme.

How do bank histories come to be written? The most common occasion is an anniversary; 50, 75 and 100 years since the founding have proved popular. The bank usually wishes to mark such a date with a record of its success. The commissioning of historians resembles that of biographers where the choice of biographer greatly influences the final product. The historian may initiate the history (Munn, 1991), but whether initiated by the historian or the bank the choice of historian is clearly of great importance. Banks are conservative and often secretive institutions, protecting both their own record and the behaviour of their customers. They therefore seek authors who are understanding and sympathetic to the bank's position.

Trust is a necessary component of banking. As Walter Bagehot said: 'A bank lives on credit. Till it is trusted it is nothing; and when it ceases to be trusted it returns to nothing'. However, they often behave as if any revelation could damage that trust and must therefore be avoided, and that seems to extend to any simple blunder, however minor, in the bank's past.

Much of the secrecy is understandable. It also explains why so many bank histories have been 'in-house' products. That can result in less objective and critical accounts than are desirable and than would be provided in different circumstances.

Theory

Historiography requires some theoretical underpinning. Historians often reject the idea of theory, certainly of explicit theory, but it is impossible to proceed without some theoretical position. Facts do not speak for themselves. The selection of data or of any archival material proceeds from some hypothesis, however deeply subconscious, that may be held. My preference is to make the theory explicit.

The first question to ask is what is it that banks do, and how is it believed that they can do that. There are different views on these questions, which is why it is a good idea for the author to be explicit. The basic theoretical framework will supply the questions that the historian wishes to answer. The criteria are then there to assess whether the bank was successful in performing its functions. The bank may also express its own objectives and can be judged in its own terms.

Banks are generally regarded as having two essential functions: to provide transaction services, and portfolio management. Another function, shared with other financial institutions, is to act as intermediary between savers and investors. What distinguishes banks from other financial intermediaries is that they supply the means of payment. A tension arises because on the one hand there is a need for competition between firms and yet there can be dangers there for the money supply. The dangers are usually thought of in terms of the default of one institution, the possibility of contagion, and the threat of a collapse of the money stock. The central question then is how do banks go about the business of providing transaction services and portfolio management while remaining careful about their wider obligations?

The additional questions the banking historian will take to the archives will also vary according to the period when the history is being written, for contemporary preoccupations are bound to intrude. That is why history is constantly being rewritten. For example a history written in 1992 in Britain (and some other countries) would doubtless have the issues of regulation or deregulation high on the agenda of the investigation, and probably also the nature of the relationship with customers during recessions. Equally, current concerns about the likely structure of European banking after 1992 would direct attention in the past to the nature of the banking system and the type of structures that were successful – say, those with large branch networks that were well diversified both geographically and by activity. This in turn would lead on to the prevailing regulatory framework. Such an approach would contrast with a history written in the 1960s, when different issues dominated.

A further function, not inherent in the definition of banking, is the promotion of enterprise. It is often asserted that this has been important in modern industrial development. In this respect finance theory, such as it is, will probably be the source, whether consciously or not, of the questions that the historian will ask of the material available. Finance theory focuses on the degree of control that the institutions exert over their customers, the nature of commitment on both sides, and the extent of monitoring by the bank of the loans that it makes. This gives rise to a number of questions. On what terms does the bank lend? What kind of collateral does it demand/obtain? How do terms and conditions vary over time and under different circumstances? Does the bank stay with its customers through all kinds of difficulties? Does it ration the credit it gives?

To answer the above questions requires the availability and accessibility of all manner of documents. Frequently these will not be available in full as there is a variety of constraints operating. The absence of free access to the archives may be one of them. Even where access is free the material may simply not be there. The historian is often confronted with this problem. However clear the ambition is, and the questions are, answers may not be realizable. The archives can dictate to a considerable extent the kind of history that can be written. In extreme form this can result in historians setting out to write about one topic and finishing up writing about another. While that is not strictly acceptable with a commissioned history, the archives nevertheless will have a considerable influence on the final product.

The historiography

So much for thoughts on what might be ideal. When we turn to the practice we find considerable divergence. First, though, there is a need for some comment on definitions. There are different usages and understandings of the term 'commercial banks'. In one sense all banks are commercial (though a distinction has been made in this colloquium between commercial and savings banks). In Britain the term is generally taken to mean the retail clearing banks, as distinct from the merchant, or investment or wholesale banks, or any other banks. But in the literature on Scandinavia the term commercial appears to be used to cover the two main activities of retail and investment banking.

Modern British banking has been established for longer than most. Some of the earliest histories date from the nineteenth century. (There was quite a flurry of hagiographical activity around the turn of the century.) It has been a growing industry in the twentieth century though the flow has necessarily been uneven. So too has the quality, ranging from the anonymous hagiographical account to the more serious academic study.

There has also been a number of different kinds of studies of the sector as a whole or of aspects of the sector: Munn on early Scottish; Checkland on Scottish; Gaskin on Scottish; Ollerenshaw on the Belfast banks; Goodhart on the London clearing banks at the turn of the century; Nevin on the London clearing banks. These all in their different ways allow each bank to be placed in the context of the sector. That is essential for giving the individual bank the proper assessment.

The same general rules about writing seem to apply throughout the century. So long as the treatment is by an insider or well-vetted outsider who plays by the rules, there are no problems other than perhaps the production of less critical history than is desirable. Difficulties do arise and have arisen when academic historians seek to produce serious history. There are several recent examples.

Many of the early histories of banks were very long, very sober and tending to the antiquarian – the kind of book that once you put down you couldn't pick up again. They were 'solid tomes as respectable and safe as the business they catalogued' (Mathias, 1991, 8). The first batch of histories of British banks were, as Mathias put it:

> . . . accurate (in the main – Hannah found some significant lapses in Matthews & Tuke on Barclays), patient accumulations of detail about branches, dates of opening, and absorptions; redolent with family pedigrees (particularly amongst the studies of Quaker banking families); documenting the banker's progress through alliances and new offspring in parallel to the family genealogies which were integral to the story. (1991, 8, 9)

This assessment diplomatically referred to the early histories but there is no doubt it could be extended to a big chunk of the whole genre.

Many of the earliest accounts, say pre-1930, were produced 'in house', or by very carefully chosen historians. This pattern has continued ever since. The results are, as could be expected, a little less than exciting. Nevertheless by the 1930s there were some important bank histories written by both employees and by academics, historians or economists.

One complaint that might be made against many, if not most, bank histories is that while they often purport to bring the story up to the time of writing, and they frequently carry finishing dates close to the date of writing, the stories usually stop many years before. There are two main ingredients to history of any kind: primary material and perspective. Commissioned business history should allow access to all available primary material. Perspective can remain a problem but not one that precludes coming up to, say, ten years or so of the time of writing. The 'great tome' tradition was certainly sustained in the first histories of the big London clearing banks.

T.E. Gregory's one hundredth anniversary history of the Westminster Bank (1936) ran to two volumes and almost 800 pages. Gregory was professor of economics at the London School of Economics. His history complied with some of the suggestions set out above, e.g. setting the monetary and banking context, but it concentrated on tracing the progress of the many constituent banks that came to make up the Westminster Bank at his time of writing. He did not really intrude on the period after the First World War. Interestingly, more than one-quarter of the book is devoted to biographies of individuals in the bank's history. There is no serious treatment of profits, profitability, lending policy, cash/deposit ratio and so on. In other words there is not much of the kind of analysis that students of banking would be looking for.

Crick and Wadsworth's *One Hundred Years of Joint Stock Banking* appeared in the same year, as a celebration of Midland's anniversary.

Both authors were internal economic advisors at the Midland and the book carried a foreword by the chairman (another common practice) in this case McKenna, a former Chancellor of the Exchequer. This too was a fairly substantial tome (460 pages) and followed a pattern not too dissimilar to Gregory's: the banking context; account of the various banks that came to make up the modern Midland; and biographical sketches of the distinguished chairmen. There was more concern in this history with analysis and that, together with its title, and possibly the pre-eminent position of the Midland in the world of banking in the 1930s, may account for its being so well known and widely used.

Fulford's history of Glyn's (1953), celebrating 200 years of the bank's history, was comparatively small (270 pages) and quite wide-ranging in subject matter, with the concentration more on business practice than on banking. This is another feature that keeps recurring and doubtless reflects the bank's preference. Once again the story stops well short of 1953, the year carried in the sub-title.

R.S. Sayers's volume on Lloyds (1957) returned to the large and serious tome (380 pages) but marked no particular occasion. Sayers was another professor from the London School of Economics and a distinguished monetary economist and modern historian. His approach was thematic, dealing with customers, employees and relations with the Bank of England (a subject on which he was a considerable authority). His particular focus, and it may have been one that the bank itself wanted, was the mergers and takeovers that led to the formation of the leading London clearer that Lloyds was by the First World War. As might be expected, writing in the 1950s rather than the interwar years he had more to say about competition. (Competition was not popular in the 1930s.) In spite of being published in 1957 the book had little of substance on the years after 1920.

There are many other histories of British banks written before 1970 but few merit any comment. Some amount to no more than a simple record of events and pictures of premises. One example is the anonymous and undated history of Glyn, Mills & Co. that dates from the 1930s. Another type is the short and well-written account exemplified by Hartley Withers, the famous journalist, in a history of the National Provincial Bank's 100 years in business up to 1933. These are essentially slight.

Post 1970

There have been comparatively few histories of British retail banks in the last twenty years. This may be partly explained by the age of the banks and the absence of significant anniversaries. The histories which have been written have not changed greatly in the way in which their authors have been chosen, or in their conception and design, from the versions of the 1930s. If there is a change of note it is that they have become shorter; that may reflect their slightly more analytical approach.

There have been several 'in-house' products, produced chiefly as public relations exercises usually but not always on an anniversary. For example Bolitho and Peel tell a good story of Drummonds (1967). The bank was founded in 1717 but Drummonds became part of the Royal Bank of Scotland in 1924, which is where this story stops. Drummonds does still retain a separate identity of a kind as a prestigious branch of the Royal. The history, though, as the authors candidly say in the preface, is a story of a branch of a noble family. 'Our concern has not been so much with the complexities of finance as with people ... '

Another example of the 'in-house' public relations product is that of Williams Deacons. In 1970 Williams Deacons was 200 years old and became part of Williams and Glyn's Bank, itself a subsidiary of the National and Commercial Banking Group. The history is anonymous, indeed it is a collection of anonymous articles written by the bank's staff and previously published in the bank's own review. Some guidance is given to the identity of the authors in the preface.

Lloyds embarked on an updating of the Sayers history at the beginning of the 1970s. Sayers's account had effectively finished in 1918 and the aim was therefore to bring the story up to date. Initially an academic historian was commissioned but that venture foundered, not without a little acrimony. Lloyds then opted instead for a less ambitious project and turned to their own employee J.R. Winton to write the account. Winton had been with Lloyds since 1933 and had risen to be economic adviser. However, the history produced was a quite brief, chronological story that revealed little that was not already known about the bank and its growth and development in the twentieth century.

More recently two histories of important banks have appeared. The first is of one of the UK's leading clearing banks, the Midland, by Holmes and Green. It provides another illustration of the caution that British banks pursue in selecting their historians. Edwin Green is the bank's archivist, and A.R. Holmes had worked for the bank in different capacities for over 40 years. The history was timed to appear on the one hundred and fiftieth anniversary of the bank and of course follows Crick and Wadsworth. It is a chronological treatment with more space given to the last 50 years, the central focus being on how management's principal strategic decisions resulted in the bank being in the position it reached in the 1970s/80s. When the history of the Midland was first written in 1936 it was the leading bank in the world and few had heard of Japanese financial institutions. Now it has fallen a long way out of the top 20, the world of banking has changed dramatically and there inevitably had to be a shift of emphasis. Holmes and Green do, however, present much of the kind of material that should be expected – data on profits, information on dividends and related policy.

The second relatively recent history is Charles Munn's history of the Clydesdale Bank. This is a little unusual in one respect. It is one of the few clear examples of a bank history being initiated by the authors. However, it was not entirely 'cold calling'. Munn had once worked for the bank and had good contacts with those who had good contacts with the bank. Nevertheless, this comes closest to the initiating outsider being given free access. Munn has produced the kind of history that historians applaud. It is essentially a chronological treatment with people in it too. Munn had complained that too many histories were told in terms of the head office, and worse, of the chairman and chief executive. He gives an extended treatment to the staff and to branches.

In 1992 a history appeared of one of England's oldest private banks, Coutts and Co. Coutts holds the accounts of the royal family and are even more nervous about searches in their archives than other banks. Although it was affiliated with the National Provincial from 1920 and is now owned by the National Westminster Bank it still retains a separate identity and control over a number of activities. Given this their choice of historian may seem positively adventurous. However, although Edna Healey is not a historian, she has written biography before, and significantly one of a Coutts family member. She is the wife of a former Chancellor of the Exchequer, albeit a Labour one. The history is a good read about business, particularly in the nineteenth century. But it is not revealing on the nature of banking and customers. Only one-eighth of the book is allowed for the last 100 years.

In summary, of all the histories of British commercial banks that have appeared there are more that disappoint than satisfy and enlighten. The banking sector has not been well served.

In progress

There has been no substantial history of Barclays since the big volume by Matthews and Tuke. In the 1950s and 1960s Barclays produced some histories for private circulation – 'Recollections' and a story of the bank in wartime – but nothing of substance. That deficiency has now been repaired. The most substantial and serious project that I know of is the history of Barclays Bank since 1945. The chosen historian is yet again a professor from the London School of Economics, Leslie Hannah. This is a commissioned history where the brief, interestingly, is to concentrate on the period after the Second World War. There are background chapters on the nineteenth century and the interwar years. Professor Hannah's chair is in business history and his interests lie primarily in management structure and performance. The emphasis is therefore on business rather than on money and banking.

A new project has also begun on the Bank of Scotland, a 300-year anniversary history, due to be published in 1995. The bank in this case also looked outside for their historian. They settled on an academic, but not a monetary or banking, historian and the suspicion must be that the preference of the bank is for an account of the business rather than an analysis of banking practice. But again we must wait and see.

Merchant banks

When we turn to merchant banks in Britain we enter a whole new realm of secretiveness. These banks promote themselves as the most prestigious institutions, supposedly with the highest quality personnel, where discretion, intellectual ability and banking expertise are thought of as genetically determined. It is a world where connections are important and introductions at a premium. Confidentiality is a virtue highly valued. All this presents a serious obstacle to good history.

It is not surprising therefore that these banks have not been welcoming to the historian. Not many genuine histories have been produced. Where a fairly remote time period has been treated these studies have been useful, but the majority are a great disappointment. Most of them have been published privately by the banks themselves – commissioned volumes, written by trusted employees or by novelists or journalists, some of them more akin to historical novels. They perpetuate the myth of mystery and cleverness surrounding financial dealings of enormous complexity.

Even a general study of the sector that was published in 1984 stopped the story in 1914 because the banks were 'unwilling to grant access to more recent records'! (Chapman)

The record of academic enterprise in this field is not good. The histories finish at points too far back to appeal to most of the potential audience. They also tend to be strong on personalities and families – family biography – and weak (for whatever reason) on banking practice. Where more serious histories have been undertaken they have often run into difficulties. For example, a distinguished professor of history from Oxford (D.C.M. Platt) was comissioned in the 1970s to write the history of Barings. But the bank took exception to some of the story that Platt produced and the project foundered. More recently Ziegler produced a history that was acceptable to the bank but is of less value to the monetary or banking historian.

Another example is the commissioned history of Kleinwort Benson, the biggest merchant bank in London, by Drs Chapman and Diaper. It was completed and delivered to the publisher (Oxford University Press) in 1983, but it has never appeared and apparently has been suppressed. The commissioned history of Schroeders, another big London name, by a highly recommended historian Dr Roberts, was a long time in the making and was even longer, it seems, in making its way through the boardroom, but it was published in November 1992, running to around 600 pages.

Dr Burk's 'biography' of Morgan Grenfell was published to celebrate the one hundred and fiftieth anniversary of the bank. Morgan's is another of London's most famous merchant banks. The author was given 'unlimited access' to the bank's papers, but the story, described as a biography in the sub-title, has its emphasis on leading personalities and much attention is given to the bank's status (which just happened to improve in the 1980s and may account for the initial enthusiasm of the bank for the project). There is not much analysis of profits or profitability and no analysis of the bank's activities that could not be found in other published forms. Burk claimed at the time that 'light has now broken through the mist of merchant banking', but as Geoffrey Jones remarked in a review her words were sadly premature. Even the publication of the history, innocuous as it is, was postponed for a period – or is that why it is innocuous? (Vincent Carosso had published a highly detailed history of the American Morgans which Burk's review had praised for its detail on corporate finance and lack of information on 'mistresses', as she puts it.)

Scandinavia

The relatively small amount of coverage given in this chapter to Scandinavian as against British banking could in part be rationalized if not quite justified by the relative importance of the two regions in the world of banking and finance. Regrettably, it has more to do with the ignorance of the author and the relative scarcity of translations of the existing Scandinavian histories.

Banking in Scandinavia has a long history. There is a central bank in Sweden that is older than the Bank of England and probably the first of its kind in the world. According to some (e.g. Sandberg) there has long been a sophisticated banking system in Sweden, some parts of which were modelled on the early and successful Scottish system. More recently though it has been suggested that compared with western Europe the financial sector of Sweden was not very well developed in the middle of the nineteenth century.

There is a difference between the two regions and that is the one alluded to at the beginning of the chapter. Commercial banks in Scandinavia developed quickly from retail banks to something closer to universal banks carrying out the whole range of retail and investment banking. However, as far as I can make out the historiography follows a similar pattern to the British, with individuals and families (notably the Wallenbergs) receiving the great bulk of the attention.

When Lars Sandberg assessed the contribution of Swedish banking to industrialization (in 1978) he attributed Sweden's rapid economic growth in part to the unusually large and efficient commercial banking system: 'In fact, at a comparable stage of development no other country, with the possible exception of Switzerland, could match the Swedish system' (Sandberg, 1978, p. 680). Sandberg's study rested a good deal on some distinguished histories of individual commercial banks: Gasslander on Stockholms Enskilda Bank before 1914 (1962) (dominated by the Wallenbergs); Hildebrand's history of the Svenska Handelsbanken (1971) that covered the period 1871–1955 (a condensed English version is available as *Banking in a growing economy)*; and Söderlund's account of the Skandinaviska Bank up to the First World War (1964). Söderlund later extended his history up to 1939 (1978). The Skandinaviska and the Svenska Handelsbanken were the two largest banks in the country and make up a substantial proportion of commercial bank activity.

More recently the history of Stockholms Enskilda Bank has been extended in two separate studies by well-known Swedish historians: Lindgren (1987) for the period 1924–45, and Olsson (1986) who covered the years 1946–71.

Other parts of the region have also been quite well served with no shortage of general histories of banking, together with accounts of particular episodes. It is a pity that the individual bank histories do not have wider circulation.

Summary

The main criticism that can be levelled against the British historiography is that with some notable exceptions the histories have not been written by economic historians. This has resulted in the absence of questions that should have been dealt with or where they are, in the economic context, inaccurately portrayed.

As a consumer I would look for discussion of profits and profitability, reserves (hidden and other), the true make-up of assets, the policy on lend-ing, and the nature and effects of regulation. History is supposed to reveal what was not previously common knowledge, but all too often these issues have been given at best a cursory treatment. Many of the British stories are very good on the amalgamation movement of the late nine-teenth century, but they do not deal with the interesting related questions. Were there economies of scale? What happened to costs and profitability?

Commercial banks have not performed well in the last 20 years or so. Perhaps part of the explanation is that they have become increasingly ignorant of their own histories and mistakes. Maybe there is a case for having non-executive directors responsible for the histories, to ensure that the whole story is told and shareholders given a better service. Against that there is a mitigating circumstance, that the last twenty years have seen the highest rates of inflation in modern history. Managing portfolios becomes much more difficult in such times.

References

Anonymous (1993), *The History of the Home of Glyn, Mills & Co.*
Anonymous (1971), *William Deacon's 1771–1970.*
Bidwell, W.H. (1900), *Annals of an East Anglia Bank.*
Bolitho, Hector and Peel, Derek (1967), *The Drummonds of Charing Cross.*
Burk, K. (1989), *Morgan Grenfell, 1838–1988,* Oxford, Oxford University Press.
Cave, C.H. (1899), *A History of Banking in Bristol.*
Chapman, S. (1984), *The Rise of Merchant Banking,* London, Allen & Unwin.
Checkland, S.G. (1975), *Scottish Banking: A History 1695–1973,* Glasgow, Collins.
Crick, W.F. and Wadsworth, J.E. (1936), *One Hundred Years of Joint Stock Banking,* London, Hodder and Stoughton.
Fulford, Roger (1953), *Glyn's 1753–1953,* London, Macmillan.
Gaskin, M. (1965), *The Scottish Banks,* London, Allen & Unwin.
Gasslander, O. (1962), *Bank och industriellt Genombrott Stockholms Enskilda Bank Kring Sekelskifiet 1900.*
Goodhart, C.A.E. (1972), *The Business of Banking,* London, Weidenfeld & Nicolson.
Gregory, T.E. (1936), *The Westminster Bank Through a Century,* Oxford, Oxford University Press.
Healey, Edna (1992), *Coutts and Co 1692–1992: The Portrait of a Private Bank,* London.

Hildebrand, K.G. (1971), *I Omvandlingens tjanst Svenska Handels-banken 1871–1955.*

Holmes A.R. and Green, E. (1986), *Midland: One Hundred and Fifty Years of Banking Business,* London, Batsford.

Larsson, Mats and Lindgren, Hakan (1992), 'The political economy of banking: retail banking and corporate finance in Sweden, 1850–1939' in Cassis, Y. (ed.), *Finance and Financiers in European History, 1880–1960,* Cambridge, Cambridge University Press.

Lindgren, H. (1987), *Bank, Investment bolag, bankirfirma. Stockholms Enskilda Bank 1924–1945.*

Mathias, Peter (1991), 'Inaugural lecture: Association of Business Historians', Glasgow.

Matthews, P.W. and Tuke, A.W. (1926), *History of Barclays Bank,* London.

Munn, C.W. (1988), *Clydesdale: The First Hundred and Fifty Years,* Glasgow, Collins.

Munn, C.W. (1991), 'Writing a bank history', *Business Archives.*

Nevin, E. and Davis, E.W. (1900), *The London Clearing Banks,* London, Elek Books.

Ollerenshaw, P. (1987) *The Belfast Banks 1826–1914,* Manchester, Manchester University Press.

Olsson, U. (1986), *Bank, familj, foretagande Stockholms Enskilda Bank 1946–1971.*

Orbell, H. (1985), *Baring Bros. A History to 1989.*

Sandberg, L.G. (1978), 'Banking and economic growth in Sweden before World War I', *Journal of Economic History.*

Saunders, P.T. (1923), *Stuckley's Bank.*

Sayers, R.S. (1957), *Lloyds Bank in the History of English Banking,* Oxford, Clarendon.

Söderlund, E. (1964), *Skandinaviska Banken 1864–1914.*

Söderlund, E. (1978), *Skandinaviska Banken i det svenska bank-vasendets historia 1914–1939.*

Tamaki, Norio (1983), *The Union Bank of Scotland 1830–1954,* Aberdeen, Aberdeen University Press.

Tuke, A.W. and Gillman, R.J.H. (1972), *Barclays Bank Limited, 1926–1969,* London.

Winton, J.R. (1982), *Lloyds Bank 1918–1969.*

Withers, Hartley (1933), *National Provincial Bank 1833–1933.*

Ziegler, Philip (1988), *The Sixth Great Power.*

CHAPTER EIGHT

On the Writing of Banking History – a Scandinavian Perspective

Ulf Olsson

It is very easy to agree with Professor Capie on most of the general description of the problems involved in the writing of banking history. Bank monographs for different audiences have been written in Norway, Denmark and Sweden, but especially in Norway and Sweden several good ones exist, as seen from our more academic point of view. How has it been possible to produce bank monographs that have been well received by bankers as well as academic research groups?

In a way it is only natural that much banking history was been written in Sweden. The Swedish commercial banks became very important and powerful institutions around 1870. A group of universal banks emerged from slightly different roots. Three of them have been dominant since then: Stockholms Enskilda Bank, Skandinaviska Banken and Svenska Handelsbanken. In addition to normal payment services and transfer of capital, they became instrumental in financing railway building and industry. In practice, they soon began to perform entrepreneurial functions in the industrialization process outside the banking sphere too. As I have described in my article 'Swedish Commercial Banking over 150 Years', which will be published by our European Association, the banks soon accounted for more than half of the total lending as well as handling the crucial imports of capital before the First World War and becoming centres for large industrial groups during the 1920s.

The leading and long-lived commercial banks have shown interest in their past and all of them have had their history written. The histories of the three largest banks were published around the 1960s, when they celebrated their centenary anniversaries. These were no 'in-house' products; they were written by established university professors of economic history. An important prerequisite for them was that the authors were given free access to the bank archives. In this respect Sweden has had very few of the traumas discussed during this colloquium.

The central position of the commercial banks also explains why they have attracted a considerable amount of interest from Swedish economic historians at our universities. This is in fact true for all the Nordic countries. Research groups meet every spring for a Nordic meeting in banking history. The most active researchers at present are from the Norwegian

School of Management in Oslo and the University of Uppsala. They are also participating in the international research project 'Bank–Industry Relations in Interwar Europe: a comparative study of Advanced Industrial Economies'. An important point here is that much of the original empirical input, at least in the Swedish part of the project, comes from the monographs. As a matter of fact the Swedish leader of the project, Hakan Lindgren, started his work by writing a commissioned history of a commercial bank. In this way, much of the material from the monographs has been 'processed' and presented to an academic audience, also in English.

The two-way traffic between the academic community and the writers of banking histories has set a certain methodological standard when it comes to source criticism and distance from the subject. This does not mean that the problems of how to write the history of a bank have been solved. There are two different traditions competing in economic history and, consequently, in banking history. On the one hand we have the historical tradition, which emphasizes the uniqueness of a research subject. All aspects of the bank should be penetrated in order to give a truly deep insight. I feel that such 'biographies' of banks have a strong explanatory power when it comes to decision making, and I am prepared to defend this 'idiographic' tradition. A good example is Karl-Gustaf Hildebrand's account of Svenska Handelsbanken, which Professor Capie mentions.

On the other hand there is the 'nomothetic' tradition, which searches for more general explanations of the role of banks in the national economy. Economists, like natural scientists, want to reveal the hidden rules behind what happens in order to get the power to monitor reality. We find very little of such explicit theoretical underpinning in the Swedish bank monographs. At most, figures for the activities of the banks have been aggregated on a national level. The two-volume work on Skandinaviska Banken by Ernst Söderlund is called *Skandinaviska Banken in the History of Swedish Banking*, which means that it is to a large extent the history of all Swedish commercial banks. Such aggregated figures have now and then been used by non-Swedes, working in the tradition of Gerschenkron or Cameron. Once they have been published in English, even rather small contributions on the role of Swedish banking attract international attention, which the case of Lars Sandberg indicates. Theory was not applied more systematically to the empirical data in Sweden until the 1980s. This fact probably also has something to do with Swedish economists, who since the 1930s have been extremely uninterested in financial history. It is significant that the economic historians in Uppsala work closely together with the Department of Business Administration but hardly at all with the Department of Economics.

The ideal bank monograph should combine the two traditions: an in-depth understanding of the subject and a clear theoretical point of departure. Such a product should be attractive to both bankers and economists.

Let me end with an example from my own experience. My history of Stockholms Enskilda Bank ends in 1971 when the bank merged with the larger Skandinaviska Banken after 115 years. It was hard to understand why the Wallenbergs took this radical decision after such a long and unbroken tradition. For more than one hundred years the inherited rules of thumb on how to run a bank worked well: concentrate on industrial customers, do not build up an expensive branch network, always keep a very high solidity, etc. Everything looked fine on the facade during the 1960s, but I could see from the books that the bank had gradually exhausted most of its hidden reserves and that the position of the bank was undermined. The environment had changed and the old recipe did not work any longer.

The income distribution of the modern welfare state made it impossible to attract sufficient deposits without a fine-meshed network of branch offices. The domestic capital market was strictly regulated and foreign exchange control was maintained after the war, which made it hard to find alternative funding. The industrial customers expanded very quickly, far more quickly than the bank itself. In addition, they used up their profits themselves and needed additional external investment capital. Enskilda could no longer satisfy these needs and the customers threatened to go to other banks for support. The late Marcus Wallenberg wanted to keep his industrial empire together, using a bank large enough as a tool. For him a merger with a larger bank was the inevitable solution. As soon as he had outmanoeuvred his elder brother as chairman of the board he carried through the traumatic operation. My own ambition in explaining what took place in 1971 was to help the reader first to understand why the bank so stubbornly kept to the old traditions. This also made it necessary to take into account the philosophy of the leading figures of the bank. Secondly I had to outline enough of the economic policy and macroeconomic background for the reader to realize that the bank had reached something of a dead end.

The readers I aimed at were the employees of the bank, the bankers and the business historians, but hopefully the questions asked were such that economists could also find the answers interesting. All theories were, however, well hidden after they were used. When a building is ready, all scaffolding should be taken away. Here is, I am afraid, a point on which I disagree with Professor Capie.

I think business history is a fruitful meeting point for agent and structure in historical writing. The history of a bank offers possibilities to explore the mechanisms of economic change as well as a fair chance of bridging the gap between history and social science. Institutions are important. To make histories of banks useful for both a more general public and the academic community there have to be meeting points. I have been working within the Institute for Research in Economic History at the Stockholm School of Economics, of which the purpose is to bring together business people and researchers, to coordinate projects and to organize seminars. In Norway, the Norwegian School of Management has moved quickly and successfully along the same lines. The initiative by the European Association for Banking History to arrange this seminar is, I am sure, an important step in the same direction.

CHAPTER NINE

Comments on Writing the History of a Commercial Bank

Edwin Green

When invited to join the panel for this session I was not certain whether to speak up as a producer or as a consumer of banking histories. Forrest Capie is clearly and rightly the customer's champion and as he has laid down something of a challenge most of my own comments are from the production point of view.

In his review of bank histories published before 1970, Forrest Capie concludes that 'few merit any comment'. Perhaps I could argue for a few more exemptions. The Scottish banks were remarkably productive between the 1920s and 1950s in producing their house histories. They shared the characteristics which Forrest identifies in their English counterparts, but the volume of new data in histories of the Union Bank, the Clydesdale and the British Linen was impressively high (Rait, 1930; Reid, 1938; and Malcolm, 1950).

I share Forrest Capie's disappointment at the 'family album' style of histories of merchant banks in the pre-1970 period but surely Ralph Hidy's *House of Baring* is an authoritative example of business history, written independently but with the consent of the firm. Amongst the smaller clearing banks surely George Chandler's *Four Centuries of Banking* also deserves an honourable mention. This two-volume history of Martins Bank is over-long but is a rich source of comparative information on bankers, customers and staff.

One of the virtues of the pre-1970, and especially the pre-1940, examples of bank histories is that they were important signs of commitment to the development of business history as a whole. The willingness of banks and insurance companies to commission substantial volumes was, for all their faults, an example which large corporations in other sectors could follow or surpass when they initiated serious business histories from the 1950s onwards. The role and influence of the banking community in the development of business history should not be overlooked.

It is often taken for granted that there was no theoretical input into this earlier generation of bank histories. This was not always the case. The example with which I am most familiar is Crick and Wadsworth's *Hundred Years of Joint Stock Banking*, a history of Midland which appeared in four editions between 1936 and 1964. Crick and

Wadsworth were not only remorseless in their pursuit of original sources but they also introduced a framework of ideas about the relationship between banking and the make-up of local, regional economies. This theme is made explicit in their history and, interestingly, the book is held in regard not only by banking historians but also by researchers in the highly theoretical discipline of historical geography.

As to the historiography as a whole, perhaps the largest omission from Forrest Capie's review is the extensive literature of British overseas banking. The Standard Bank produced its earliest history in 1914 (Amphlett) and published another in 1963 (Henry); Barclays DCO followed suit in 1936 (Anon.) and 1975 (Crossley and Blandford). A scholarly history of BOLSA by David Joslin was published in 1962 and Richard Fry's useful study of the British Bank of West Africa appeared in 1976. Above all, however, we have Geoffrey Jones's two-volume history of the British Bank of the Middle East (1986, 1987) and Frank King's four-volume history of the Hongkong and Shanghai Banking Corporation (1987–91). Both of these projects surely meet Forrest Capie's criteria for an explicit framework, a clear understanding of the political and economic context, and an appreciation of the banks' objectives and relative performance.

These additions and revisions to our shopping list of histories suggest that British banks have been more productive and thoughtful than seems at first sight. Yet the quality of the output is crucially affected by the design of each project, in particular the decisions which are made about readership and the choice of author. It must be made plain here that, in cases where a bank is taking the initiative or sponsoring the project, the interests of historians and economists are rarely the first concern. Fortunately many British banks have been persuaded of the long-term value of producing a text which can be used for teaching and research as well as for presentation. The needs of the historian are nevertheless in a minority; the commissioning bank is much more likely to be influenced by the expectations of its staff, shareholders, customers, regulators, correspondent banks, the media and investment analysts.

The choice of author is certainly an area of high risk. It is also an area of quixotic decisions, depending upon the bankers' perception of the craft of 'writing'. The Chartered Bank, for example, turned to the novelist Compton Mackenzie in 1954. Another old-established house chose its authors on the grounds that one of them wrote children's books and fantasies – an interesting choice for a study of the intricacies of the London money markets.

If a bank is more concerned with the type of balance which Forrest Capie recommends, then there is still likely to be a problem in deciding on an insider or an outsider. In an ideal world the choice would fall upon the well-informed and experienced outsider. From a more practical point

of view there are arguments in favour of the insider with suitable creden-
tials, as a collaborator if not as an author:

1.   The insider will bring advantages in terms of access to sources, not
     just in terms of confidentiality but also in identifying sources.
2.   Most bank histories are incredibly long projects which demand
     arduous political negotiations within the organization. It is not
     enough to have a mentor at head office; it is vital to have staff conti-
     nuity and back-up.
3.   Forrest Capie is understandably concerned about the caution with
     which banks have selected their authors in the last 20 years, but he
     also pinpoints a key historical factor: banking history, as with other
     types of business history, has seen its share of disputes and litigation.
4.   Caution need not be synonymous with lack of criticism or innova-
     tion.

For these different reasons the judgement that 'the banking sector has
not been well served' seems unduly harsh. Few sectors have taken their
histories as seriously as the banking community in the United Kingdom.
Notwithstanding some indifferent work, the literature of British banking
compares well with that of other business sectors or that of other
financial centres. Not least, banking history in the United Kingdom has
been an important example – and a fertile ground for historians – in the
wider development of business history.

References

Amphlett, G.T. (1914), *History of the Standard Bank of South Africa.*
Anonymous, *A Banking Centenary. Barclays Bank (Dominion, Colonial
    and Overseas) 1836–1936.*
Chandler, G. (1964, 1968) *Four Centuries of Banking,* 2 vols.
Crick, W.F. and Wadsworth, J.E. (1936), *A Hundred Years of Joint
    Stock Banking.*
Crossley, J. and Blandford, J. (1975), *The DCO Story.*
Fry, R. (1976), *The Story of the Bank of British West Africa Limited.*
Henry, J.A. (1963), *The First One Hundred Years of the Standard Bank.*
Hidy, R.W. (1949), *The House of Baring in American Trade and
    Finance. English Merchant Bankers at Work, 1763–1861.*
Jones, G. (1986, 1987), *The History of the British Bank of the Middle
    East,* 2 vols.
Joslin, D.M. (1962), *A Century of Banking in Latin America. The Bank
    of London and South America 1862–1962.*

King, F. (1987–91), *The History of the Hongkong and Shanghai Banking Corporation*, 4 vols.

Mackenzie, C. (1954), *Realms of Silver. One Hundred Years of Banking in the East.*

Malcolm, C.A. (1950), *The History of the British Linen Bank.*

Rait, R.S. (1930), *The History of the Union Bank of Scotland.*

Reid, J.M. (1938), *The History of the Clydesdale Bank 1838–1938.*

CHAPTER TEN

Comment

Philip L. Cottrell

These remarks will be concerned with only a limited number of points, given the ground admirably covered both by Professor Capie's paper and the other commentaries. Whilst making these observations, it is perhaps necessary to point out that they will be received first by an audience comprised of professional banking historians, banking archivists and practical bankers. Therefore, there is a real danger of appearing to be in the position of 'teaching your grandmother to suck eggs'. This is no way intended; rather the purpose is merely to put forward some thoughts provoked primarily by Capie's paper, many of which will probably occur to any of its readers.

Archival records

When writing a history of a bank, the foundation for such a work is the institution's historic archive, although perhaps supplemented by oral history work for the contemporary period. There may, too, be available documentary evidence elsewhere, especially when the institution has made a substantial impact upon the broader dimensions of humankind's experience. Most British banks have depositories of their accumulated papers,[1] although of varying sizes, whereas the inception of a history project, especially if it is commissioned by the institution, may stimulate a further search for historic records. In the case of one leading British bank its historian commented after writing the history of it, that he thought not a single piece of paper had ever been idly thrown away by its staff. Although some historians have raised doubts about the writing of twentieth-century history, because of the impact of the telephone, telegram and cable, my experience would suggest that these advances in communications have not created the 'holes' in the archives that have often been feared. In the institutions with which I have been concerned, happily in nearly every case, communication by 'wire' was confirmed by letter and, with respect to one particular bank, the 'gist' of telephone conversations was promptly written down to provide a permanent record. Such a welter of accumulating paper poses one problem for the archivist – storage – and another for the putative historian – selection. A history is more than a mere summary of the institution's physical paper holdings.

Having now stressed the weight of evidence that a historian is likely to have to struggle with, it is important also to enter a few notes of caution. One arises from the concern to establish statistical series, particularly if these are then to be employed for econometric analysis. Such basic material is available but as the historian reaches back, so it becomes more idiosyncratic and patchy. Testament to this is Professor Capie's own Herculean struggle to establish monetary series for the United Kingdom for the period after 1870 out of material available in banking archives, together with that contained within official publications.[2] So much so that the estimation of deposits held by British banks has become a fully established branch of academic endeavour in its own right.[3] Another illustration arises from the attempts to discern more clearly the lending activity of British banks. Here the archival record is equally patchy, with documentation ranging from full schedules of overdrafts at one extreme to teasing out answers from a general manager's general jottings book at the other. Frequently within this source material the rate of interest on such provision of banking accommodation is rarely noted and another only too real frustration for a historian pursuing such an avenue of research arises from trying to discover whether a loan, an overdraft, or a discount facility was renewed, rolled over, or called in. During the mid-nineteenth century, it is often only with the banks' more difficult customers – those in extremis – that some concerted account of the bank/customer relationship can be established from the primary archival record.[4] Consequently 'large' archives, in a physical sense, will not necessarily mean that they contain the requisite material to provide the answers to all the questions that a current banking historian would like to pose.

Secrecy

What should aid the formulation of the questions that a banking historian would ask? This raises more general questions about the nature of 'history' and its construction by historians. It is not my intention here to explore this large area of methodology, which again is a subject in itself. The purpose of raising this point is to illustrate some special and particular features of 'writing a history of a bank'. One arises from populist attitudes towards banking, money and finance, whether from the right or left of the political spectrum. Second, even amongst historians there is a particular excitement generated by banking records. They are many times seen (often by those who should know better) as secret sources, sometimes all-knowing secret sources, containing special information which will cast a particular illumination upon humankind's affairs. Implicit here are notions arising from the crudest variants of 'conspiracy theory'. It would be odd not to find the occasional nugget of such a philosopher's stone for a historian; that is the general point of turning to primary sources. Usually, however, their contents are mundane or amorphous, requiring considerable probing and shaping by the historian at work. Secrecy arises for different reasons: out of the particular relationship between banker and client, constituting so much of the bank's accumulating goodwill, and out of perhaps understandable guardedness, regarding past managerial miscalculations, plain wrong decisions and, of course, 'bad luck'. They are common enough to the 'general' business historian, but none the less the banker is more than frequently regarded as the common archetype of the capitalist, more so than the industrialist, and especially during periods of economic strain. During a recession, depression or slump, it is more likely for the blame to be put at the doors of the bankers than at the feet of the captains of industry.

Methodologies of approach

Capie has argued cogently that the approach to writing banking history should stem from questions arising from economic theory and, in particular, from microeconomics. Quite simply, how profitable was banking, and to what extent were profits related either to the particular decisions of the managements of individual institutions, or to the structure of banking as a whole? But that, in turn, raises questions about the very nature of the historical development of English banking.

Until the beginning of the twentieth century, the English banking system (unlike the Scottish or Irish) was composed of a multitude of institutions, largely local or regional concerns. Nationwide banks were the exception, rather than the norm. Furthermore, there was extreme specialization of function, to the extent of the 'system' being a very good example of Adam Smith's concept of the 'division of labour'. This gave rise, for example, to a unique money market within the 'City' of London, in which the principals were the discount houses. Furthermore, this specialization of function, hardly touched by continental European notions of 'universal banking' stemming from the Crédit Mobilier, meant that overseas banking was conducted by an almost separate group of financial institutions – the 'Anglo-International' and 'Imperial' banks together with the private merchant banks.

Microeconomic theory can be applied, and properly so, when attempting to write a history of one of the institutions within this system, but modern corporate/managerial theory will find itself in a strange land, certainly before the 1890s and probably even before the 1950s and 1960s. Much of English banking was a personal business, with all the

strengths and weaknesses which that entailed, and this gave rise to organizational structures and decision-making processes which were decid-
edly 'uncorporate' in nature. As with the English economic establishment
in general, although the outward trappings of a corporate economy
emerged from the 1890s, and at a growing pace during the interwar
period, senior management remained in essence based more on the attitudes and ambience of the 'club', than the corporate boardroom.

It is more than probable that this historical inertia ultimately resulted
in failings, yet it may mean that the application of current economic
theory may be, in some respects, inappropriate to constructing the 'early'
and 'middle' history of a modern English bank. The historian will certainly find answers by asking questions arising from such an approach,
but may thereby leave many other aspects of the historical development
of the nature of his subject unilluminated. In fact, the application of
sociology and the techniques of social history, and the specific questions
that they prompt, may be equally as important to the writer of a history
of an English bank before the 1880s. Many, if not most, of the English
banks of the mid-nineteenth century were particular reflections of the
local and regional societies that they had been established to serve. Indeed
they were products of those communities, with often a substantial degree
of overlap between their shareholders and their borrowing customers.
Professor John, many years ago, rightly called the provincial joint stock
banks of the period 1830 to 1880 'middle class loan clubs' and, as such,
the application of, say, social network analysis may be as fruitful, if not
more so, than the theory of the firm in developing an understanding of the
emergence and early growth of many English banks. That may be important for the provincial progenitors of the current 'Big Four': if the subject
for the historian was an eighteenth- or nineteenth-century constituent of
the 'City', then some application of the sociology of minority ethnic, and
religious, groups may have a considerable role to play.

There are 'even' questions of gender, if only arising because women
constituted so many of the shareholders of mid-nineteenth-century
English joint stock banks. Sex also played its role in the conduct of the
business affairs of at least some English banks with, for instance, George
Carr Glyn reminding his agent Seymour of the influence of Mme de Barry
within the Habsburg Court when seeking the concession for the Anglo-
Austrian Bank in the early 1860s.[5]

Other problems, regarding the methodology of the approach to be
taken, arise in the case of private banks. During the mid-nineteenth
century and especially in the provinces, the number of such constituted
banks was diminishing rapidly, but as both domestic commercial institutions and merchant banks they continued to be a leading force within the
'City' until after the First World War. In the case of merchant banks,

particularly, many of these institutions were family concerns and this gives rise immediately to the question of where the affairs of the bank came to an end, and those of the family began. Making this remark brings to the forefront the example of Anthony Gibbs, a London merchant bank, in the mid-1860s. Having then just lost the monopoly of the Peruvian guano concession and, as a result, searching for new business directions, the situation of this family merchant bank would seem readily amenable to some of the concepts of 'corporate analysis'. Yet its letter books, held by the Archive of the Guildhall Library, an important public depository of British financial history, reveal a complete absence of a central 'corporate' concern. The problems of this bank are clearly revealed in the letters that various family partners wrote to one another, but their individual commentaries on their position are heavily intermixed with other family concerns – the estates and what should be done about timber and the grain harvest – along with understandable concern for the health of elderly relations. Here the bank, with its branch houses in Latin America and its associated shipping interests, are but one aspect of a spectrum of family affairs. Furthermore, retaining a significant interest in the rural economy was then not without its advantages to a banker. One Governor of the Bank of England, Bonamy Dobree, during the late 1850s and early 1860s used his estates steward's report of the harvest to gauge the likelihood of English corn imports and their consequences for international bullion flows.

There are other reasons for extending the methodological viewpoint of the putative historian of an English bank. As with business history in general, so with banking history in particular: too often the scope of the history being developed is restricted to the affairs of entrepreneurs of the firm or institution in question – partners, directors and senior managers. That partly arises from aspects of selectivity in order to make the history manageable for the author, but it omits much, for the average customer of a bank dealt on a day-to-day basis, from the 1860s, with a clerk, or a branch manager. Unless they rose from the ranks to reach the parlour or the boardroom, these important historical actors are seldom considered, beyond perhaps general questions of recruitment and training. The bank manager, especially in small towns, was an important part of the local élite, being an opinion maker and formulator. Bank staff, with their relatively above-average education and relatively above-average pay, formed an important section of the skilled workforce, hovering somewhere between the working classes and the burgeoning middle class in the changing social hierarchy. In the case of British overseas banks, ethnicity once more arises, as frequently their branches were disproportionately staffed by the Scots. As middle-rank English overseas bankers swelled in number, they often came from the public schools and replicated in bank messes and guesthouses many of their earlier adolescent experiences, even down to the menus they preferred. Taking this wider global view of English banking also raises questions about the employment of local personnel and the functions to which they were put, supervised by the bank's expatriate 'white' staff.

There are grounds for suspecting that much of the burden of Professor Capie's remarks stems from an impatience with some of the fruits of the work of past English bank historians. There is some justification for this in that, on the one hand, there is often an over-dwelling upon the qualities of the most senior of a bank's management to the extent of approaching hagiography, while on the other hand, words such as 'profits' may rarely feature in the history's index. In conclusion my own vexation arises from the frequently made general statement to the effect that the institution concerned made an important contribution to industrialization, but then is followed by little substantiation in the continuing text. Nonetheless, it has always to be remembered that our efforts are only too frequently erected on the edifice of past work and, here, I would like to take the opportunity to pay tribute to the enduring qualities of one of the pioneering English bank histories, namely Crick and Wadsworth's study of the first hundred years of the Midland Bank.[6]

Notes

1.   Pressnell, L.S. and Orbell, J. (1985), *A guide to the historical records of British banking*, Aldershot.
2.   Capie, F. and Weber, A. (1985), *A Monetary History of the United Kingdom, 1870–1982, I, Data, Sources, Methods*, London.
3.   Higgonet, R.P. (1957), 'Bank Deposits in the United Kingdom, 1870–1914', *Quarterly Journal of Economics*, LXXI; Sheppard, D.K. (1971), *The Growth and Role of the UK Financial Institutions 1880–1962*; Nishimura, S. (1976), 'Bank Deposits in the U.K., 1880–1913', unpublished discussion paper, Hosei University, Tokyo; Bordo, M.D. (1981), 'The U.K. Money Supply 1870–1914', *Research in Economic History*, VI; Collins, M. (1983), 'Long Term Growth of the English Banking Sector and Money Stock, 1844–80', *Economic History Review*, XXXVI; Capie, F. And Webber, A. (1984), 'Bank deposits and the Quantity of Money in the U.K., 1870–1921', *Research in Economic History*.
4.   These remarks arise from undertaking the underlying research in bank archives for the discussion of bank lending in Cottrell, P.L. (1980), *Industrial Finance 1830–1914*.
5.   Cottrell, P.L. (1969), 'London Financiers and Austria 1863–1875: The Anglo-Austrian Bank'. *Business History*, XI, reprinted in Jones, G. (ed.) (1992), *Multinational and International Banking*, Aldershot.
6.   Crick, W.F. and Wadsworth, J.E. (1936 and numerous subsequent reprints), *A Hundred Years of Joint-Stock Banking*. This work was written while both the authors constituted the Economic Advisory Staff of the Midland Bank.

Further, their endeavours largely brought together the historic archive of Midland, in particular the papers of its various nineteenth-century progenitors. Unhappily, Wadsworth died at Christmas 1992.

CHAPTER ELEVEN

How to Write the History of a Bank – Belgium, Holland, Germany, Luxemburg, Switzerland

Richard Tilly

Introduction

The conference title would seem to call for country reports which carry on a dialogue between what one wants to know about a given country's banking history and what one does or can know about that history. It might have been helpful to have had at the outset a specification of desired knowledge, say, on the religion of bank founders, on banking regulation laws, on liquidity ratios, etc. In lieu of such specification I have opted for the following strategy: I first reflect on what users of the producers' good, bank history, might reasonably wish to have more of. For me, that means choosing a paradigm, or possibly a set of paradigms. Then I look at the available stock of such goods (for my assigned countries) and attempt to describe how well it satisfies my specified needs.

I readily admit, however, that the proposed strategy may sound better than it is. For the truth is, my inventory of the 'available stock' of the producers' good is biased strongly toward items I have found useful in the past, and is not a random sample of the 'true population'. In particular, I must mention two limitations: first, the period of history covered only begins with the nineteenth century, and that rules out consideration of pre-industrial origins and problems. Second, country coverage is strongly biased toward German developments, with Switzerland and Belgium running a poor second and third, and Holland and Luxemburg getting no more than an honourable mention. I do not believe that these limitations vitiate my survey, but they must be borne in mind.

Paradigms

My survey builds on a hierarchy of paradigms, old and not-so-old. The central paradigm relates institutional change to informational problems and economic backwardness to economic development. Subsidiary ones involve the capital-asset-pricing-model and the theory of credit creation. Banks may be viewed as institutions specialized in the acquisition and processing of information concerning the availability of surplus funds on the one hand, and investment opportunities on the other. Economies of scale in this information activity give banks an edge over non-specialized finance and the ability to realize diversification gains, higher real returns per unit of risk. But information asymmetry remains. Borrowers know more about their own ability and willingness to service their debt, i.e. their own creditworthiness, than do lenders; and creditworthiness will vary among such borrowers, particularly in the context of industrialization where the range of risky investment opportunities is wide. Theory suggests that atomistically competitive markets operating by prices and quantity adjustments alone would fail to properly identify such quality differences and tend to generate a discrepancy between market value and market price. 'High quality' borrowers would withdraw from such markets, and the latter, 'markets for lemons', in George Akerlof's words, would tend to disappear (Akerlof, 1970). Capital shortages could develop and even perpetuate themselves. However, before that happened, institutions could emerge to overcome informational asymmetries. Credit banks, for example, could acquire decision-making powers in the management of borrower enterprises, or credits could be linked to certain turnover minima of current account balances held by borrowers with the lending banks. By such means, borrowers could offer credible commitments to honour their debt obligations and an adequate flow of credit could be maintained. In addition, banks could organize secondary markets for trading securitized forms of their customers' debt, i.e., forge direct links between bank credit and capital market transactions. Such directness meant lower information costs than would have characterized 'external' capital markets and, given the credible commitments bank debtors offered, lower perceived risk for the ultimate investors.

There is a catch here, to be sure. The institutional mechanisms just described represented bank power *vis-à-vis* their customers. That means that the 'social savings' associated with such informational intermediation – the result of a better allocation of savings across available investment opportunities than would otherwise prevail – could be largely appropriated by the banks themselves. Nevertheless, the ultimate investors could still end up with a better return per unit of risk than would have been obtained in a competitive financial market with asymmetric information.[1] This is an empirical issue worth coming back to.

The institutional mechanisms just described are precisely the mechanisms developed by the 'mixed' or 'universal' banks in nineteenth-century Europe. Indeed, viewing my country sample from a late-twentieth-century, Anglo-American perspective, I find the institutional predominance of universal banking to be one of its main unifying characteristics. The foregoing argument suggests that there are good economic reasons for such institutions. Nevertheless, history was and is important; and it is part of my central paradigm. In this connection I draw on Alexander Gerschenkron's well-known typology of industrialization. According to Gerschenkron late industrializers faced significantly larger capital demands relative to savings than had the pioneer country, Great Britain, and they found the latter's relatively atomized and decentralized credit and capital markets inadequate. They innovated, in a sense, organizational substitutes for those markets, e.g. on the Continent the 'universal' banks, or in more extreme cases (such as Tsarist Russia), state institutions (Gerschenkron, 1962). In general, this development was marked by the emergence of larger decision units, or as some scholars have pointed out, by hierarchies increasingly substituting for markets (Daems, 1975). The key features of this historical paradigm would seem to be relative capital shortage and a stress on large-scale enterprise. However, other historical influences may also be at work here, for example, the inertia of past institutions, regulations affecting bank operations having no clear link to backwardness or capital shortage.[2] They also deserve consideration.

A sample of banking history I: the rise of universal banking

It may be useful to point out that this sample does not build on the individual bank and banker biographies alone, but also on those studies which purport to treat commercial banks as a system or sector of the economy. Such studies, I believe, must be an integral part of any attempt to reconstruct the history of European banking. The story of special interest here begins to the 1830s in the small, new country of Belgium. It centres on the pioneering development of 'mixed' (later 'universal') banks in that country, initially through the expansion of the Dutch creation, the Algemeene Nederlandsche Maatschappij ter begunstiging van de Volksvlijt founded in 1822, into the Belgian Société Générale. This institution, along with a similarly constructed rival, the Banque de Belgique, may be seen as a response to imperfections in the then existing Belgian capital market, imperfections related to the capital-intensive character of Belgian growth sectors as this time (coal mining, iron and steel, and transportation) and to the reluctance of Belgian wealthholders to invest in those industries directly. Initially, interestingly, these institutions were truly 'mixed' banks, combining note issue and investment banking activities. Difficulties experienced in the crises of 1838 and 1848, however, forced them to abandon the note-issuing business. In the

1830s and 1840s, moreover, the Belgian 'industrial' or 'mixed' banks had already launched a new institution, the investment trust or holding company (1835: Société de Commerce de Bruxelles; and Société Nationale pour les Entreprises industrielles et commerciales) (Cameron, 1967, 135), to stimulate, as it were, indirect public investment in Belgian industrial companies. By the 1860s and 1870s, the Belgian mixed banks, despite these creations, had themselves become very largely holding companies, with well over half of the Société Générale's entire portfolio consisting of industrial securities (Cameron, 1967, 147; also Daems, 1975, 38–9). The banking business, at least before 1870, was subsidiary to the holding function.

This period in banking history offers support for the Gerschenkronian typology. It also contains some useful concrete lessons for the conference's topic. Exemplary is the careful attention bestowed on the relationship between bank loans to industrial enterprise and long-term participation in the latter, above all the good documentation of the initially unintended character of the Société Générale's cultivation of investment banking (Van der Wee and Goossens, 1991, drawing on Durviaux, 1947 and De Troyer, 1974).[3] The discussion of liquidity problems and of the subsequent abandonment of note issue by the mixed banks is also laudable. I also found the rise of the holding company instructive, though puzzling. Could it have something to do with the behaviour of the National Bank of Belgium? Or does it reflect the peculiar financial needs and resources of Belgium's non-financial enterprises? Could the interesting demise of the Banque de Belgique shed light on such questions?

I have little to say on Dutch banking history. Projects for mixed banks, modelled on the French Crédit Mobilier, appeared in the 1850s, were turned down, reappeared in the 1860s and led then to the founding of four new banks (Cameron, 1961, 163–4 and Hirschfeld, 1923). They do not appear to have had great impact on the domestic economy, however, and it has been argued that true universal banking only became characteristic of Dutch commercial banks after the Second World War (Baasch, 1927, vol. II, 559–68; Siemers, 1981, 20–21). One of the reasons for their tardy development in Holland may have been the relative abundance of capital there – a suggestion which offers negative support of the Gerschenkron interpretation. However, the positive early role of foreign capital in Dutch railroads casts some doubt on this hypothesis (Baasch, 1927, 510–11).

Luxemburg may also deserve more attention than I can give. Unfortunately, my biased stock of knowledge can support no more than one observation. Luxemburg appears to have served as a base for German operations in the 1850s, one which was free of onerous German restrictions. In 1856 the Banque International à Luxembourg represented the response of Prussian bankers to Prussian (and other German state) restrictions on banks of issue – a response aimed at satisfying demands in the Prussian and other German money markets (Cameron, 1961; Tilly, 1966, 42).[4] A little more than a hundred years later the move to Luxemburg by German banks followed analogous motives, though they were more clearly international in scope than their nineteenth-century predecessor (Tilly, 1991).

'Mixed' or 'universal' banking attained its purest form in nineteenth-century Germany. As with Belgian investment banks, German 'mixed' banks were a response to capital market imperfections and began to grow in the 1830s and 1840s in association with the development of the railroads and the heavy industrial complex spawned by railroad building, i.e. in response to the growth of relatively capital-intensive sectors. As early as the 1830s and 1840s one finds private bankers linked to the enterprises they had founded through the use of proxy shareholder voting rights, through holding directorships in these companies, as well as through close monitoring of their current account payment flows. If long-term refunding of current account debt was deemed necessary, the banks organized the required capital market transactions themselves. In a sense, therefore, 'mixed' (or industrial) banking was pioneered by private bankers before joint-stock banks appeared upon the scene. The limits of their own resources (and difficulties experienced in organizing collective cooperative organizations) encouraged private banking firms to organize joint-stock banks with limited liability. By the 1850s a number of these institutions were in place, and they gradually became independent of the private bankers who had founded them. Indeed, by the 1870s, they began competing the latter out of existence (Pohl, 1982). Nevertheless, they followed the same 'mixed' banking programme.

But more than relative capital scarcity was at work here. Political history played a significant role. In most German states and in Prussia, by far the most important state, the issue of bank notes was recognized as a kind of money creation having a 'public good' character and one offering the possibility of seigniorage gains. Moreover, the movement toward economic integration among the several German states (the Zollverein) called for monetary regulation and relatively stringent state control over note issue (Holtfrerich, 1989). The historical result was a division of labour which left most pure payments and short-term trade credit business of the economy to the government bank of issue and most of the industrial credit and also the security issue business to the private bankers and their protégés, the corporate 'mixed' banks. In addition, the latter found themselves increasingly able to turn to the former for payments services, cash, and for short-term discount credits when the need arose.

This encouraged the latter to concentrate more heavily on the relatively risky, illiquid industrial business than they would have done had their liabilities been dominated by 'quick claims' such as bank notes redeemable at sight (instead of the deposits of wealthy rentiers or large industrial customers whose payment habits were more predictable). This separation of note issue and industrial banking, so pronounced in the German case, became generally characteristic of most continental countries.

A general point on this literature is worth stressing here. It emphasizes the potential importance of the relationship between the state's central banking policy, on the one hand, and commercial banks' liquidity and portfolio strategies, on the other. This raises a number of interesting questions, one of which concerns the extent to which money creation by commercial banks was complementary to, or a substitute for, the supply of government or central bank money. Another concerns the security portfolio intermediated by the banks. Was it riskier than that held by all German investors? How risky was it for the banks themselves? Dealing with such questions, however, would be greatly facilitated if one were able to establish the social and economic identity of banks' owners, creditors and debtors. Despite a good deal of research, there is not much precise information on this critical variable of bank behaviour.

Historians seem to agree that through most of the nineteenth century, Switzerland enjoyed a relative abundance of capital (Cassis and Tanner, 1992; Mottet, 1987). Nevertheless, the spread of 'mixed' banking institutions under French Crédit Mobilier influence in the 1850s affected Switzerland too.[5] Perhaps this was because existing institutions had initially neglected the new needs of railroad building and the possibilities of the joint-stock company business form (Cameron, 1961, 161-2; Ritzmann, 1973, 58 ff; Mottet, 1987, 77-8 and 211-15). One of the most significant results of this movement, at least in the long-run perspective, was the founding of the Schweizerische Credit-Anstalt (Crédit Suisse) – interestingly enough with substantial help from a group of German bankers (Wehrli in Mottet, 1987; Cameron, 1961, 161-2; Jöhr, 1956)! Like their counterparts in Germany and Belgium, these banks became active agents in the growth of large-scale enterprise in transportation and industry, and developed close connections with these enterprises. There are many success stories, well documented (see, e.g. Jöhr, 1956; Cassis and Tanner, 1992). Unlike mixed banks in those countries, however, their development initially did not benefit from a strong central bank of issue which could provide them with efficient payments services and emergency credit support. In fact, Swiss currency conditions were so unstable until the early twentieth century, that one must register surprise that the Swiss banks performed so well; and one really needs to know how the commercial banks managed their payments business (Ritzmann, 1973, esp. 89–102; and Blaum, 1908). This is an intriguing aspect of Swiss banking history which deserves more attention.

One last general remark on Crédit Mobilier banking is in order. These Crédit Mobilier banks were never purely 'industrial' banks, for the bulk of their business was in railway finance, and a good deal in government funds as well. Moreover, so far as they were long-run successes, they practised considerable diversification across sectors of the economy as well as across industries. This was true of Germany, where more exclusively industrial banks such as the Schaaffhausen'sche Bankverein (West German heavy industry) fell behind and more highly diversified institutions like the Deutsche Bank forged ahead. It was true of other countries also, e.g. Switzerland, where the more successful 'mixed' banks were those which followed a policy of diversification involving the financing of domestic and international trade, foreign portfolio investment, government bonds as well as domestic industry (Ritzmann, 1973, 49–88). In a sense, therefore, 'industrial' banks is more apt as a description of one important part of the business of the continental commercial banks than as a synonym for the latter. In the long run, very few purely industrial banks survived.

A sample of banking history II: universal banking since the 1870s

In this section the historical focus shifts away from the development of universal banking in the context of industrialization and economic backwardness to universal banks as going concerns, as a problem of concentration of economic power and industrial control, as vehicles of international financial flows, and as contributors to aggregate economic growth and stability. This also means, in effect, a temporal shift toward the period covering the last one hundred years or so. The presentation here also changes slightly, proceeding collectively, instead of country by country.

In most of our countries in the period observed commercial banks underwent marked   concentration, though the pace was uneven and varied from country to country. Were we to limit our attention to the large, mixed banks in Belgium, for example, we could find the Société Générale at the zenith of its power in the early 1880s, and concentration in the sense of monopoly power declining, accompanied by the growing weight of deposits and related banking business relative to the holding function (Van der Wee and Goossens, 1991; Kurgan-van Hentenryk, 1992). In Germany, similar tendencies were observable, but their timing was more strongly affected by the First World War and especially the great inflation which followed it (Born, 1983, 54).

Concentration in the sense of market shares is not identical with degree of competition, to be sure, and one can well agree with contemporary bankers' contentions – e.g. as argued by Jacob Riesser in the early 1900s – that competition among the few could be intense competition indeed (Riesser, 1910). Nevertheless, closely documenting and measuring this process of concentration has been and remains an important task for banking history. It means examining the micro- and macroeconomic conditions which led to mergers or takeovers of individual banks. Was it the negative threat of rising costs and falling profits which was decisive? Answering this question, in turn, means, among other things, identifying and unravelling the ownership and market-sharing connections between ostensibly independent banking firms. It also implies discussion of the important comparative question of why some banks survive and prosper while others stagnate and disappear. Important work has been done in this area; but there is still more to do (Pohl, 1982; Feldman, 1992; Kurgan-van Hentenryk, 1992; Cassis and Tanner, 1992).

Similar arguments apply to the question of banks' links with non-bank enterprises, especially industrial ones. An important issue frequently raised in discussions of the 'universal' banks concerns their monopoly power and the degree of competition characteristic of industrial finance. It has been alleged, particularly in the German case, that banks exercised considerable power over their industrial clients. Indeed, according to Rudolf Hilferding, the very organizational structure of Germany's leading industries (around 1900) reflected bank power, and it was the German industry which formed the basis of his theory of 'finance capital' (Hilferding, 1910). Hilferding's idea was good, but his analysis, which he saw as a revision of Marxist doctrine, became encumbered in dialogue with the latter's value theory. In its modern variants, the argument sees banks first as possessors of more information about the relative productivities of an industry's firms than those firms themselves and, by virtue of discretionary power in writing loan contracts, of the ability to steer those industrial firms toward a profit-maximizing output for the industry as a whole; and second, as low-cost suppliers of diversification opportunities to holders of liquid funds (Cable, 1985; Pecchenino, 1988; Daems, 1975).

These remarks suggest the importance of research into control mechanisms, particularly into the alleged discretionary power of banks to write loan contracts which could effectively constrain their industrial customers. Research in the field has not produced much direct evidence of such contracts, but the empirical–historical evidence of financial control of industry is abundant, if controversial. That industrial banks of the Belgian, French or German type consciously and actively pursued the goal of controlling the railroads and industrial enterprises they financed is documented in hundreds of individual episodes (Cameron, 1961; Lévy-Leboyer, 1964; Landes, 1969; Tilly, 1966; März, 1968; Pohl, 1982; Kocka, 1978). German examples range from the steel rail cartel formed by West German steel companies in 1876 – on the insistence of creditor banks and against the wishes of important producers such as Krupp – to the reorganization of the electrical engineering firm, Siemens & Halske, in 1897 at the behest of the Deutsche Bank (Wengenroth, 1986; Kocka, 1969). Industry control by means of representation in the key decision-making organs of the companies concerned has been studied extensively, somewhat less so the related question of ownership and control of voting shares.

This is not the place for comprehensive survey, but two points of detail may be of interest, one related to Belgian and German evidence and one to the German case only. First, representation in German top management control organs has involved both bankers in industry and vice versa. However, the bulk of evidence suggests that bankers held more important positions in industry than industrialists did in banks; and this is true today (Jeidels, 1905; Riesser, 1910; Kocka, 1978; Pappi, Kappelhoff and Melbeck, 1987). The observation is of interest since a revisionist school of thought has long existed which downplays the power of the bankers with the help of the 'mutual power' argument. It has stressed the fact that (a) many prominent industrialists occupied positions on the supervisory boards of the larger banks and that (b) quite a number of case studies show harmony, rather than conflict between banks and industry as characteristic. For Belgium in the postwar period, the best evidence shows holding company directors occupying strategic positions in that country's corporate sector, rather than being controlled by directors of enterprises in other branches (Daems, 1975). Second, since the nineteenth century, German bankers have had easy access to the voting rights of shares held on deposit with them ('Depotstimmrecht'). This meant that bankers rarely had to devote a significant proportion of their own resources to mobilize the desired number of votes in important shareholders' meetings. Of course, the trust of their customers was not unrelated to the banks' past performance as intermediaries of desirable securities and this itself required large equity capitals. In recent decades this practice has been restricted, but it still exists.

In all the countries in the period observed internationalization of commercial banking operations proceeded apace. In part this resulted from banks expanding their international business as part of their own countries' growing foreign commerce, in part from cooperative agreements with banks of other countries and, finally, by means of the establishment of subsidiaries abroad. An important product (or accompaniment) of these developments was foreign investment. In all the sample countries foreign portfolio investment intermediated by commercial banks and private bankers expanded significantly in the 1870–1913 period. And in this period those same institutions also intermediated growing flows of short-term capital across national borders. Indeed, the integration of international capital markets in these years is one of the most striking financial achievements of the period;[6] and it is one which is still only poorly understood. How large, for example, were the short-term flows? How 'efficient' were banks' own portfolios (in the sense of observable gaps in yields or rates of return among alternative investment opportunities, e.g. between domestic and foreign securities)? How large were the write-offs on foreign loans? Banking history in the countries surveyed gives us some answers to these questions but more should be possible. It should be possible, for example, to discover how finely tuned commercial bankers were to arbitrage opportunities in the market for short- and long-term capital, to determine more clearly to what extent bank success depended upon correct assessment of relative interest and exchange rate movements.[7] It goes without saying, and there is no space for adequate treatment here, that the international character of commercial bank operations in the sample countries remains evident throughout the interwar and postwar periods, though in varying degrees and with a sign shifting first to negative and then becoming positive again after 1945.

A last perspective concerns the contribution of universal banks to economic growth and stability. Banking history in the narrow sense will not itself provide answers to such questions, but it is one of their conditions *sine qua non*. German banking history, to begin there, contains many well-known and instructive case studies which strongly suggest a positive growth contribution. Take the risky railroad finance intermediated by Cologne bankers in the 1830s and 1840s, for instance. In the absence of banker readiness to advance funds, one can conjecture that the Rhenish railway network would have come into profitable operation significantly later than it in fact did (Tilly, 1966). Then we have the classic cases taken from the history of the Deutsche Bank: its sustained and crucial support of the Mannesmann Company in the 1890s, its intervention in the reorganization of the Siemens & Halske firm in the same decade, its leading role in the creation of Germany's largest nineteenth-century foreign enterprise, the German Overseas Electricity Company (the Deutsche-Überseeische-Elektrizitäts-Gesellschaft) (Seidenzahl, 1970; but see also Wessel, 1990, esp. 70–80). Or to take another case, one can cite banker support – especially by Jakob Landau & Co. and the Nationalbank für Deutschland – of the early and critical years of the Emil Rathenau's Deutsche Edisongesellschaft, the forerunner of the great A.E.G. (Pinner, 1918, 92–9; and Fürstenberg, 1931, 169–82). Cartel formation offers another set of examples. It now seems certain that banks forced reluctant steel producers into the first steel rail cartel in the 1870s (Wengenroth, 1986). The weight of bank influence in the establishment of the Rhenish-Westphalian Coal Syndicate in 1893 or the renewal of the steel cartel in 1904 is unclear, but that they participated in the relevant decision-making processes is not (Wellhöner, 1989; Jeidels, 1905, etc.). In any case, such facts can be combined with empirical investigations of industrial performance and joined to comparisons with a hypothetical development path without cartels. These suggest a positive net contribution to economic growth (Webb, 1980; Wengenroth, 1986). A similar approach is to look at such samples of industrial enterprise development and combine them with accounts and indicators of banking influence as well as with consideration of non-financial influences upon enterprise performance. Such studies also suggest, though not unanimously, that the mixed banks did have net positive effects on the performance monitored (Feldenkirchen, 1985; Kennedy, 1976 and 1985; Tilly, 1991; and Wellhöner, 1989). And finally, the capital market performance of bank-intermediated security issues has been investigated in a comparative context. One result suggests that the bank-created portfolio of industrial sectors in the 1880–1913 period reflected relatively high growth rates and high risks, but was at the same time much more efficient in the sense of proximity to the economy's optimal yield–risk position (or 'frontier') than was the portfolio favoured by the British capital market in the same period (Kennedy, 1985; and Tilly, 1986). That is a measure of performance analogous to comparison between *ex post* results and hypothetical alternatives.[8]

For obvious reasons, German banking history of the interwar period has produced fewer positive case studies, though the history of non-bank enterprise does point to a few (Chandler, 1990, 515–16). The postwar period offers a contrast of overall success, but such an abundance of explanatory hypotheses that commercial banks have not received much attention. Here one might cite the role of commercial banks in allocating Marshall Plan counterpart funds as funnelled through the Kreditanstalt für Wiederaufbau, or the example of the reorganization of the West German steel industry in 1962–63 as suggestive of success stories, and an important econometric study covering a somewhat later period (1968–72) identifies universal banking control mechanisms (labelled 'internal capital market') as positive factors. Once again, however, such suggestions have not yet been incorporated in micro-studies of the commercial banks.

Monetary stability is a 'public good' which has more to do with central banking than with commercial banks. Nevertheless, the latter are and have been an important part of the stability story. Indeed, in a sense, they are and have been intermediaries between central banks and non-bank enterprises, and have thus been viewed as 'transmission belts' for monetary (and central bank) policy. Nineteenth-century banking history in the broad sense offers some interesting, though conflicting, possibilities. On the one hand, if we look at German business cycle history (as constructed, for example, by Spree), we find that almost every upper turning point coincides with a more than negligible financial crisis reflecting rapid expansion and contraction of commercial bank credit (Spree, 1977; see also Kindleberger, 1978). On the other hand, a comparative study of German monetary history for the 1880–1913 period reveals extraordinary stability (McGouldrick, 1984). Looking at our sample countries, it is arguable that the close ties between universal-type commercial banks and their non-bank customers, perhaps also the degree of diversification realized through the growth of a broadly based network of branches, could have helped to contribute to this result. These, however, are largely speculations which have not yet been confronted with banking history in the narrow sense.

The financial crisis of the 1930s, in contrast, has benefited from such confrontation. For Germany, the case has been made that the crisis was in part endogenous, produced by an intensive, indeed hyper-intensive competitive scramble for business among the commercial banks in the 1920s (Born, 1968 and 1983; James, 1985). This is likely to have been true of other countries as well, e.g. Belgium, and especially Switzerland,[9] though special conditions undoubtedly played an important role in Germany, e.g. the capital-weakening of the banks which resulted from inflation and its aftermath. In this connection it is interesting to note that Dutch commercial banks reportedly escaped severe crisis in the early 1930s, a fact which has been attributed to the absence of industrial-type universal banking there (Siemers, 1981). This need not contradict the observation that 'true' universal banks performed better than more specialized ones (White, 1986). In any case, careful work on the credit policy of the individual banks is largely missing and would be most welcome, if only to help us see beyond the conventional view that keeping a bank liquid and solvent in a crisis situation is more than a matter of proper preventive caution and sound judgement (Seidenzahl, 1970).

Summary and conclusions

This survey of country experience, which draws on both individual and collective histories of commercial bank operations, may be summed up in the following observations:

1.   The available literature clearly documents the origination and early

development of 'mixed' or universal banks. It provides a good picture of the motivation behind their founding, some notion of the political resistance they faced and some plausible hypotheses concerning the determinants of their success.

2. Individual banking histories have provided much valuable information on the social background and personalities of the commercial bankers themselves. They have also done well in the task of describing key transactions such as mergers and large-scale financial projects, accompanied by related contemporary judgements on their riskiness and profitability. It is true, to be sure, that these studies are marked by an obvious, if unfortunate, bias toward ultimately successful projects.[10]

3. This literature on banking history in the narrow and the broader sense has also produced a clear picture of the long-run quantitative development of both individual banks and of the commercial banking sector as a whole. Such data – which generally include total assets as well as a structural breakdown for both sides of the balance sheet – have permitted assessment of a number of significant aspects of banking history, e.g. the importance of mergers and takeover or long-run enterprise growth. This positive judgement, however, does not extend to the matter of bank profitability. Shifts and differences in standards of financial reporting, across time and countries, make reasonable *ex post* assessment difficult. One possibility which could be pushed further is (for publicly quoted companies) the estimation of rates of return based on dividends and stock market prices. But inside data remain indispensable here, to the extent they can be made available.[11]

4. Some persistent deficits must also be mentioned. The banking history literature has given us no more than a very incomplete picture of inside, or 'micro' operations, of banks. We need more information concerning the socio-economic composition of banks' owners and shareholders, their creditors and their debtors, our need ascending in the order given. We also have only a rough notion of the development of bank lending. Not only do we need to distinguish between new lending and net changes in loans outstanding, but we need more information on how loan contracts developed over time, how they may have varied cyclically, how automatic their renewal was, to what extent they reflected quantity as opposed to price rationing, in what degree they reflected longevity and continuity of bank–customer relationships, to what extent they required minimum deposits maintained with the lender, etc. Such matters lie at the concrete centre of banking operations and represent the means by which past banking operations and performance can be made

replicable for the present. Is it too much to hope for significant improvement in the source basis of the banking history of the countries surveyed here? One hopes not.

Notes

1. For a largely theoretical discussion of these matters, see Stiglitz (1985).
2. Such influences obviously accentuated national differences in banking systems – a point stressed by Rondo Cameron in his many publications. See, for example, Cameron (1967), Introduction, and Cameron (1972), Introduction.
3. One would like to know more about the character of the Société Générale's portfolio, its 'efficiency' in the sense of yield–risk mixture compared with Belgian investors as a whole. Is a study of the kind Daems (1975) offered for the postwar Belgian economy feasible for the earlier periods?
4. The Banque International's original plans called for the issue of notes in several currencies, Prussian taler, francs, Dutch gulden, etc. The note-issuing side, however, had but short-lived success. Nevertheless, the Banque International is alleged to have played a significantly positive role in financing Luxemburg's industrial development (see Hansen, 1906, 661–3).
5. In all of the countries surveyed here one notes the simultaneous presence of considerable foreign portfolio investment and the exploitation of domestic investment opportunities by foreign capital. That is capital exports and capital imports, or to put it differently, capital surplus and capital shortage. In any case, I readily acknowledge that 'capital shortage' is a problematical concept.
6. For a summary of some recent work and further possibilities see Neal (1985); for Germany's part in this see Tilly (1991b). I also have a conference paper offering further documentation of the point: Tilly (1992).
7. Paul Wallich's recollections of Berlin banker participation in the short-term market in the early 1900s are most interesting and provoke curiosity as to available archival documentation for the relationships. See Wallich (1978, esp. 404–16).
8. The empirical experiment mentioned in the text utilized sectoral rates of growth as returns, but the same thing could be done with financial rates of return. An investigation of the individual bank portfolios, despite obvious source problems, might be useful.
9. For an excellent study of Swiss bank difficulties in the crisis of the 1930s illustrating points in the text see Scheuss (1960). In Switzerland, in contrast to Germany, the problem lay in foreign loans which went bad.
10. A welcome exception to this rule is to be found in the recent Festschrift for the Cologne private bank, Sal. Oppenheim Jr & Cie, where the awful consequences of financing an expensive innovation which failed – embodied in the 'International Compressed Air and Electricity Company' founded in 1890 – are clearly discussed Stürmer, Teichmann and Treue (1989, 296–303).
11. In this connection it may be in order to make a plea for the mobilization of more data on the profitability of individual sets of transactions, e.g. new issues of securities and syndicate operations. Such data would be most welcome as a means of reconstructing bank capital market performance.

References

Akerlof, G. (1970), 'The Market for Lemons. Quality Uncertainty and the Market Mechanism', *Quarterly Journal of Economics* (84), pp. 448–500.

Baasch, E. (1927), *Holländische Wirtschaftsgeschichte*, 2 vols, Jena.

Blaum, K. (1908), 'Das Geldwesen der Schweiz seit 1798', in *Abhandlungen aus dem staatswissenschaftlichen Seminar zu Strassburg i. E.*, XXIV, Strasburg.

Born, K.-E. (1968), *Die deutsche Bankenkrise*, München.

Born, K.-E. (1983), 'Vom Beginn des Ersten Weltkrieges bis zum Ende der Weimarer Republik (1914–1933)', in Institut für bankhistorische Forschung (ed.), *Deutsche Bankengeschichte*, III, Frankfurt am Main.

Cable, J. (1985), 'Capital Market Information and Industrial Performance: the Role of West German Banks', *Economic Journal* (95), pp. 118–32.

Cameron, R. (1961), *France and the Economic Development of Europe*, Princeton, Princeton University Press,.

Cameron, R. (1967), *Banking in the Early Stages of Industrialization*, New York and London, Oxford University Press.

Cameron, R. (1972), *Banking and Economic Development: Some Lessons of History*, New York, Oxford University Press.

Cassis, Y. and Tanner, J. (1992), 'Finance and Financiers in Switzerland, 1880–1960', in Cassis, Y. (ed.), *Finance and Financiers in European History 1880–1960*, Cambridge and New York, Cambridge University Press, pp. 293–316.

Chandler, A. (1990), *Scale and Scope. The Dynamics of Industrial Capitalism*, Cambridge, Mass.

Daems, H. (1975), *The Holding Company. Essays on Financial Intermediation. Concentration and Capital Market Imperfections in the Belgian Economy*, Leuven, Catholic University of Leuven, Faculty of Economics, no. 16.

Feldenkirchen, W. (1985), 'Zur Finanzierung von Großunternehmen in der chemischen und elektrotechnischen Industrie Deutschlands vor dem Ersten Weltkrieg', in Tilly, R. (ed.), *Beiträge zur quantitativen Unternehmensgeschichte*, Stuttgart.

Feldman, G. (1992), 'Banks and Banking in Germany after the First World War: Strategies of Defence', in Cassis, Y. (ed.), *Finance and Financiers in European History 1880–1960*, Cambridge, Cambridge University Press, pp. 243–62.

Fürstenberg, H. (1931), *Carl Fürstenberg. Die Lebensgeschichte eines deutschen Bankiers 1870–1914*, Berlin, Ullstein.

Gerschenkron, A. (1962), title essay of: *Economic Backwardness in Historical Perspective*, Cambridge, Mass., Harvard.

Greenwald, B. and Stiglitz, J. (1992), 'Information, Finance, and Markets. The Architecture of Allocative Mechanisms', in *Industrial and Corporate Change* (1), pp. 37–63.

Hansen, Josef (1906), *Gustav von Mevissen. Ein rheinisches Lebensbild*, 2 vols, Berlin.

Hilferding, R. (1910), *Das Finanzkapital*, Vienna, Brand.

Hirschfeld, H.M. (1923), 'Der Credit-Mobilier-Gedanke mit besonderer Berücksichtigung seines Einflusses in den Niederlanden', in *Zeitschrift für Volkswirtschaft und Politik*, III, pp. 438–65.

Holtfrerich, C.-L. (1989), 'The Monetary Unification Process in 19th Century Germany: relevance and lessons for Europe today', in De Cecco, M. and Giovannini, A. (eds), *A European Central Bank? Perspectives on monetary unification after 10 years of EMS*, Cambridge.

James, H. (1985), 'The Causes of the German Banking Crisis of 1931', in *Econ. Hist. Rev.*, 2 series, bd. 37, no. 1.

Jeidels, O. (1905), *Das Verhältnis der deutschen Großbanken zur Industrie, mit bes. Berücksichtigung der Eisenindustrie*, Leipzig.

Jöhr, W. (1956), *Schweizerische Kreditanstalt 1856–1956. Hundert Jahre im Dienste der schweizerischen Volkswirtschaft*, Schweizerische Kreditanstalt, Zürich.

Kennedy, W.P. (1976), 'Institutional Response to Economic Growth: Capital Markets in Britain to 1914', in Hannah, L. (ed.), *Management Strategy and Business Development*, London, Macmillan.

Kennedy, W.P. and Britton, R. (1985), 'Portfolioverhalten und wirtschaftliche Entwicklung im späten 19. Jahrhundert. Ein Vergleich zwischen Großbritannien und Deutschland. Hypothesen und Spekulationen', in Tilly, R. (ed.), *Beiträge zur quantitativen vergleichenden Unternehmensgeschichte*, Stuttgart.

Kindleberger, C. (1978), *Manias, Panics and Crashes. A History of Financial Crises*, New York, Basic.

Kocka, J. (1969), Unternehmensverwaltung und Angestelltenschaft, Stuttgart.

Kocka, J. (1978), 'Entrepreneurs and Managers in German Industrialization', in Mathias, P. and Postan, M.M. (eds), *Cambridge Economic History of Europe*, vol. 7, Cambridge, England.

Kurgan-van Hentenryk, G. (1992), 'Finance and Financiers in Belgium 1880–1940', in Cassis, Y. (ed.), *Finance and Financiers in European History 1880–1940*, Cambridge, Cambridge University Press, pp. 317–35.

Landes, D. (1969), *The Unbound Prometheus*, Cambridge, Mass., Cambridge University Press.

Lévy-Leboyer, M. (1964), *Les Banques Européennes et L'industrialisation internationale dans la première moitié du XIXe siècle*, Paris, Presses Universitaires de France.

März, E. (1968), *Österreichische Industrie- und Bankpolitik in der Zeit Franz-Josephs*, Frankfurt and Zürich.

McGouldrick, P. (1984), 'Operations of the German Central Bank and the Rules of the Game, 1876–1913', in Bordo, M. and Schwartz, A. (eds), *A Retrospective View on the Classical Gold Standard, 1821–1931*, Chicago.

Mottet, L. (ed.) (1987), 'Geschichte der Schweizer Banken. Bankier-Persönlichkeiten aus fünf Jahrhunderten', *Neue Zürcher Zeitung*, Zürich.

Neal, L. (1985), 'Integration of International Capital Markets: Quantitative Evidence from the Eighteenth to Twentieth Centuries', in *Journal of Economic History* (45), pp. 219–26.

Pappi, U., Kappelhoff, P. and Melbeck, C. (1987), 'Die Struktur der Unternehmensverflechtung in der Bundesrepublik', *Kölner Zeitschrift für Soziologie und Sozialpsychologie* (39), pp. 693–717.

Pecchenino, R. (1988), 'The Loan Contract: Mechanism of Financial Control', *Economic Journal* (98), pp. 126–37.

Pinner, F. (1918), *Emil Rathenau und das elektrische Zeitalter*, Leipzig.

Pohl, M. (1982), *Konzentration im deutschen Bankwesen, 1848–1980*, Frankfurt am Main, Fritz Knapp.

Riesser, J. (1910), *Die deutschen Großbanken und ihre Konzentration*, Jena, Gustav Fischer.

Ritzmann, F. (1973), *Die Schweizer Banken. Geschichte – Theorie – Statistik*, Bern and Stuttgart, Paul Haupt.

Scheuss, W. (1960), *Der Zusammenbruch und die Liquidation der schweizerischen Diskontbank*, Winterthur.

Seidenzahl, F, (1970), *Hundert Jahre Deutsche Bank, 1870–1970*, Frankfurt am Main.

Siemers, M. (1981), *Struktur des Bankwesens in den Niederlanden*, Frankfurt am Main.

Spree, R. (1977), *Die Wachstumszyklen der deutschen Wirtschaft, 1840–1880*, Berlin.

Stiglitz, J. (1985), 'Credit Markets and the Control of Capital', *Journal of Money, Credit and Banking* (17), pp. 133–52.

Stürmer, M., Teichmann, G. and Treue, W. (1989), *Wagen und Wägen. Sal. Oppenheim jr. & Cie. Geschichte einer Bank und einer Familie*, München and Zürich, Piper.

Tilly, R. (1966), *Financial Institutions and Industrialization in the Rhineland, 1815–1870*, Madison, University of Wisconsin Press.

Tilly, R. (1986), 'German Banking 1850–1914: Development Assistance to the Strong', *Journal of European Economic History* (15), pp. 113–52.

Tilly, R. (1991a), 'Geschäftsbanken und Wirtschaft in Westdeutschland seit dem zweiten Weltkrieg', unpublished conference paper, Dortmund.

Tilly, R. (1991b), 'International Aspects of the Development of German Banking', in Cameron, R. and Bovykin, V.I. (eds), *International Banking, 1870–1914*, Oxford University Press.

Tilly, R. (1992), 'German Banks and Foreign Investment in Eastern and Central Europe Before 1939', unpublished conference paper, Minneapolis.

Van der Wee, H. and Goossens, M. (1991), 'Belgium', in Cameron, R. and Bovykin, V.I. (eds), *International Banking 1870–1914*, New York and Oxford, Oxford University Press.

Wallich, H. and P. (1978), *Zwei Generationen im deutschen Bankwesen, 1833–1914*, Frankfurt am Main, Fritz Knapp.

Webb, S. (1980), 'Tariffs, Cartels, Technology and Growth in the German Steel Industry, 1879 to 1914', *Journal of Economic History* (40), pp. 309–29.

Wellhöner, U. (1989), *Großbanken und Großindustrie im Kaiserreich*, Göttingen.

Wengenroth, U. (1986), *Unternehmensstrategien und technischer Fortschritt. Die deutsche und britische Stahlindustrie 1865–1895*, Göttingen and Zürich, Vandenhoeck & Ruprecht.

Wessel, H.A. (1990), *Kontinuität im Wandel. 100 Jahre Mannesmann 1890–1990*, Düsseldorf, Mannesmann.

White, E. (1986), 'Before the Glass-Steagall Act: An Analysis of the Investment Banking Activities of National Banks', in *Explorations in Economic History* (23), pp. 33–55.

CHAPTER TWELVE

How to Write the History of a Commercial Bank

Josefine Stevens

The question of how to write something of this nature presupposes that the question why it should be written has already been satisfactorily answered. For a profit-oriented organization, the standard viewpoint of the point or usefulness of history is not just theoretical, but also a practical one of expense. I should therefore like to start by looking at the history of Commerzbank and at the significance which a leading bank, and Commerzbank in particular, attaches to its history. I shall then discuss source material and finally the criteria governing what is to be included in the history of a commercial bank.

History of Commerzbank

Commerzbank was founded in 1870, that is to say during the second major period in which joint-stock banks were established in Germany. The name chosen, Commerz- und Disconto-Bank in Hamburg, indicated the main objectives of the bank, which were to provide a new source of funds to the Hamburg business sector and to facilitate trade. During its early years, Commerz- und Disconto-Bank was also involved in placing Hamburg, Prussian and German government bonds. From the very beginning, Commerzbank regarded itself as a universal bank, and was active in setting up new business enterprises. Close ties were established with the shipping industry and the young electricity sector.

The bank was very internationally oriented, as could be expected in view of Hamburg's significance in the world of trade. Commerz- und Disconto-Bank was one of the founders in 1872 of the London and Hanseatic Bank, London, with a 50 per cent holding in it. And close contacts were established with banks in northern Europe, Russia and Austria.

The bank had branches in Berlin and Frankfurt as of 1897, and its head office moved to the capital city in 1905. The next expansionary phase began towards the end of the First World War. The merger in 1920 with the Mitteldeutsche Privat-Bank, a regional bank whose activities were concentrated in Saxony-Anhalt, Saxony and Thuringia, was an important development. Business activities in Hesse and Thuringia were intensified when the bank joined forces in 1929 with the Mitteldeutsche Creditbank. The 1931 banking crisis led the German government to decree in 1932 that Commerz- und Privat-Bank, as it was now called, merge with Barmer Bank-Verein Hinsborg, Fischer & Comp., a leading regional bank in western Germany.

Prior to 1945, Commerzbank, like other big banks, was involved in mergers and acquisitions with small and medium-sized banks, at the same time establishing numerous branches (there were 169 in 1910, 392 in 1930 and 359 in 1940). Similar developments have taken place at German big banks in the postwar period.

Like the others, Commerzbank has stepped up its private customer business since the late 1950s; the 1960s saw a move towards the inter-nationalization of banking activities via the acquisition of holdings, setting up subsidiaries and opening branches abroad. It was during this decade that Commerzbank went from being just a joint-stock company to becoming the parent bank of a group; this meanwhile covers not only banking but also home loans, real-estate, insurance, business consultancy and information services. So much for the bank's own history.

One good reason for a company to establish its own archives and to publish historical literature is the benefit in terms of public relations. The bank's history of over 120 years, from its foundation on a local basis in Hamburg to a worldwide group organization, is a powerful factor in promoting its image and in customer acquisition. The long existence of a company, in the face of competition and crises, can boost the confidence of shareholders, customers and the public in it, an aspect which is of particular importance in the credit field. This longevity is also good publicity.

A topical example is the unification of the two German states. When opening new branches in eastern Germany, Commerzbank has been able to remind the public of its significance in the region prior to 1945. An additional function of historical publications is to meet the growing demand on the part of the public for greater transparency, without, of course, exposing material of a confidential nature. This informative role is vital in a free market economy. In addition to furthering public re-lations, an archive also has a contribution to make to scientific research; a bank can either provide access to its records, or compile its own studies.

The internal corporate identity of a company is also an aspect to be considered within a historical framework. Many members of staff are very interested in the history of 'their' bank, or have their interest awak-ened by publications or exhibitions. In both instances, historical archives can help personnel to identify with the company for which they work.

In recent years, there has been some discussion of the extent to which archive staff in the economic sector should become involved in policy-making and decision-making. The large number of queries addressed to the Commerzbank archive staff on internal matters would seem to indicate that the historical link should not be overlooked in the process of decision-making.

Source material

The state of the documentation available is unfortunately very fragmented, as a result of losses during the Second World War and the immediate postwar years. A large number of files in the bank's Berlin headquarters were destroyed in air-raids in November 1943, and a number of files were also removed for safe-keeping elsewhere. As far as is known, neither these nor the documentation kept in Berlin have survived. Only the records of branches taken over after 1945 by the newly established state banks and provincial banks are now available in archives in eastern Germany.

Since 1945 there have been a number of publications on the bank's history, and many attempts have been made to obtain further documentary material. These activities were intensified in the early 1960s, with the approach of Commerzbank's hundredth anniversary in 1970. The core of the bank's archives consists of the collection started by the economics department in Düsseldorf. After the anniversary celebrations, there was just one member of staff responsible for the archives, on a part-time basis only. Not until 1988 was a permanent job for a historian created. The archives form part of the documentary services section of the bank's research and communication department in Frankfurt am Main.

Professor Tilly expressed the desire for a significant improvement in the source basis of banking history. I hope to have illustrated how limited this is in our own particular case, owing to both internal and external influences. We are taking steps, though, as you have heard, towards meeting Professor Tilly's expectations.

Past and future publications

So much on the background to historical writing at a commercial bank. Our actual topic is how to write such a history. Commerzbank's hundredth anniversary was commemorated by the publication of a work entitled '100 years Commerzbank'. It took the form of a chronological account, covering the foundation of the bank, the development of its equity capital and balance-sheet total, the branch network, the acquisition of other banks, changes in the supervisory board and the board of managing directors, and important new issues and innovations in banking business. This approach must be seen as the desire to reconstruct the history of Commerzbank as a whole, following the loss of its branches in central and eastern Germany after the war and the division of the bank under Allied authority into a number of smaller units which were only reunited in 1958.

In 1995, Commerzbank will be able to look back over 125 years' existence. We do not wish to repeat the 1970 publication, but are thinking of a complementary work concentrating on postwar developments and taking stock of our current position.

Professor Tilly also expressed regret that the role of the commercial banks in the postwar period is a sadly neglected topic. Our publication is intended to reflect Commerzbank's position as a global bank with an international outlook. Both internal and external authors will contribute chapters on the various structural, social and business dimensions of the bank. They will cover such topics as developments from decentralization to current group status, changes in personnel such as the increase in the number of female employees, technical progress in the workplace and a breakdown of the bank's shareholders. Activities such as corpo-rate customer and private customer services, international business, invest-ment banking and innovations in banking will of course also be examined.

In this connection, topics such as the role of a leading bank in the economy as a whole, its business policy within the framework of monetary and financial policy, public relations activities, bank advertis-ing and bank architecture will be dealt with. In this way, we hope to give the general public a clearer picture of the highly complex structure of a big bank.

CHAPTER THIRTEEN

Comment

Carl-Ludwig Holtfrerich

I find Richard Tilly's paper extremely helpful, because it pinpoints uncharted territory in banking history, mainly in Germany, but in its neighbouring countries as well. And it comes from an experienced expert, who started his life of academic prominence with a book on *Financial Institutions and Industrialization in the Rhineland, 1815–1870* (1966) and has kept on researching and publishing on banks and banking history ever since.

Tilly's view is well balanced. It presents theoretical issues at the outset and confronts these with empirical evidence on the emergence and further development of 'universal' banking, first during the early industrialization in the nineteenth century and second, from the 1870s well into the twentieth century.

The central paradigm relates institutional change, that is the emergence and development of universal banks, to informational problems and to Gerschenkron's thesis of economic backwardness of the five continental countries of Europe *vis-à-vis* Great Britain. With capital needs (and the riskiness of investment) relatively greater for latecomers in industrialization, great credit banks, collecting surplus funds nationwide to promote business enterprises by short-term and long-term lending as well as by the security business and direct participation, would seem to be a rational choice of answer to the problem. By diversification they could realize higher returns per unit of risk. And as information-processing agencies they would be better equipped to activate surplus funds, on the one hand, and locate investment opportunities, on the other, better than an anonymous capital market providing only for direct links between individual investors and investing businesses. Diversification and information processing would both be the basis for economies of scale (and scope). In addition, the control that universal banks acquired over business firms through direct participation and proxy shareholder voting rights would further improve the informational stock of the banks, reduce the risks of investment, and generate additional economies of scale.

Economies of scale are a bonanza that we would all like to have and exploit. Viewing the economy as a whole, it produces 'social savings', in Tilly's words, or productivity gains. Tilly correctly raises the important question: which group benefits from these gains within the economy? As to the economies of scale in banking he comes to the conclusion that these gains 'could be largely appropriated by the banks themselves'. Following Joseph Stiglitz (1985) he regards this as a positive contribution to economic development and maintains that 'the ultimate investor could still end up with a better return per unit of risk than would have obtained in a competitive financial market with asymmetric information'.

The issue of economies of scale raises an even more important question that Tilly has not elaborated on. How do economies of scale affect the functioning of competition among banks? Or how have they done so in the past? Once large credit banks have realized substantial economies of scale and have established themselves on the market, do outsiders still have a chance to enter the market and compete? If not, two issues arise. First, in static distributional terms, will an oligopolistic market structure with established universal banks be beneficial not only to the banks and investors, but also to the rest of the economy, especially when cartels, not only among banks, but among their industrial clients, are formed? And, second, in dynamic terms, if competition among banks should indeed have become a victim of economies of scale, what does this mean for the innovative capacity of the banking sector, on the one hand, and – via its controlling influence on industry – of the economy at large, on the other? In other words, will economic growth be slowed as a result of encrusted markets? Perhaps this has a bearing on Germany's relative stagnation in the interwar period, when concentration and cartellization reached new heights, especially in the banking sector as a result of Germany's great inflation.

One variable that could catch the dynamic aspect of competition and therefore deserves greater attention from banking historians is the interest-rate spread ('Zinsmarge') and its development over time. In my view, no other quantitative variable can measure the productivity effect of dynamic competition in banking on the rest of the economy as well as this one. When conventional measures of productivity development in banking, like output or turnover per employed person or per man/woman-hour show an improvement, but the interest-rate spread between the asset and liability side of the balance sheet does not narrow, the employees and owners of the banking sector alone appropriate the 'social savings' from productivity growth. The rest of the economy might then benefit indirectly from their increased purchasing power, but not from a lower price of financial intermediation, i.e. from innovation in banking that has reduced the costs of using financial intermediation as an input for production outside the banking sector. The latter effect, desirable from a macroeconomic (not from a banking-sector) perspective, can only be realized more or less, in as much as the invisible hand of competition in banking is allowed to play its role.

In sum, I plead for banking history with special regard for the development of competitive structures in the banking sector (and via the banking sector in the economy at large) and for the consequences of the expansion or restriction of competition.

I regard banks as core elements of capitalistic–industrial societies and developments based on private property and competitive market structures. Banks, it seems to me, have always been visible and forceful defenders of the institution of private property, but have not acquired a reputation for defending and preserving competitive market structures. The reasons for this should be closely scrutinized by banking historians.

CHAPTER FOURTEEN

Comment s'est Ecrite l'Histoire Internationale de la Générale de Banque?

Isabelle Wybo-Wehrli

Au cours de mon intervention, je voudrais tout d'abord vous décrire brièvement la genèse de la fonction d'historien à la Générale de Banque. Ensuite nous verrons comment, une fois la fonction créée, je me suis attelée à écrire l'histoire internationale de la Banque, les méthodes auxquelles j'ai recouru et les problèmes que j'ai rencontrés. Enfin, je voudrais vous livrer, en guise de conclusion, quelques réflexions personnelles sur les vicissitudes et la nécessité de la fonction historique dans nos institutions financières.

Si nous nous replaçons au tout début des années 80, nous constatons qu'il n'existait, à ce qui était à l'époque la Société Générale de Banque, aucune espèce de fonction historique. La préoccupation de connaître et de reconstituer le passé de l'institution n'était pas formellement éprouvée ni reconnue. Concrètement, cela signifiait qu'aucun service, qu'aucune personne n'avait pour mission d'écrire l'histoire de la Banque et que personne ne se sentait responsable de cette tâche. Bien plus, les moyens nécessaires pour mener à bien une telle tâche, aurait-on voulu la prendre en charge, faisaient largement défaut: en particulier, il n'existait pas de centralisation systématique ni, à fortiori, de gestion ordonnée – pour ne pas dire scientifique – des documents qui, par leur nature et leur importance, constituent naturellement les archives de base nécessaires au travail de l'historien.

C'est un peu fortuitement, à la suite d'une série de demandes ponctuelles qu'a pris corps progressivement la conscience du besoin d'affecter quelqu'un à l'histoire de l'institution. Le rédacteur en chef de notre revue d'entreprise, le *G-Magazine*, souhaitait publier une série d'articles sur le passé de plusieurs de nos bâtiments, situés précisément dans un quartier de Bruxelles chargé d'histoire. Ne sachant à qui s'adresser, il jeta son dévolu sur la cellule culturelle, responsable de l'organisation d'expositions de prestige. Comme je faisais partie à l'époque de cette cellule, je me vis confier le soin de rassembler la documentation nécessaire et d'écrire des articles souhaités. Ce fut un premier pas. Peu après, compte tenu de l'intérêt qu'avaient témoigné de nombreux cadres et membres du personnel pour ces enquêtes historiques, la rédaction du *G-Magazine* me demanda de m'atteler à la réalisation d'une histoire de la présence international de la Banque depuis l'époque de sa fondation. Il apparut cette fois clairement que le travail demandé dépassait le cadre d'une mission ponctuelle et spécifique et ce, à maints égards: ampleur des recherches à effectuer, diversité et dispersion des documents à consulter, réflexion sur la finalité d'une telle entreprise et sur la diffusion à donner à la publication. La portée de ce travail et sa vocation à intéresser un public externe autant qu'interne, firent que la fonction historique fut enfin jugée digne de recevoir une reconnaissance structurelle. Compte tenu de mes prestations antérieures, la fonction me fut attribuée.

La bonne compréhension de la suite du récit exige que je vous résume à présent en quelques mots l'histoire internationale de notre banque. L'expansion de son réseau est intimement liée au développement des industries belges à l'étranger; la création, en 1902, de la Banque Sino-Belge en constitue le véritable point de départ. A la suite de la révolte des Boxers, qui avaient assiégé les légations étrangères et endommagé la ligne de chemin de fer Pékin-Hankow construite par notre groupe, la Chine se vit contrainte de payer une indemnité de 450 millions de taels aux pays occidentaux; la Belgique en reçut huit. Payée sous forme d'annuités, cette indemnité fut l'occasion d'installer en Chine une banque belge. Celle-ci devint en 1913 la Banque Belge pour l'Etranger, en élargissant son champ d'action à l'Egypte, où les tramways du Caire ne sont qu'un exemple du dynamisme industriel belge en ces lieux; vers la même époque ou un peu plus tard, elle s'implanta également dans les Balkans, à Londres, à Paris, à New York, au Portugal et dans les pays qui avaient formé l'Empire austro-hongrois. Parallèlement, nous avions participé à la création en 1909 de la Banque du Congo Belge, destinée à appuyer le développement économique de notre colonie. Enfin, la Banque Brésilienne Italo-Belge, constituée en 1911 avec une banque italienne, trouva son origine directe dans l'opération de valorisation des cafés, entreprise par le Gouvernement brésilien; cette banque étendit bientôt ses activités à plusieurs autres pays de l'Amérique latine.

Ce long périple autour du monde – que j'ai intentionnellement fort résumé – se réduisait toutefois à peu de chose sur les étagères de nos archives historiques, ou plutôt de leur embryon. La disparition de quelques filiales au siège d'exploitation lointain, la fermeture parfois précipitée, pour des raisons politiques, de certaines de nos succursales ajoutaient à cela de grands vides.

Cette constatation, jointe aux impératifs que m'imposait l'éthique de ma fonction, me dictèrent un texte essentiellement neutre et factuel; il en résulta une histoire institutionnelle et strictement chronologique de nos multiples implantations à l'étranger, sans trop de pourquoi ni de comment, proche du style de nos anciens rapports annuels, qui furent d'ailleurs la source principale de mes recherches. Je profite ici de l'occasion pour lancer un appel aux rédacteurs de ces rapports dans les différentes institutions représentées et pour souligner l'importance de leur tâche aux yeux de l'histoire. Comme ces rapports annuels sont appelés à devenir une référence essentielle, qu'ils ne soient avares ni de précisions quant à la date exacte d'un événement, ni de justifications concernant les décisions prises. Ceci afin d'éviter le genre de phrase: 'C'est au cours de cet exercice que nous avons fait telle ou telle chose': l'exercice pouvant être, le cas échéant, à cheval sur deux années.

Très rapidement je fus confrontée à un autre problème – et pas des moindres – à savoir citer ou ne pas citer le nom des différents protagonistes qui, tout au long de notre expansion à l'étranger, avaient animé nos activités aux quatre coins du globe. J'avais pu constater, dans mes recherches, la présence dans la maison de véritables dynasties de dirigeants et de clients. L'idée de commettre un impair peut-être irréparable, en oubliant d'en nommer l'un ou l'autre, m'incita à ne citer que les personnages de notre société dont la stature historique était indiscutable . . . Je fus confortée dans cette décision à la suite des quelques interviews que j'avais sollicitées auprès de nos cadres de direction. Ces rencontres ne fournirent qu'un nombre réduit d'informations véritablement significatives; elles révélèrent en revanche quelques réactions de fierté, pour ne pas dire de vanité personnelle, qu'une longue carrière, loin du pouvoir central, pouvait sans doute expliquer.

Vu le foisonnement des succursales, sans compter la complexité de nos participations, il m'apparut par ailleurs indispensable de résumer chaque chapitre par un tableau synoptique, évitant ainsi au lecteur une gymnastique mentale fatigante. En plus de ces tableaux, des cartes géographiques facilitaient la visualisation de nos implantations.

Vous voudrez bien m'excuser, je l'espère, d'avoir évoqué uniquement mon expérience personnelle à la Générale de Banque, mais je pense que c'est ce type de témoignage d'une praticienne que vous attendiez. Je voudrais maintenant conclure en vous livrant quelques réflexions –oserais-je dire – philosophiques que m'a inspirées mon bref parcours. Elles me ramènent aux vicissitudes et à la nécessité de l'exercice de la fonction d'historien au sein d'une banque commerciale.

Les vicissitudes d'abord. En premier lieu, il faut bien constater que l'historien de banque souffre d'un certain manque de compréhension au coeur même de l'institution qu'il entend servir. Et cela est en quelque sorte normal, car il représente des valeurs culturelles, non-marchandes, dans un organisme à vocation marchande par excellence. Il se consacre au passé dans un milieu où tout est axé sur l'avenir. Il est un vecteur de réflexion et d'analyse là où la place d'honneur revient à l'action. Bref, les préoccupations de l'historien sont aux antipodes de celles du financier. Même si celui-ci reconnaît le rôle spécifique de l'historien, son utilité, sa valeur ajoutée – pour reprendre la terminologie économique – restent obscures de prime abord: c'est vrai d'ailleurs que l'histoire d'une banque n'a pas de valeur d'enseignement ou d'enracinement comme peut l'avoir l'histoire d'un pays ou d'une religion. La plupart des Belges peuvent citer le nom de leurs 5 rois, mais rares sont les employés d'une banque capable de citer le nom des 5 derniers présidents . . . Les impératifs, ou le prétexte, de la confidentialité sont une autre contrainte qui pèse parfois lourdement. Les considérations d'opportunité inspirées par la politique générale de l'institution peuvent aussi constituer un écueil redoutable. Enfin, sachons le reconnaître, la démarche historique se trouve un peu en porte-à-faux par rapport à l'esprit de ce temps; de ce temps où l'éphémère, voire l'évanescent, est bien plus à l'honneur que le durable; de ce temps où, pour vendre, la nouveauté est souvent un meilleur argument que la tradition.

Et à tout prendre pourtant, la fonction historique est indispensable, y compris dans une banque commerciale. Sa genèse chez nous, telle que je vous l'ai contée, ne montre-t-elle pas qu'elle répond à un besoin réel, encore qu'inconscient, de ceux-là mêmes qui forment l'institution? Mais surtout j'ai l'intime conviction que, pour un organisme financier, il n'est pas de meilleur gage de sa solidité financière, de son utilité sociale et de son enracinement dans l'économie nationale que l'evocation publique et sans complexes d'un passé bien ancré dans l'histoire, riche et diversifié. En ce sens, l'image de l'institution est admirablement servie par son histoire.

CHAPTER FIFTEEN

How to Write the History of a Commercial Bank – the French Case

Maurice Lévy-Leboyer

To write the history of a French commercial bank is not an easy task, for the obvious reason that any historian who might be tempted to do so does not simply have to build a narrative and add some economic or social themes in order to illustrate the development of a family concern or of a public institution. First and foremost, he has to overcome the many prejudices that have accumulated in the country against money lending and financial profit. Such prejudices have their roots in religion and culture, however, because it has been taught for quite a long time that the growth of the economy has been marred by capital exports, by discriminatory policies (in favour of the larger firms) and by the high cost of credit which is supposed to have been maintained in the past by private bankers. There is no historical textbook that would not mention, with true sympathy, the 1860s campaign waged by Emile and Isaac Péreire against the Bank of France and the Haute Banque, which they accused of rationing credit at the risk of causing 'the ruin of all our industries'. The lectures and press articles, published around 1900–1905 by A.E. Sayous, Eugène Letailleur (Lysis) and others, to condemn the banking community they made responsible for 'the paralysis of trade and national industries', are also among classical texts used in some classrooms to discredit bankers.

Of course, these ideas, which were the product of slow growth periods, should have been discarded with the next upturn in the economy. However, they found new roots, partly because quantitative history has shown that banks' achievements have been uncertain: the share of bank deposits, to take one example, edged up at best to 45 per cent of the money stock in 1913, half the proportion one could find at that time in anglo-American countries. Those collected by the four leading banks kept depressed for some fifteen years, during the war and the postwar periods, to such an extent that they did not regain their real level of 1913 until 1928, in spite of a 40 per cent increase in industrial production; and, as an upsurge of bank notes took place in the next two decades, the shrinkage of deposits went on (up to 35–7 per cent of M 2 in 1939 and 1945) and so did the commercial banks' ability to promote a revival in the economy. Banks were dependent upon the liquid funds they collected, and in those circumstances they could not and did not build a credit structure equivalent to those of leading industrial countries. To sum up the point, the arguments advanced by the Péreires in their quarrel with the old bank might not stand up to too close an analysis, but one has the feeling that their general attitude was right.

This explains many of the ambiguities that the writing of individual banks' histories has added to the debate and the doubts that were currently expressed, at times, as to their capacity to bring about a true industrial change. Two points have attracted attention. Firstly, the banks' unequal size and the fact that the larger ones – the Comptoir National d'Escompte, founded in 1848, the CIC, i.e. the Crédit Industriel et Commercial, the Crédit Lyonnais and the Société Générale, all three of which date from 1859–64 – started at an early date and remained in the lead, with more than 60–65 per cent of all the banks' balances that were published in 1891–1901, and still with 51 per cent of them in 1913, as if money had been accumulated steadily over time by the same banks in a most uncompetitive way. Secondly, one would question the use that was made of these resources. Although investment banks and commercial banks were to specialize and complement each other, the credit operations of the latter have often been critically assessed. The Crédit Lyonnais, in particular, although the third largest bank in the world by 1913, was regularly blamed at the time for its cautiousness and its negative attitude toward the financing of industry. Criticisms, in fact, went one step further in the mid-1960s, with the publication of Jean Bouvier's doctoral dissertation, 'The Crédit Lyonnais in its formative years – from 1863 to 1882', and his later works. Under his influence, it was held that the development of a branch network by this bank and other commercial establishments drained away liquid funds, hastening the decline of regional activities for the benefit of a few key cities and increasing *pari passu* the intensity of panics, since the Crédit Lyonnais became 'overloaded with funds' which it moved abroad or else used at home, financing stock market speculation rather than industrial investment.

It was partly to mitigate these views that centenary volumes were published by the Crédit Lyonnais (1963) and the Société Générale (1964). They emphasized both the contributions the two banks had made towards modernization of the economy, the way they had diffused low cost and low denomination credits among business firms, whatever their size, how they had assisted the new industrial sectors, etc. Their success, however, was limited, if one may judge from later works and from the contradictory views that are presented, using the same lines of arguments, in the two recent histories of the Banque de l'Indochine: one, by Yasuo Gonjo (1985), takes issue with the bank's disregard for the credit needs of local peasants and local entrepreneurs, its tendency to move capital out of the country through the financing of foreign trade and Chinese business ventures, etc.; and the other, by Marc Meuleau (1990), calls attention to the public works, the plantations and the industries that were developed locally with the assistance of the bank, and reminds the reader of the primitive state of Asiatic countries at the turn of the century – the absence of a land code, a prerequisite for opening credits to peasants, the low level of foreign trade and the absence of return cargoes that compelled the bank to enter circuitous operations through Hong Kong and London to remit homebound funds, etc.

The fact that these problems are still being debated endlessly is a proof that considerably more histories of French commercial banks should be written, and in far greater detail. It is not possible to provide clear answers until we have better knowledge of how the banks actually worked and the true constraints they faced. But, in the meantime, three issues should be clarified. Were the leading banks equivalent from the start to the industrial oligopolies that came to dominate the American domestic market in the 1880s, as described by business historians? Were they an obstacle to growth, in so far as they failed to duplicate the model set up by the German universal banks? And since the economy did actually expand twice in the twentieth century – in the first third of the century and again in the post-Second World War years – were these periods of steady growth the result of an improvement in the banks' strategy and structure or simply one aspect of the smooth working that state controls impart to the functioning of the market?

What banks?

There is a general tendency among French historians to concentrate on the subject of the larger banks, in part for the sake of convenience. These firms published their accounts and they were well covered in the press, as far as their general policy was concerned, while the rest of the profession tended to be left in oblivion. Their position, in spatial terms, was also easier to follow through the country – the three leaders had almost 200 branches (permanent and temporary) in 1880, some 260 in 1897, 1,500 in 1913 (more than 80 per cent of these had been opened in the 20 years that preceded the war), probably 2,600 in 1930, etc. Moreover, since mergers with smaller institutions were actively used to intensify this network, it is often assumed that banking went through two stages.

The first was extreme dispersion: in the early part of the century, until markets were unified by railroads, payment and credit operations were handled, on a seasonal basis, by a multitude of petty bankers and discounters scattered over the country and loosely connected with correspondents located in major cities; they were in charge of discounting their bills, of holding their spare funds, of remitting them in the autumn and of supplying extra credits in times of strain, etc.

The second stage, which was one of large-scale urbanization and amalgamation, logically should have led to the disappearance of the system just described. At least this is the impression one has, when following the rise of the four leaders. In 1901 their bill holdings were to reach more than 70 per cent of the total registered in published balance sheets (Table 15.1). And the funds they held on deposit were bound to increase with the number of their customers: while a private house, like the Neuflize's, had only 650 accounts in the 1860s, with an average of FFr14,600 each, both the two new leading commercial banks already had 10 to 15,000 depositors in 1870, who left some FFr2,200 on average. The four leaders had then collected a total of FFr180 million, brought in by 32,700 customers; 40 years later, on the eve of the war, the total amount collected on deposit was to reach FFr5.6 billion, a figure which means that they perhaps had some 2–2.5 million customers, on the assumption that one can divide the total sum of deposits by three over this period. The Crédit Lyonnais was credited with 230,000 accounts in 1897 and almost 700,000 accounts in 1914, a fair indication of its command over the market.

Table 15.1   Share of the four largest establishments in some sections of banks' published balances, 1891–1937

	1891	1901	1913	1929	1937
Number of banks reporting accounts	42	64	132	276	187
Four banks' share (%):					
Deposits	68	72	59	37	45
Bill portfolios	66	71	63	–	–
Profits	51	54	39	–	–

Source: Bouvier, J. (1973), Un siècle de banque française, Paris, Hachette, pp. 122–5. The four banks are the CIC, the Comptoir National d'Escompte, the Crédit Lyonnais and the Société Générale.

Is this, however, a fair way to write history? As the country did not experience any sort of commercial revolution, in spite of its railroads and its department stores – 60 per cent of the population was still living in small towns and villages up to the Second World War – one would have expected the new banking system not to supersede the old ones, but simply to keep operating along with it, both catering for the credit needs of two different categories of customers. In other words, was competition impossible, because of the sheer size of the big banks? Or did the smaller banks survive?

As a matter of fact, the dispersion of banks' sizes and locations remained fairly high. There were still some 1,000–1,300 banking establishments at the turn of the century, plus a group of discounting houses equivalent in size (Nakagawa, 1986). And, contrary to expectations, the total number doubled between 1906 and 1921, according to data compiled by Nishimura (1992): the larger banks of more than 500 employees increased in number from 11 to 59, and the medium ones (with a workforce of 20–500) to almost 2,200, while stability prevailed with the 2,000 very small units (of less than 20 employees). In other words, the real break came not through the amalgamation process and the transfer of cash funds to key money-centres, but with the depression of the 1930s when 670 banks suspended payments – a fact that is confirmed by the trend in the number of reporting banks, as it kept rising during the expansion of the early twentieth century, but fell by one-third in the post-1929 period (Table 15.1).

Credits on current account, which were more flexible to use and lower in cost than discounts, and so more important for small firms which had no access to capital markets, are supposed to have been slow to develop, because of the big banks' negative attitude towards them. The ratio of discounts to overdraft facilities at the four largest banks was 15:10 over the 1865–95 period; but it rose to 25:10 in 1905–13 and to 35:10 during the First World War and the early 1920s, their portfolios being swollen further with Treasury bills, to such an extent that private bills (in constant prices) did not amount then to more than 15–20 per cent of their 1913 level (Plessis, 1992). But this view should be somewhat qualified in two ways: firstly, the provincial banks which still held the great majority of offices followed a reverse pattern, the same ratio of discounts to current credits falling, with them, from 30:10 to 8:10 between 1890 and 1910, a sign that credit facilities were still available locally for small business firms. Secondly, the Bank of France, whose rediscounts had helped the big banks to get started, lost their custom in the 1880s when they stopped discounting their portfolio. So from 1897, under the guidance of Georges Pallain, the new governor, the bank turned around: it started opening new agencies (there were more than 500 in 1910, holding some 100,000 accounts), to compete with the larger banks, opening current and discount accounts to second-rank firms (and taking in paper bearing only two signatures), while supplying the smaller banks in remote centres, which were not serviced by the leading banks, with the same rediscounting facilities.

Yet, there might have been a gap in the system, if all the banks, organized as 'sociétés anonymes', had still had to submit to the restrictive
rules that were rigidly imposed by the Council of State, when being
applied for banking privilege early in the nineteenth century. However,
with the law of 1867 which opened the way to free company formation,
the regional banks started revising their statutes, a process that was interrupted by the 1870 war, but that was quickly taken up again, giving them
the possibility of diversifying their services, of opening credit lines on
current account, of issuing stocks, of taking shares in new ventures, etc.
In many cities, but foremost in Lille, Nancy and Grenoble, they built
local networks in order to collect working capital (deposits were multi-
plied by eleven at the Crédit du Nord in 1890–1913), and they were able
to cooperate with firms in new sectors such as the steel and electricity
industries which required long-term credits and external capital. In
Bordeaux and Marseilles, where banks had to reckon with fewer open-
ings and with British competition (in the field of foreign acceptance business), they limited their operations, for a time, to short-term commercial
credit and the issue of colonial and domestic securities, often for the
account of their Paris correspondents.

In short, it might be misleading, in the case of France, to concentrate
on the history of one of the leading commercial banks and to adopt too
critical an attitude. As already stated, there was a wide variety of banks,
according to periods and regions. During the expansion period that
started in the 1890s, in particular, most banks were innovative, upgrad-
ing their bonds and equities, strengthening their ties with other institutions, expanding locally through amalgamation (including in the
Mediterranean area on the eve of the war), and eventually merging into
new national entities, such as the Société Centrale des Banques de
Province, which was founded between 1909 and 1913. It may well be
that no history of individual banks should be written in isolation, but in
relation to other establishments, in order to take a broader view of the
sector's development.

What services?

Leading banks did not present the sort of bold and imaginative policies
that were followed, for instance, by the German and Italian commercial
banks after the 1890s. The rule set forth in March 1882 and still re-
iterated 20 years later by Henri Germain, the founder and long-term
president of the Crédit Lyonnais, was that the establishment had to be
transformed, out of concern for its customers' safety, into a pure bank of
deposit, 'a second Bank of France, but without the constraint of its

cumbersome regulations'. Or, to put it in more concrete terms, that 'all demand deposits and current accounts be set apart and tally exactly with the cash funds and the other assets that could readily be sold'. But with the unforeseen result that, in a period of slower economic growth and low interest rates, as in the 1880s and the early 1890s, when the scheme was first applied, the bank, as well as the Société Générale and the Comptoir National d'Escompte, had to submit to very low returns on capital – their share of profits fell strikingly between 1900 and 1913 (Table 15.1); there was a vicious circle whereby the fall in profits made these firms more dependent on sight deposits (the search for time deposits was discontinued), and, as a consequence, on short-term lending. Thus even though they were able to sell new shares, on a substantial scale, after the turn of the century and in the later part of the 1920s, once inflation had been halted, their margin of diversification (i.e. that part of their assets that was not tied up in cash, in interbank accounts and short bills) fell steadily from 55 per cent in the 1870s to 40–45 per cent in 1910–12 (compared with 65 per cent at the Deutsche Bank, 75 per cent at the Dresdner Bank, etc.), and then to 33 per cent in 1929 and 23 per cent in 1939 (Table 15.2). The financial services that the leading commercial banks should have provided to industry may well have been close to minimal.

Table 15.2   Main sections of the four leading banks' accounts
1875–1939 (%)

	Capital	Liabilities		Other	Cash	Assets			Holdgs
		Deposits		items	etc.	Bills	Credits		
		demand	time			overdft	med-t		
	(1)	(2)	(3)	(4)	(5)	(6)	(7)	(8)	(9)
1875	24.9	49.6	16.4	9.1	6.7	36.9	28.0	18.3	10.1
1895	18.0	64.5	10.4	7.1	8.7	40.7	23.9	19.2	7.5
1913	15.2	76.9	4.9	3.9	7.0	51.2	22.5	17.1	2.2
1925	5.2	89.3	1.5	4.1	13.8	61.6	18.3	5.6	0.7
1929	7.0	83.6	3.4	6.0	12.4	54.5	26.2	6.4	0.5
1935	8.9	84.0	2.0	3.7	17.5	49.4	26.4	6.1	0.6
1939	5.8	82.0	1.2	4.2	16.1	60.6	19.3	3.7	0.4

Source: General Assemblies. Other items (4) are made up of 6.6 per cent bills payable and acceptances, and 2.5 per cent comptes d'ordre in 1875, 1.3 and 3.4 per cent on the average thereafter. Cash (5) includes specie, money with correspondents, at the Treasury and the Bank. Overdrafts (7) and medium-term credits (8) are set apart. Holdings (9) include securities and business participations.

But this 'minimal' was far from negligible, because of the close cooperation and interlocking directorates that developed between business
firms and banking establishments, whenever large and lumpy investments required long-term facilities. In fact, it is the high level of demand
for capital, in each period of expansion, that called for innovations and
eventually led to the foundation of new institutions. Economic growth
brought in new creations. During the railway boom of the mid-nineteenth century, the large commercial banks were started as mixed banks
by business promoters, coming from such sectors as railroads, urban
constructions and the heavy industries. The Société Générale (the full
name read 'General Society for the Development of Trade and Industry')
belonged to that group. In the 1860s and 1870s the bank was to finance
large firms, such as the Mining Company of Mokta El Hadid, the iron-
works of Denain-Anzin and La Marine, and coal mines near Charleroi,
all being run by the same body of directors. In the mid-1860s the Crédit
Lyonnais had, in its turn, a share in la Fuschine, one of the first artificial
dyeworks, in a Gaz company in Saragosse, etc., but with less satisfactory
results and, so, with less incentive to carry on other financial operations.
In other words, up to the 1880s, there were no important differences
between 'les banques d'affaires' and the commercial banks, except that
the first tended to be created by private banking firms and the second by
business managers.

Twenty years later, when the second industrialization set in, the same
pattern did not exactly apply, since business units in the forward sectors
were still small and could operate with retained profits and the facilities
they received from local bankers. But electricity and the basic industries
required large outlays of fixed capital and therefore had to be financed
externally. They were supplied once more by the older banking establishments, e.g. the Société Générale, which contributed, among other
ventures, to the development of steel plants at Commentry, Senelle-
Maubeuge, Longwy, Denain, and in southern Russia. They were also
supplied by the Comptoir d'Escompte. After 1903, when Emile Mercet, a
private banker and former President of Thomson-Housten, became
president, it built up an exclusive network of customers, especially in the
electrical sector. Regional banks provided similar services, especially
when business managers had joined the board and redirected their
operations: Th. Favarger, a director of Hotchkiss, and Ad. Salles, of the
Eiffel group, among other cases, were to transform the CCF (Crédit
Commercial de France), then a small institution that had been founded in
1894, with only FFr1 million capital, by bankers from Basle and Zurich,
into one of the leading industrial banks in the country.

The same process recurred in the 1920s, though on a larger scale,
because corporations in the new industries that had matured over time

were still short of funds and also because many firms in the armament industry, plagued with unused capacities from the war, still had to be converted. These were the two investment lines that were followed up by the BNC (Banque Nationale de Crédit), again a small bank, when it started in 1913 – with, among its assets, the French branch network of the Comptoir d'Escompte de Mulhouse (then a German bank) which had been granted autonomy; the BNC was to develop forcibly in the 1920s, under René Boudon, an investment banker who organized its merger with the BFCI (Banque Française pour le Commerce et l'Industrie), and under André Vincent, the president of a number of large industrial concerns and, later, of the bank itself. In 1930, the BNC already had a total of 750 branches, half the number held by the Crédit Lyonnais, and FFr5.5 billion assets, a figure that compared favourably with the assets of the Crédit du Nord and the CCF, then of the order of 2.5–3 billion, and with the 10–15 billion that were held by each of the three leaders. In short, there had been two periods of rapid growth and two waves of bank formation, and so, except in the inflation period of the 1920s, no deficiency in bank services.

Nevertheless, one element was missing in the system. The larger banks, because of their ability to sell securities through their branch network, kept for themselves the larger part of the business of stock issues; the Société Générale was responsible for one-fifth of the sales of securities that were realized in 1913. But they did not hold them long. The rule was to keep their participation in the corporations they assisted to a minimum: the portfolio of the BNC in 1930 accounted for 1.2 per cent of its assets; it was less than one per cent, 320 million out of 50.5 billion, in the case of the six largest banks. Moreover, they did not require these firms to abstain from having other bankers. So, even though they had representatives in many directors' boards, their influence upon management could not have been as decisive as that of a universal bank. However, it was not to be neglected. Banks were a main source of short- and medium-term credits, they organized syndicates with other banks and corporations, and they often kept some control interest by setting up holding companies.

The Crédit Mobilier had experimented with syndicates and holding companies as early as the 1850s when it was trying to expand its real estate operations in Paris and Marseilles. They were taken up again by half a dozen banks including the Crédit Lyonnais during the building boom of 1879–81; the latter launched two corporations, la Lyonnaise des Eaux et de l'Eclairage, which is still one of the leading public utility companies and still an 8–9 per cent subsidiary of the bank, and la Foncière Lyonnaise, keeping at that time a 60 and 80 per cent interest in both. But the system was made general, later on in the century, for a twofold purpose. Firstly, to assist corporations in capital-intensive sectors, such as the electrical industries, where self-financing out of profits could not match investments: Thomson-Houston and the CGE (Cie Générale d'Electricité) were founded in 1893 and 1898 as holding companies by private bankers, with the strong backing of commercial banks; and so it was, at a later date, with the financial subsidiaries they set up, when they became full-fledged manufacturing entities. Secondly, some of the banks that had entered joint ventures in the modern sectors of industry set up holding companies to keep and eventually to finance their participations and to protect themselves against the risk of tying up too many resources: la Société d'Applications Industrielles acted in such capacity from 1896 for the CCF; the Compagnie Technique et Financière has had a similar position at the BNC since 1923.

In fact the shortage of capital that developed in the 1920s prompted many industrial groups to open a financial branch, in order to issue bonds and equities in foreign markets, to help them to diversify by selecting investments in the forward sectors, and compete with the commercial banks. In each period of monetary stability, however, the latter returned to their former policy and set up specialized institutions, often on a collective basis, such as UCINA (Union pour le Crédit à l'Industrie Nationale), which started in 1919 as an offspring of the Crédit Lyonnaise and the Comptoir d'Escompte; CALIF (Société de Crédit à l'Industrie Française) in 1928 with the Société Générale, the CCF and the BNC among its founders; OFINA (Omnium Financier pour l'Industrie Nationale) in 1929, with the assistance of a greater number of banking establishments, etc.

From this brief review, one may conclude that banks were in no way as inactive as suggested by some authors, although a more concrete presentation of what was achieved would be desirable. One would expect historians to push further the analysis of the members of the banks' personnel, their experience, purpose and career, generation by generation; our knowledge of the structure of credit facilities, of the rules that guided the banks when they assessed the risks involved in selecting projects, the negotiation and implementation of contracts should also be improved; and so should their end-results, from a financial point of view. These are all aspects that are well covered for many of the great merchant-bank houses in the nineteenth century, but that are still unknown for most of the commercial banks. From a more general point of view, one would also hope that bank historians would explain why the competitive advantage that the French establishments enjoyed at a time in the past did not mature. Why is it that the large establishments increased in number, rather than in market share? Why did they tend to divide risks, instead of entering new markets, taking up new opportunities and the

chance of new profits, as in other countries? In spite of many achievements, French banks lost in ranking. The Crédit Lyonnais was almost
equal to the Midland Bank and Lloyds Bank in 1913, but it fell steadily,
with only one-fifth of their assets by 1930; a few years later, according to
R.J. Truptil's figures, the five big banks' deposits in England reached
FFr135 billion, at the 1934 rate of exchange, against FFr40 billion for
their French counterparts; their respective share was equivalent to 89 and
43 per cent of the two countries' total deposits; and the gap increased in
the 1930s. Of course, there are many possible explanations: the fact that
the market was not truly unified; that large corporations were too few;
that inflation cost one-quarter of the deposits (in constant prices) held by
the six larger banks over the 1913–26 period; and also that there was some
unfair competition on the part of the public sector – deposits were divided
in a 51:49 ratio between private and public banks in 1913, but in a percentage of 36:64 in 1936, etc. The writing of bank histories should be conducted both at a micro and at a macro-level, so as to clarify these issues.

What risks?

No mention has been made so far of the impact of panics, even though
borrowing short and lending at long term were bound to play havoc
among commercial banks. Money withdrawals, ill-advised credits and
frozen assets that lost in value were most common incidents in the banking history of any country, including France. They explain much of the
outright or near downfalls of all the leading banks, at one time during
their past history. It was the case of the Péreires' Crédit Mobilier under
the impact of a crash in the stock market; the same occurred in1882 at
the Union Générale and many other banks, including the Crédit
Lyonnais, in 1889 and 1905 at the Comptoir d'Escompte and the Société
Générale, after ill-fated attempts by some of their customers to corner the
copper and sugar markets; the BNC's stoppage in January 1932, in spite
of a massive two-year rescue operation by public agencies, was probably
the worst, with a fall of almost FFr4 billion (out of FFr4.6 billion)
deposits. All these were severe setbacks, accompanied by great losses that
had to be covered from the banks' reserve accounts and new capital
issues, and also by large-scale dismissals of employees; one-fifth of the
personnel was laid off at the Crédit Lyonnais in the 1880s, and 50 per
cent at the BNC between 1932 and 1935, while one out of every three
branches was closed. However, in contrast to past narratives, there is a
tendency to side-step such incidents, probably because of what has been
written of the recovery of each of the large banks thereafter, of the
stability of their profits over time, and of the rule they are said to have

imposed upon themselves to limit their operations to the discounting of self-liquidating paper and other safe credits. Historians may feel there is no need to dwell upon cycles and crises, since commercial banks do not run risks any longer.

But it might be misleading to limit the study of bank policies to that of the flow of funds. The large banks kept enlarging their operations and their personnel over time. And as such, they should be studied in terms of strategy and structure, the way it is done for any large-scale corporation in the manufacturing sector: the BNC, under its new names – BNCI from 1932 and BNP after 1966 – had no more than 5,000 employees in 1935, just after the crash, but 15,000 in 1942, 20,000 in 1965, 45,000 in the next fifteen years (twice that size for some other establishments). This should justify new research into the bank's internal organization, beyond the analysis of their balance sheet. Further, after a period of falling profits, due to the economic environment of the interwar period, banks had to face a surge of operations and so of fixed costs, which raised problems of economies of scale (to keep gross profits above increasing costs), of levels of paid-up capital (because of their tendency to keep permanent funds at a minimum to hedge against the fall in returns), of their financial autonomy (against unforeseen accidents), etc. There are many more questions to be raised than there are answers in the present state of bank history.

It may be possible to sketch out some sort of chronology by drawing a distinction between defensive and offensive periods. In the first stages from the 1870s to the 1940s, the opening of branch networks raised specific problems, since the large banking establishments became loose federations of unit banks, trying to cover the whole range of services, to accommodate local customers without delay, but generating huge volumes of daily documents, heavy costs, including those for the storage of securities and coupon payments, and the registration of interbranch commissions and interests; they were often overstaffed and required, after a period of trial and error, rationalization and leaner structures. Thus, usually under the pressures created by financial panics, every bank tried to enforce stricter managerial procedures by setting up permanent committees and supervisory commissions to oversee the allocation and monitoring of credit. At the Comptoir National d'Escompte, regional or intermediate units were set up in 1889–90 which were placed in charge of managing accounting procedures and portfolio services in order to save on local personnel and costs and improve the ability of the staff to plan and control the bank's overall operations.

Similar measures had been taken at the Crédit Lyonnais in the 1880s and were to be taken at the BNCI in the 1930s. In the latter case, eight to nine such administrative centres were in operation before the Second

World War, each of which supervised some 40–50 branches. There was, in fact, a continuous process of centralization that benefited, in the 1930s, from the use of new accounting machines for the registration of commercial operations and the handling of securities. The drawback of the institutionalization of these procedures for dealing with commercial operations and the handling of securities was that a gap developed between managerial staff and the personnel performing these increasingly routinized tasks because those in charge of managerial functions asked for and had to be offered higher pay since they were recruited according to higher standards required by their greater responsibilities. At the same time, the status and salaries of regular personnel diminished. This problem was solved in part, at the BNCI, by developing social services and family allowances during the war, by granting housing credit facilities from 1948, and after 1939, by gradually opening paths to the internal promotion of individuals, through adult occupational training and the use of psychotechnical laboratories.

With the revival of market activity, in the 1960s and 1970s, cutting fixed costs became less of a binding rule among commercial banks. Competition was revived, and from 1966 banks were granted, by law, the possibility of opening new branches, of merging and acquiring new establishments, of canvassing for new customers, etc. Demand deposits, that had remained stable (in constant prices) at their 1929 level up to the mid-1950s, were to increase fourfold in the next 25 years. And with this new start, strategies were revised so as to include retail banking, medium-term credits for enterprises and private households, more diversified products to finance the new sectors of activity, but also to finance older ones, such as the construction industry and foreign trade operations. The stagnation of almost two generations thus came to an end. The rigid structures, which were based on strict lines of authority and control between a central and intermediate staff and which had ended up depriving operating units of much of their ability to initiate new operations, however, became obsolete. This was because the balance between 'production' and 'administration' had to be shifted back to central staff in order to meet local competition and adapt to market demand without delay. The employment of computers and other data-processing equipment toward these ends changed lines of control and authority relationships. At the BNCI a status of autonomy had been given in the 1950s and 1960s to overseas and foreign branches and to a few departments working in special areas; but the true decentralization of banking operations was a long-term process. Experiments in decentralization were first undertaken in two regions in 1974–78 and then generally instituted through the creation of a divisional structure. Eleven domestic and international regional groups replaced the old branch networks, each of which had specialized departments to deal with specific types of customers (large-scale corporations, industrial firms, etc.) or with specialized internal functions.

This brief sketch does not do justice to French commercial banks. Its sole purpose is to bring more life to their past history, by calling attention of course to achievements and personalities, but also to some of the real problems of the profession that tend to be overlooked, i.e. the risks, profits and losses they faced, the strategies and structures they had to adopt, and the better assessment they deserve of their contribution to the development of the country.

CHAPTER SIXTEEN

Comment

Corry van Renselaar

Lévy-Leboyer's report, an interesting and well-balanced inventory of French commercial banking history, is in fact a strong plea for more and in-depth research. Rightly so, I think. As in the Netherlands, some fundamental problems in French banking history have not yet been solved. One of the main issues, as mentioned, is the contribution of banks to the modernization of the economy in the nineteenth and twentieth century, more specific to industrial growth.

I fully agree that concentrating on the history of large banks is not only an unfair way to write history, but presents a rather misleading view on the actual state of affairs. Both France and the Netherlands knew a variety of banks and financial institutions in time and region, whose contribution to industrial development was 'minimal but not negligible'.

'Not negligible', a crucial but unsatisfactory notion, has to be dealt with by a more detailed examination of the records of individual banks and more research on the financial services supplied on a local basis.

Some four years ago, on the occasion of the 250th anniversary of Van Lanschot's, a well-established bank in Den Bosch, a valuable collection of essays was published entitled *Bankieren in Brabant*. Brabant, as you know, is one of our southern provinces. This book contains some very interesting articles by the economic historians Veraghtert and Van den Eerenbeemt. In one of his contributions Veraghtert questions the importance of capital as a crucial variable in the industrialization of Brabant. Its role, he says, was limited, even in the beginning of the twentieth century. Brabant's slow and gradual transition from artisan to mechanized industry was covered by retained profits, short- and medium-term credit by local commercial banks, credit on current accounts and family funding. Rather interesting in this respect are Veraghtert's remarks on local notaries public who often operated as cashiers and bankers. As such they were in a way one of the trailblazers of commercial banks. Notaries public as financial key figures in small communities deserve more attention by historians. They may well have played an equally important role in the emerging industrialization of rural France.

Veraghtert's article is followed by a review of the activities of the commercial and industrial banks in nineteenth-century Brabant, by Van den

Eerenbeemt, who must have spent quite some time in local archives. It has been a true fact-finding mission and a vital impetus to further research Brabant's commercial banking history.

As such *Bankieren in Brabant* – to which Professor Van der Wee made an important contribution as well – is just one example of a more scientific approach to commercial banking history, which has been dominated too long by the occasional anniversary book.

In recent years we have not only seen a modest flow of books and articles on the subject, but the publication of a thorough review of source material as well. Earlier this year NEHA, the Netherlands Economic History Archive, presented *Dutch Banking, its history and sources*.

This publication is a *mer à boire* for economic historians, one of whom may present a paper to a future colloquium on 'How to write an even better history of a bank'.

CHAPTER SEVENTEEN

Writing the History of Commercial Banks in Spain – Problems and Perspectives

Gabriel Tortella

There are serious problems for the scholar who tries to write the history of a private bank in Spain. The first and main problem is that access to private bank archives is extremely difficult, if not impossible, as Teresa Tortella reported recently to the European Colloquium on Bank Archives.[1] The second and related problem is that private banks rarely manifest an interest in their own history and seldom retain the services of a business historian to research and write about their past. It is true that, as was mentioned in the debate subsequent to Tortella's paper, some private banks have published volumes on the occasion of their anniversaries.[2] But these books, although occasionally offering very interesting information for the historian, are usually of little scientific value, either because they deal with peripheral matters (reportage, hagiographical biography, anecdote) or because, when they do engage in banking history, they tend to be rather loose on method (inadequate reporting of sources, poor or non-existent statistics and/or theoretical apparatus, etc.). The result of all this is that, although there exists a group of banking historians in Spain who are doing their best to carry out research in the field, and although they devise new and ingenious methods to develop their task, the history of Spanish commercial banks is largely virgin territory.

Spanish banking history has had to adapt itself to the possibilities. This is why we know much more about public than about private banks, and more about the evolution of the banking sector as a whole (its macroeconomic history) than about its individuals (its business or microeconomic history). There are two reasons for this. First, public banks have been readier than private banks to open their archives and to fund research into their own history. Second, while access to bank archives is difficult, banking statistics are more accessible. Official statistics have been published at least yearly since the early 1920s and, thanks to the efforts of the Bank of Spain and those of some researchers, banking and monetary statistical series have been reconstructed for the period starting around 1850.[3]

Problems in the past

All this does not mean that there is no serious banking history in Spain. Although no definitive history of the Bank of Spain has been written, there are several books and articles which study partial aspects of its history.[4] It is, not surprisingly, and in spite of the many gaps, the best studied bank in Spanish history. Other public or official banks have been studied, such as the Banco de Crédito Industrial and the Banco Hipotecario.[5] To my knowledge, only a smaller surviving private bank has been studied, the Banco Herrero; most of the other private banks studied are already extinct, such as the Banco de Oviedo, and Banco de Barcelona, the Banco Hispano-Colonial, the Banco de Cataluña, etc.[6] An illustration of the frustrations of the Spanish banking historian is the case of the archive of the Banco Urquijo. This bank, created as a private merchant bank in the mid-nineteenth century, was incorporated in 1918 and became the leading industrial bank until its demise in 1981. The Urquijo also had a tradition of supporting research in economics and in history: it sponsored scientific seminars, had its own scholarly journal and publishing house, and also asked a professional archivist to make an inventory of its archive.[7] That professional archivist happens to be my mother. Perusal of this inventory makes clear that the Banco Urquijo had a leading role in the development of Spain's industry and that its archives are an important source not only of the bank's history, but also of the economic history of twentieth-century Spain. The Urquijo archive, however, is now inaccessible to historians, as the bank's assets have been sold several times over the last few years and its papers transferred from one institution to another; and not only inaccessible, but impossible to trace. The only systematic use of the inventory and archive was made in the late seventies and early eighties by Alfonso de Otazu, who eventually published a history of the early years of the Rothschild branch in Madrid (where the founder of the Banco Urquijo learned his trade).[8]

The causes of this depressing situation are only too familiar: lack of interest if not outright mistrust of researchers on the part of the banks (justified to some extent by the anti-capitalist bias and hostility towards business of some historians) and a certain passivity on the part of the state, which could certainly do more to prod private institutions into making their papers more accessible. As you can see, all parts have some share of the blame for this historiographical void, although the main responsibility, of course, falls upon the banks themselves who are, after all, the owners of the main historical source, their papers. There is no doubt an understandable mistrust towards historians on the part of banks; as Forrest Capie says in this volume, caution is the banks' second nature, and so it should be. However, the banks' fears may be exaggerated. In the first place, the extant literature on Spanish banking history has been generally objective and balanced. Furthermore, there are some recent business history studies in Spain which have vindicated firms and individuals that were originally under a cloud of suspicion: this is the case with the former King Alfonso XIII and with the Rio Tinto Company.[9] The popular image of banks is critical in Spain, probably due to a centuries-old anti-capitalist prejudice, to the almost universal envy that wealth and power provoke, and to the cosy relationship most big banks had with the Franco dictatorship. In fact, research may show things to have been less simple: among other things, it is a fact that not all big banks were sympathetic to the Franco régime. Spanish bankers should realize their image is so bad that research could hardly worsen it, and it may very possibly make it look better.

In spite of the sombre picture just sketched, there are a few things one can say about the Spanish private, commercial banking sector, with the help of the better known macroeconomic series. Figures 17.1–17.4 tell us several things about the Spanish banking system in the twentieth century.[10]

First, the Spanish private banking system took off around the First World War. This is shown by:

- the growth of banking assets relative to national income after 1915, and
- the growth of private bank deposits as a percentage of the money supply after about the same date.

This is not to deny that there was interesting banking history in nineteenth-century Spain.[11] In the nineteenth century, however, Spanish industry and commerce were but a relatively small part of national income and the private banking sector remained very small indeed. This becomes clear when we bring the fact to mind that by the century's end, three-quarters of all banking deposits were held by the Bank of Spain. This proportion fell fast during the early twentieth century, so that by 1935 it was down to 20 per cent. The growth of the private banking sector to maturity, therefore, took place in the early twentieth century.

Second, the growth of the private banking system is also reflected, among other things, in a decrease of the velocity of circulation of money. It is interesting that, in spite of not being on the gold standard, Spain carried out deflationary policies in the period prior to the Spanish civil war (with the only exception the First World War period, and this for reasons largely out of the government's control). This can be clearly seen in Figure 17.2, which shows practically no growth of the money supply in

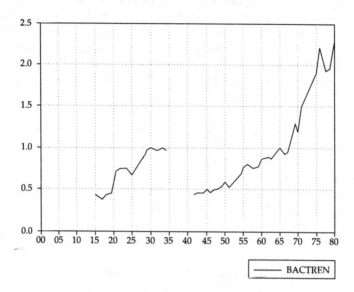

Figure 17.1   Ratio of banking assets/national income

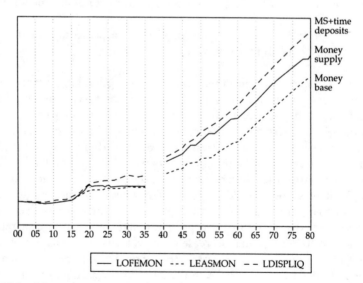

Figure 17.2   Monetary aggregates (log scale)

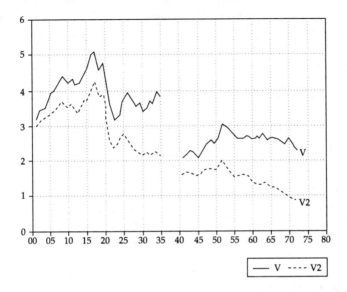

Figure 17.3 Velocity of money circulation: two versions. V-Y/M1; V2-Y/M2

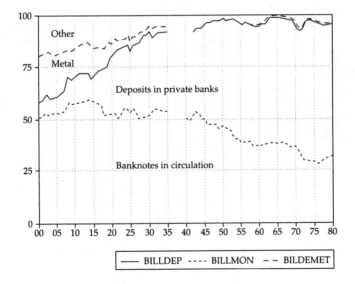

Figure 17.4 Money supply components in percentages

1900–15 and 1920–35. The result of this was a surprising increase in the velocity of circulation from the 1880s until around 1917 (Figure 17.3).[12] Although velocity has shown a normal downward trend from 1917 on, there have been periods of upward or stagnating trend, such as 1922–35 and 1941–51. The first of these upward-trend stages is due to tight monetary policies at a time of real-income growth. In the second stage what obtains is general economic regression shown, among other things, by a fall of the banking-assets/national-income ratio (Figure 17.1). This is a period of intense 'repression' of the financial system and heavy-handed government intervention in the economy,[13] which produced stagnation both in real and in financial variables.

I will close with a few 'additional reflections' on the methodological problems encountered by me and my colleagues while in the preliminary stages of a research project on the history of two leading Spanish banks, the Banco Central and the Banco Hispano Americano, which have merged recently to form the Banco Central Hispano.

Approaches in the future

We are trying to combine two distinct, different approaches: the micro approach (which could be called 'Chandlerian') and the macro approach (no need to give it a name). We are still not sure that we will not end up writing two books instead of one (or perhaps four, two for each bank).

The micro approach would try to answer questions such as: why did the bank grow? In turn we will investigate two types of factors, external and internal. The investigation of external factors will take us mostly into secondary literature and published statistics: we will have to deal with the growth of the general economy, the growth of markets and of sectors such as industry and commerce, and other elements in demand for credit and banking services. We know a certain amount about these things (some of them have been referred to in the preceding pages), and the general answer is that there was growth, and therefore external factors were conducive to the development of banks in general.

The investigation of internal factors would try to compare the growth of the bank with that of the banking sector as a whole and again to explain why the bank had grown relatively (if the bank had not experienced relative growth we probably would not be studying it). We certainly will be looking for some kind of Schumpeterian innovation (which includes tapping new markets and carrying out organizational improvements) to explain the success of the bank. In the case of the Banco Hispano Americano this innovation probably consisted in its own specialization in commercial banking, a choice that was avoided by most other large banks in Spain. It appears that this was a very conscious choice by the bank's founder and early inspirer, Antonio Basagoiti.

A related internal question is that of how growth affected the structure of the bank. Did the bank retain its basic initial structure? Did it grow in one or several markets? The answer to the last question is easy: the Banco Hispano Americano grew in several different geographical markets, as it was one of the early developers of branch banking in Spain. Now this posed new challenges, essentially problems of communication between central headquarters and the branches, with attendant accounting difficulties. It seems that a solution was found to these problems by a new man imported from the Midland Bank in the late 1920s, Andrés Moreno.[14] The problem of 'overspecialization' in commercial banking was solved by means of a pact (Pacto de 'Las Jarillas') with the Banco Urquijo in 1944, whereby the two banks would cooperate: the Urquijo would specialize even more in industrial finance while the Hispano Americano would remain commercial and be an occasional lender to the normally more cash-strapped Urquijo.

The Banco Central gave very different solutions to these problems. To start with, the Central was the product of the fusion in 1919 of a number of smaller provincial banks (hence its name). The Banco Central clearly chose to become a 'mixed' bank; and be the holder of controlling share packages in a series of big industrial and banking companies. This industrial specialization, plus some additional problems carried over from the 1920s, seriously affected the Central during the Great Depression (unlike the vast majority of Spanish banks, whose most frequent complaint at the time was that of an excess of liquidity).[15]

The macro approach would have as its main question, how and what did the bank contribute to the economy as a whole? In the case of a central bank the standards are obvious, and most of this part of the study would consist of the application of monetary-policy criteria to the historical record of the bank in question. Since we are dealing with commercial, or private, banks, this need concern us no further.

In the case of a private bank we should look at how successful it has been in the provision of banking services. Of course, there is a problem in defining what it is that banks produce, i.e. what their output is.[16] Without going into that question, we can take a bank's market share, as measured by its deposits, as a proxy for its output. Now, interestingly enough, the market share (bank's deposits relative to the sector's combined total) of the Banco Hispano Americano and the Banco Central evolved in very different ways. The Hispano Americano's share can be seen to follow a bell-shaped curve: a rapid increase to the mid-1930s and 1940s (the series has a long gap in the late 1930s and early 1940s due to the Spanish civil war), and then a gradual decline. At its maximum, the

Hispano Americano's share was over 35 per cent. It then went down gradually to hover at about 12 per cent in 1980. The Banco Central, in contrast, had a share of under 5 per cent in the 1920s and 1930s. In the following decades its share remained at around 10 per cent and then in the 1970s it inched upward towards 13 per cent, so that by 1980 it had overtaken the Hispano Americano (and it remained ahead until their recent merger). Their race looks very much like that of the tortoise and the hare. After a fast start, the Hispano Americano rested on its laurels for about forty years and in the end it lost.

This performance raises a series of questions, the most obvious being, what caused the relative decline of the Hispano Americano? Blaming simply the expansion in the number of banks is not enough, for two reasons. First, the Central's share did not shrink, rather it expanded, so the Hispano Americano's decline was not inevitable. Second, the number of banks increased much more rapidly during the 1920s and 1930s, when the Hispano's share was growing, than after 1940, when its share went down. The conclusion seems inescapable: the Hispano Americano did something wrong, if only by omission. Everything points to excessive conservatism in its management, perhaps caused or abetted by the 'Las Jarillas' pact which, by establishing a clear division of labour between the Urquijo and the Hispano Americano, possibly discouraged innovation or competitiveness in the latter.

We now return to the more general question, what did the banks contribute to the Spanish economy? There seems little doubt that they were instrumental in financing the industrialization of Spain, a twentieth-century phenomenon. Spanish commercial banks followed, knowingly or not, the German model of 'universal' banks. This is how Ignacio Villalonga, then president of the Banco Central, justified in the very early 1960s what in Spain is known as 'mixed' banking:

> . . . the Spanish economy can be considered as underdeveloped by comparison with that of the other countries of Western Europe [. . .] three civil wars in little over one hundred years, plus the colonial wars, have exhausted the country and have considerably retarded its development. In Spain, whatever one may say, there is no rich bourgeoisie, no powerful middle class, except in regions such as Catalonia, the Basque provinces and, in part, Valencia [. . .] and therefore, Spain lacks a sufficient capacity of saving and capital [formation . . .]. In this situation it was indispensable, if one wanted the economic recovery of Spain without foreign intervention – which in the nineteenth century became a veritable colonization – or without state socialism, something very costly, inefficient, and against the Spanish spirit, there was no other recourse in order to set the country in movement but to employ a part of the resources entrusted to the commercial and deposit banks; that is to say, to opt for what is known as mixed banking, because it is a combination of commercial

banking and business banking; and it was thus that in the economic and banking recovery of Spain in the twentieth century, Spanish banks, impelled by necessity and not by a technical, scientific, and deliberate plan, assumed the character of mixed banks, thus rendering the country a service of such magnitude that nobody can honestly deny it. [. . .] Had it not been for the existence of a mixed banking system in Spain, capital formation in the country would have been sensibly less [. . .][17]

Of course Villalonga omitted to say that the state deserved a great part of the credit (if credit was due) for this condition of things, since mixed banking was largely a consequence of the relationship between the Bank of Spain, the Ministry of Finance, and the private banking sector, as defined by legislation and favoured by political and administrative practice. In particular, private banks could hold sizeable quantities of industrial bonds and shares in their portfolios because the Bank of Spain acted as lender of last resort, a role facilitated by the absence of a gold standard.

In summary, the history of Spanish commercial banks is still largely virgin territory. Although we know something about the timing of the sector's growth and about the macroeconomic determinants of this timing and the shape development took, the individual, microeconomic perspective is largely missing. It is to be hoped that bankers, scholars and the state will soon contribute to remedy this situation and that the new knowledge will help us to understand Spanish economic history and general banking history better.

Notes

1. Tortella (1992) and literature cited there.
2. Banco de Bilbao (1857); Banco de Santander (1957); Banco Hispano Americano (1951). Even in the nineteenth century the Bank of Barcelona published what possibly was the first of this kind of books, see Banco de Barcelona (1894).
3. Martín Aceña in Carreras (1989); Martín Aceña in Sánchez-Albornoz (1985); Martín Aceña (1985); Tortella (1974).
4. Tedde (1988); Santillán (1865); Tortella (1970); Anes in Tortella (1974); Galvarriato (1921 and 1923); Robledo (1988); Sardá (1970).
5. Tortella and Jiménez (1986); Lacomba and Ruiz (1990).
6. Anes and Otazu (1987); Cabana (1965, 1972 and 1978); García López (1989).
7. Casares (n.d.).
8. Otazu (1987). A manuscript sketch of the history of the Banco Urquijo also exists: see Beltrán (n.d.).
9. Gortázar (1986); Harvey (1981); for a fuller explanation see Coll and Tortella (1992).
10. More on these topics in Tortella (1994).

11. The interested reader can consult a few items in English: Tortella (1972 and 1977).
12. See also Tortella (1983), pp. 134–6.
13. Lukauskas (1992), esp. ch. 4.
14. *The Midland Venture*, July 1929, p. 256. I am grateful for this information to Edwin Green, archivist of the Midland Group, and to Jorge Hay, adjunct director general of the Banco Central Hispano.
15. Tortella and Palafox (1984), esp. pp. 105–11.
16. For a review of the problems involved see Gorman (1969) and Tortella (1985).
17. Villalonga (1961), pp. 103–4.

References

Alvarez Llano, R. and Andreu, J.M. (1982), *Una historia de la banca privada en España*, Madrid, Banco de Bilbao.

Anes Alvarez, Rafael (1974), 'El Banco de España (1874–1914): Un banco nacional', in Tortella et al. (1974).

Anes Alvarez, Rafael and Otazu Llana, Alfonso (1987), *El Banco Herrero. 75 años de historia*, Oviedo, Banco Herrero.

Banco de Barcelona (1894), *Memoria que la Junta de Gobierno presenta a la General Extraordinaria de Accionistas en 20 de mayo de 1894. Quincuagésimo aniversario de su creación*, Barcelona, Imprenta Heinrich y Cía.

Banco de Bilbao (1957), *Un siglo en la vida del Banco de Bilbao. Primer centenario (1857–1957)*, Bilbao, Talleres tipográficos de Espasa Calpe SA.

Banco de Santander (1957), *Aportación al estudio de la historia económica de la Montaña*, Santander, Talleres tipográficos de Editorial Cantabria SA.

Banco Hispano Americano (1951), *El primero medio siglo de su historia*, Madrid, Imprenta Maestre.

Banco de España (1970), *El Banco de España: Una historia económica*, Madrid, Banco de España.

Beltrán Florez, Lucas (n.d.), 'Notas sobre la historia del Banco Urquijo', mimeo.

Cabana, Francesc (1965), *La banca a Catalunya. Apunts per a una historia*, Barcelona, Edicions 62.

Cabana, Francesc (1972), *Bancs i banquers a Catalunya. Capítols per a une historia*, Barcelona, Edicions 62.

Cabana, Francesc (1978), *Historia del Banc de Barcelona*, Barcelona, Edicions 62.

Cameron, Rondo (1961), *France and the Economic Development of Europe, 1800–1914*, Princeton, N.J., Princeton University Press.

Cameron, Rondo, (ed.) (1972), *Banking and Economic Development. Some Lessons of History*, New York, Oxford University Press.

Carreras, Albert, (ed.) (1989), *Estadísticas históricas de España*, Madrid, Banco Exterior.

Casares, María Teresa (n.d.), 'Banco Urquijo. Inventario topográfico de la documentación antigua', ms.

Coll, Sebastián and Tortella, Gabriel (1992), 'Reflexiones sobre la historia empresarial: estado de la cuestión en España', *Información Comercial Española* (708–9), pp. 13–24.

Cuervo, Alvaro (1988), *La crisis bancaria en España, 1977–1985*, Barcelona, Ariel.

Fanjul, Oscar and Maravall, Fernando (1985), *La eficiencia del sistema bancario español*, Madrid, Alianza.

Fremdling, Rainer and O'Brien, Patrick K. (eds) (1983), *Productivity in the Economies of Europe*, Stuttgart, Klett-Cotta.

Fuchs, Victor R. (ed.) (1969), *Production and Productivity in the Service Industries*, New York, National Bureau of Economic Research.

Galvarriato, Juan Antonio (1921), *El Banco de España. Síntesis de su labor*, Madrid, Imprenta Espinosa.

Galvarriato, Juan Antonio (1923), *El Banco de España. Momentos culminantes de su vida*, Madrid, Imprenta Espinosa.

García López, José Ramón (1989), *El Banco de Oviedo, 1864–1874. Historia económica de un banco de emisión*, Gijón, Mases Ediciones.

Gorman, John A. (1969), 'Alternative measures of the Real Output and Productivity of Commercial Banks', in Fuchs (1969), pp. 155–89.

Gortázar, Guillermo (1986), *Alfonso XIII, hombre de negocios. Persistencia del Antiguo Régimen, modernización económica y crisis política*, Madrid, Alianza.

Hamilton, Earl J. (1970), 'El Banco Nacional de San Carlos (1782–1829)', in Banco de España (1970).

Harvey, Charles E. (1981), *The Rio Tinto Company: An Economic History of a Leading Mining Concern, 1873–1954*, Penzance, Cornwall, Alison Hodge.

Lacomba, Juan Antonio and Ruiz, Gumersindo (1990), *Historia del Banco Hipotecario*, Madrid, Alianza.

Lukauskas, Arvid (1992), *The Political Economy of Financial Deregulation: The Case of Spain*, Doctoral dissertation, University of Pennsylvania.

Martín Aceña, Pablo (1984), *La política monetaria en España, 1919–1935*, Madrid, Instituto de Estudios Fiscales.

Martín Aceña, Pablo (1985), *La cantidad de dinero en España, 1900–1935*, Madrid, Banco de España.

Muñoz, Juan (1969), *El poder de la banca en España*, Algorta, Vizcaya, Zero.

Otazu, Alfonso de (1987), *Los Rothschild y sus socios españoles (1820–1850)*, Madrid, O.Hs. Ediciones.

Pohl, Manfred (ed.) (1992), *The situation of bank archives in west European countries. First European Colloquium on Bank Archives*, Frankfurt am Main, Verlag Waldemar Kramer.

Pohl, Manfred (ed.) (1994), *Handbook on the History of European Banks*, European Association for Banking History e.V., Aldershot, Edward Elgar.

Robledo, Ricardo (1988), '¿Quiénes eran los accionistas del Banco de España', *Revista de Historia Económica*, VI, 3, pp. 557–91.

Sanchez-Albornoz, Nicolás (ed.) (1985), *La modernización económica de España*, Madrid, Alianza.

Santillan, Ramón (1865), *Memoria histórica sobre los bancos ...*, Madrid, Est. Tip.

T. Fortanet (Facsimile Edition, ed. by Pedro Tedde de Lorca, Madrid, Banco de España, 1982).

Sardá Dexeus, Juan (1970), 'El Banco de España (1931–1962)', in Banco de España (1970).

Tedde de Lorca, Pedro (1988), *El Banco de San Carlos (1782–1829)*, Madrid, Banco de España/Alianza.

Tortella, Gabriel (1970), 'El Banco de España entre 1829–1929. La formación de un banco central', in Banco de España (1970).

Tortella, Gabriel (1972), 'Spain, 1829–1874', in Cameron (1972).

Tortella, Gabriel et al. (1974), *La banca española en la Restauración*, 2 vols, Madrid, Banco de España.

Tortella, Gabriel (1977), *Banking, Railroads and Industry in Spain, 1829–1874*, New York, Arno Press.

Tortella, Gabriel (1983), 'National Income Estimation by Means of Monetary Variables, the Case of Spain, 1772–1972. Some Preliminary Results', in Fremdling and O'Brien (1983).

Tortella, Gabriel and Palafox, Jordi (1984), 'Banking and Industry in Spain, 1918–1936', *The Journal of European Economic History*, vol. 13, no. 2, special issue on *Banks and Industry in the Interwar Period*.

Tortella, Gabriel (1985), 'El Producto (valor añadido bruto) del sector bancario español, 1856–1935: una primera aproximación', ms.

Tortella, Gabriel and Jiménez, Juan Carlos (1986), *Una historia del Banco de Crédito Industrial*, Madrid, Alianza.

Tortella, Gabriel (1994), 'Spanish Banking History, 1782 to the present', in Pohl (1994), pp. 865–74.

Tortella, Teresa (1992), 'Les archives bancaires espagnoles à l'heure actuelle', in Pohl (1992).

Villalonga Villalba, Ignacio (1961), 'La banca española en lo que va de siglo', *Arbor*, 189–90, pp. 93–111.

CHAPTER EIGHTEEN

Commercial (Universal) Banking in Central Europe – from Cisleithania to the Successor States

Alice Teichova

During the research work in the countries under investigation (which began in 1986) many practical and theoretical problems had to be overcome, such as access to material, coping with the enormous, sometimes patchy, and often disparate source material both in national archives and in individual archives of commercial banks, applying and coordinating quantitative and comparative methods, and finding solutions to problems of interpretation through personal contacts and frequent workshops. However, I suppose that similar questions will have been the subject of presentations and debate in previous sections. Therefore I propose to concentrate on questions concerning Cisleithania, the Austrian part of the Habsburg Monarchy and, after its collapse, the two most advanced successor states, Austria and Czechoslovakia. A more detailed statement about the Hungarian case (Transleithania and Hungary) will be made by Dr Pogány (Chapter 20).

Since the turn of the century the role of banks in economic development has been the subject of debate: in terms of either furthering or hindering industrialization, with regard to their function in the process of concentration, and their general impact upon both the course of business cycles and economic growth. This discussion gained a further impulse in the mid-1960s with Alexander Gerschenkron's essay on relative economic backwardness in historical perspective in which he ascribed a missionary role to banks through helping latecomer economies to overcome the initial scarcity of capital. More recently the rediscovery of Rudolf Hilferding's *Finance capital. A study of the latest phase of capitalist development* (published in English for the first time in 1981) had brought the question of the interaction between banking and industrial capital again to our attention. The persuasiveness of the approaches taken by Gerschenkron and Hilferding, which closely resemble each other but differ substantially in their general conclusions, has influenced thinking not only among academics, but also – in Hilferding's case – amidst a wider politically-minded public.

Cisleithania

The present state of research permits a more comprehensive approach to the development of commercial banking in the economies of the Danube Basin (that is in the Cisleithanian area of the Habsburg Monarchy until 1918 and in its successor states thereafter) as part of the rise of large-scale enterprise, monopolistic and oligopolistic formations and cartels. This furthered the activities of universal banks – those institutions which combine the short-term business of deposit banking with the long-term credit-financing of investments and which also provide stockbroking services, manage their clients' portfolios, and acquire shares and voting rights for their own and their customers' stock at general meetings of joint-stock companies. This type of banking became prevalent throughout Europe during the phase of the buoyant expansion of capitalism from the 1880s to 1914.

In Central Europe cartelization and the union of banking and industry was very marked. This was relatively soon realized by contemporaries as documented by the very first book on cartels by Friedrich Kleinwächter which was published in Innsbruck in 1883. It may seem improbable that the very first systematic description of concentration in industry, trade and finance should appear on the territory of the Habsburg Monarchy which was held to be severely lagging behind in industrialization. But there has been a tendency to overstate the backwardness of Austria-Hungary in macroeconomic assessments. This view endures mainly because the uneven economic development of this multinational empire has not sufficiently been taken into account, particularly not the historical fact that – parallel to harbouring some of the most economically backward regions of Europe in its southeastern parts – its western regions (Bohemia, Moravia, Silesia and Austria) experienced an industrial revolution similar to western European countries. Also the first attempt to analyse bank–industry relations emanated from this part of the world: Rudolf Hilferding's *Finanzkapital* published in Vienna in 1910 was influenced by conditions in the author's homeland. He himself says 'Austria . . . provides the clearest example of the direct and deliberate influence of bank capital upon cartelization'. Contrary to the widespread assumption that, after the failure of the Crédit Mobilier in France, Germany became the home of universal banking par excellence, it is actually to be found in its purest form in the Habsburg Monarchy.

Most typically this was expressed by the foundation in 1855 of the K.K. privilegierte Österreichische Credit-Anstalt für Handel und Gewerbe (further Credit-Anstalt) as a joint-stock bank on the pattern of the Paris brothers Pereire's Crédit Mobilier but adapted to Austrian conditions. This bank has until recently received the greatest attention from publicists, economists and historians who wrote about certain episodes in its development, especially its spectacular crash in 1931. Dieter Stiefel conjectured in his book that its collapse at the beginning of the world economic crisis is related to the end of finance capitalism (Stiefel, 1989). But its definitive history is contained in the two volumes written by Eduard März who, before his death, related the story in the framework of Austrian economic and social history from the mid-nineteenth century to 1923 (März, 1968, 1981). It is being continued by Fritz Weber.

Important private banking houses had existed before the foundation of the Credit-Anstalt but they were mainly concerned with government finance as well as providing credit for the estates of the high aristocracy, and only to a lesser degree with promoting companies. Also the Österreichische Nationalbank, founded in 1816, conducted some regular banking business which in the long run was unable to satisfy the rising demand for credit. (For the official history of the Österreichische Nationalbank from its foundation to 1938, see Preßburger in 7 volumes, 1959–76 and Kernbauer, 1991.) In 1853 the Niederösterreichische Escompte-Gesellschaft received imperial permission to provide trade and industry in Lower Austria with money by discounting bills of exchange. But the Credit-Anstalt remained the only universal banking institute operating throughout the whole Habsburg Monarchy until the mid-1860s. In 1863 the Allgemeine Österreichische Boden-Credit-Anstalt (further Boden-Credit-Anstalt) was founded which combined mortgage business with commercial banking. It derived its privileged position among the Viennese banks from acting as the banker of the imperial family and the court. As a mediator between the financial centres of London and Vienna the Anglo-Österreichische Bank started its activities in 1864 (Cottrell, 1969). Somewhat later, in 1869, the Wiener Bank-Verein was established as an associate of the Boden-Credit-Anstalt, but its business took off only after 1881. These were to become the most famous of the great Vienna banks, whose individual histories have yet to be written. Fritz Weber's history of the big commercial banks of Vienna during the First World War and the postwar period to approximately 1934 is to appear soon.

Until the late nineteenth century the large Viennese commercial banks did not fulfil the expectations placed in them as promoters of industry. As 'profit-maximizers and risk-minimizers' they preferred the funding of railway construction and public borrowing to financing of industry. Only after overcoming the Great Depression of the 1870s, after the railway boom had run its course, and after profits especially from handling government loans began to decline, did the Vienna banks begin cautiously to turn to industrial lending. From their very beginnings they did not see their role in encouraging entrepreneurial spirit when promoting industrial enterprises, but directed their business to well-established firms (Rudolph, 1976). Neither were they in the forefront of founding new industrial ventures but they preferred to convert profitable enterprises into public limited companies. In the light of empirical evidence none of the big banks performed the 'missionary' task in furthering industrialization accorded to them by Alexander Gerschenkron.

The Austrian banking system performed the usual functions of accumulating and mobilizing capital like that of other developed economies, but it played a much greater active role in employing resources in industry and trade. Since there were no legal limits to share-ownership by banks, they secured their credits by acquiring shares preferably in the largest and soundest enterprises; they strengthened their supervision of client companies by interlocking directorships, they were initiators or mediators of mergers and they encouraged cartelization. The banks performed marketing functions for enterprises belonging to their sphere of influence through sales departments and they acted as cartel bureaux for whole sections of industry, as in the case of sugar, coal and wood.

By the eve of the First World War the eight great Vienna banks held about two-thirds of the total capital of all financial institutions of the empire, they had secured strategic positions in most branches of industry and their influence reached from Vienna to all Habsburg territories. In the Hungarian part of the dual monarchy only one bank could be compared to the leading Viennese banks, the Hungarian General Credit Bank, which itself was linked to the Austrian Credit-Anstalt (Ránki, 1983), while in the Czech Lands the only bank which exceeded the size of a provincial bank with its capital resources and business operations was the Živnostenská banka of Prague (Lacina, 1983, 1990).

At the time of the break-up of the Habsburg Monarchy the big Viennese universal banks found themselves suddenly standing at the centre of multinational diversified concerns. During the short period from 1919 to 1923 the leading Vienna banks were penetrated by international capital and two of them – the Österreichische Länderbank and the Anglo-Österreichische Bank – had become fully foreign-owned Paris- and London-based institutes (Teichova, 1979; Cottrell, 1983).

Despite these sudden transformations, the further evolution of the banking system in the successor states during the interwar period was strongly marked by the prewar system. Accordingly, a parallel development of the bank–industry structure in Austria, Czechoslovakia, Hungary, Italy, Poland and Yugoslavia occurred after the dissolution of constitutional ties. In briefly summing up the common features of this banking system, inherited by each successor state, the following points can be made. The tradition of the universal banks as the source of finance for industrial enterprises continued unbroken. Domestic deposits were mostly insufficient and, towards the end of the 1920s, decreased. Liquidity problems arose perennially, the banks defaulted on their enormous debts in the crisis of the 1930s, and concentration within banking, through mergers, intensified. At the end of the interwar period (1937) 75 per cent of the equity of commercial banks in Romania and Yugoslavia, and at least 30 per cent in Poland and Bulgaria were in foreign, mainly western hands. While foreign shareholding was comparatively high in the case of Austrian banks (although no precise figures are known), no more than 15 per cent of the total capital of all joint-stock banks in Czechoslovakia was foreign-owned (Teichova, 1974).

Czechoslovakia

In many respects the development of the Czech banking system in the Habsburg Monarchy and during the existence of the independent Czechoslovak state between 1918 and 1938 differed from that of the other successor states. As early as the upswing in the business cycle between 1907 and 1912 the Czech banks had achieved a dominating position on the domestic/local (Bohemian, Moravian and Silesian) money market. The strongest among them, especially the Živnostenská banka, penetrated the traditional markets of the Viennese financial institutions. In their competitive expansion into the areas of the Austro-Hungarian Empire populated by Slavs they employed the nationalist slogan of 'mutual Slavonic interests' against the established Vienna and Budapest banks. Although by the outbreak of the Great War the capital of the 22 largest Viennese banks still amounted to 71.4 per cent of the total banking capital of Cisleithania (the Austrian part of the Dual Monarchy), that of the Czech banks had increased its share from four banks and 7.9 per cent in 1900 to 13 banks and 13.3 per cent of the total banking capital in 1913 (Nečas, 1987).

In comparison with the post-1918 Austria where the savings banks sector hardly provided domestic resources for the commercial banks and was only centralized in the Girovereinigung der Sparkassen as late as December 1937, the Czech savings institutes had already founded the Ústřední banka českých spořitelen (Sporobanka) (Central Bank of the Czech Savings Institutes) in June 1903, which became a constant source of funds for the big Czech banks (Hájek, 1986). While the Czech banking system was not immune to the vagaries of crises in the interwar period, in comparison with the Austrian case it had avoided crashes and, above all, the Živnostenská banka's business policy was more cautious than that of the great universal banks of Vienna in granting credit facilities to industrial enterprises, in paying out dividends, and more farsighted in building up reserves. Professor Faltus will most probably comment on the specific story of Slovak banking within the Transleithanian and the Czechoslovak framework (Faltus, 1993).

Austria

In the case of Vienna, the former financial centre of the Danube Basin, bank–industry relations were dramatically affected by the disintegration of the empire, although the big Viennese commercial banks attempted to carry on 'business as usual', but in very much changed circumstances. In the expectation of recovering their role as the financial leaders the Viennese banks retained a hand in credit-financing at least a part of the former empire's business. This policy was pursued, despite the severance of most of their branches (of the 143 branches the 10 biggest Vienna banks possessed outside Austria in 1918 only 9 had remained by 1924). Large sections of their subsidiary enterprises were lost through the application of the process of nostrification within the successor states which involved the transfer of head offices of companies from Vienna to the new nations. Above all, the Viennese banks lost control of their most profitable industrial enterprises, now located beyond the Czechoslovak border.

Unlike German banks which after 1918 opposed foreign penetration the Viennese banks were anxious to attract capital from the countries of the Entente. As with the Austrian government, the bankers assumed that the shrunken Austrian economy would be unviable without external support. During the inflation of the early 1920s industrial demand for credit rose steeply and was met by the banks, but at the price of plunging the Austrian financial sector increasingly into foreign debt. This, eventually dire, situation arose because a prerequisite for the expansion of bank advances to industry was a steadily growing indebtedness on the part of the Viennese banks to western Europe and the USA. With respect to only the short-term foreign indebtedness of the biggest Viennese banks, this liability increased approximately threefold from 1924 to 1930, rising from AS 370 million to AS 980 million (Weber, 1985; Kernbauer and Weber, 1986).

As compared with before 1913 industry became dependent to a much higher degree on bank loans while, in turn, the banks increased their share ownership of dependent client companies. The banks' credit-financing came to rely to a growing extent on borrowing short abroad, but then relending funds on a longer-term basis (Cottrell, 1992). The banks hoped for an upswing in business, but this proved to be illusory and, further, Vienna never regained its regional leadership in finance and trade.

As in other economies, mergers between the Austrian banks took place from the mid-1920s, but to a much greater degree. These fusions occurred after rampant speculation, which marked the period until 1924, and which had been unchecked, since there was no effective banking legislation (Teichova, 1992). In the chaos of hyperinflation, a Banking Commission was established by the Austrian Government in 1922 and charged with the preparation of legislation both to control banking practices and restrict fraudulent dealing on the stock exchange. However, its work was stymied and, eventually, the Commission was disbanded in 1926 without result (Enderle-Burcel, 1992).

Crashes and crises continued and led to more amalgamations. In 1929 only four banks remained out of the eight Viennese institutions. In every case the surviving bank had a greater number of dependent industrial enterprises and more packets of unsaleable shares. The merger movement peaked in 1929 when the Credit-Anstalt absorbed the Boden-Credit-Anstalt, after having digested the Anglo-Österreichische Bank in 1926. Yet it was no solution as the Credit-Anstalt itself crashed spectacularly in May 1931. This sent out shock waves and exacerbated the international banking crisis. The whole Austrian economy, already strained by general depression, was plunged even more deeply into crisis conditions. An article on the industrial shareholdings of the Credit-Anstalt and the debts of its subsidiary enterprises in the early 1930s was published by Mosser and Teichova (1991).

The Austrian government and the Austrian National Bank mounted a rescue operation for the Credit-Anstalt which, by 'socializing' the bank's enormous losses, both satisfied the foreign creditors and eventually after the fusion with the Wiener Bankverein led in 1934 to the establishment of practically a 'One Bank System'. As in Germany this state support was not the application of a policy of nationalization for the banking system, but a state-aided reconstruction exercise. Under it, the debt burden of the insolvent banking system was shouldered by the state. Government financial guarantees indirectly also rescued the bank's industrial enterprises, as most of their debts were written off (Stiefel, 1983, 1989).

The state became the majority shareholder in the Credit-Anstalt, which continued to function as the leading bank, though at a much reduced level, in a system which from 1934 was composed of three big banks, but the other two were the Viennese offices of a Czechoslovak institution, the strong filial of the Prague Živnostenská banka, and the Länderbank controlled by the Paris Banque des Pays de l'Europe Centrale. The consequential implicit underlying shrinkage of the banking system has been termed 'Austrification', because not only were the domestic industrial holdings slimmed down, but all the foreign holdings of the Credit-Anstalt were transferred to its foreign creditors. Unlike in

Germany, the bank was not reprivatized, the majority of it shares continuing to remain with what ultimately became the Austrofascist state. By the time of the Anschluß in March 1938, the Austrian banking system had resumed profitability, but was then fully integrated into the German Reich (Matis and Weber, 1992).

Without a 'lender of last resort' universal banks were unable to cope with the crisis of the 1930s. The 'Great Slump' marked an end to the form of 'mixed' banking which had functioned since the 1880s. Across central and eastern Europe the state was forced to intervene and mount rescue actions: everywhere the losses of the big credit banks and their large industrial clients were 'socialized', everywhere the state took over such banks, either outright or through majority shareholdings. However, this did not usher in socialism, as Hilferding had expected; on the contrary, these actions succeeded in rescuing capitalism and buttressed highly concentrated structures within banking and industry.

In Czechoslovakia the banking system was first essentially taken over by Nazi Germany after the occupation of the Czech Lands (15 March 1939), and then nationalized by the post-1945 and dismantled by the post-1948 communist régimes. It is now in the process of reconstruction.

In Austria, universal banking had outlasted all changes. While the banking organization after the Anschluß remained essentially unaltered except for the replacement of Jewish by German directors, its business was directed to serve the Third Reich's war finances. During the Second World War Austria was recognized as 'the first victim of Nazi aggression' by the Allies (1943) and in the wake of Germany's defeat it recovered its status of independence. The banks were nationalized in 1946 to avoid being taken over as German property by the Allies. After a decade of allied four-power occupation Austria gained neutrality in 1955. Since 1957 the banking system has undergone partial privatization. It has functioned effectively in rebuilding the mixed economy of the Second Austrian Republic. Since the collapse of communism in 1989 the Austrian banks have shown vigorous interest in the recently opened investment opportunities in central and southeast Europe where, in historical content, their traditional market has been.

There are large and numerous gaps in the history of central European commercial banking and even more so in the history of individual commercial banks. While books on the subject are scarce, the number of articles has steadily increased, not least because of the encouragement provided by the ongoing research projects. The references, which lay no claim to completeness, are designed to give an impression of the state of the historiography of commercial banking in Austria and Czechoslovakia.

Note

The research project 'Bank–Industry Relations in Interwar Europe: Austria, Czechoslovakia, Hungary and Sweden', under the direction of Alice Teichova, began in October 1986. Since 1 January 1990 it has been supported by the British Economic and Social Research Council (ESRC) for which I wish to express my warmest thanks. Those involved comprise: Elisabeth Boross (Budapest), Philip L. Cottrell (Leicester), Mats Larsson, Håkan Lindgren, Ragnhild Lundström, Jan Ottosson, Hans Sjögren (Uppsala), Herbert Matis, Alois Mosser, Desirée Verdonk, Fritz Weber (Vienna), György Ránki (until his sudden untimely death), György Köver and Agnes Pogány (Budapest), Jan Hájek, Vlastislav Lacina, Jiří Novotný and Jaroslav Pátek (Prague), Josef Faltus (Bratislava).

References

Ausch, K. (1968), *Als die Banken fielen*, Vienna.

Cottrell, P.L. (1969), 'London financiers and Austria 1863–1875: The Anglo-Austrian Bank', *Business History*, XI.

Cottrell, P.L. (1983), 'Aspects of Western equity investment in the banking systems of East Central Europe', in Teichova, A. and Cottrell, P.L. (eds), *International Business and Central Europe 1918–1939*, Leicester and New York, pp. 309–47.

Cottrell, P.L. with Stone, C.J. (1992), 'Credits, and deposits to finance credits', in Cottrell, P.L., Lindgren, H. and Teichova, A. (eds), *European Industry and Banking, 1920–39: A Review of Bank Industry relations*, Leicester, pp. 43–78.

Cottrell, P.L., Lindgren, H. and Teichova, A. (eds) (1992), *European Industry and Banking, 1920–1939: A Review of Bank Industry Relations*, Leicester.

Enderle-Burcel, G. (1992), 'The Austrian Workers' bank: a financial institution for the community or simply another profit-oriented institution?', in *European Industry and Banking*, pp. 95–108.

Federn, Walther (1928), 'Die österreichischen Banken', in Federn, W. (ed.), *10 Jahre Nachfolgestaaten*, Vienna.

Gerschenkron, A. (1965), *Economic Backwardness in Historical Perspective*, New York.

Gerschenkron, A. (1977), *An economic spurt that failed*, Princeton.

Hilferding, R. (1981), *Finance capital. A study of the latest phase of capitalist development*, London.

Kernbauer, H. (1991), *Währungspolitik in der Zwischenkriegszeit. Geschichte der Oesterreichischen Nationalbank von 1923 bis 1938*, Das österreichische Noteninstitut, Dritter Teil, Erster Band, Vienna.

Kernbauer, H. and Weber, F. (1984), 'Die Wiener Großbanken in der Zeit der Kriegs- und Nachkriegsinflation', in Feldman, Gerald D. et al.

(eds), *Die Erfahrungen der Inflation im internationalen Zusammenhang und Vergleich*, Berlin.

Kernbauer, H. and Weber, F. (1986), 'Multinational Banking in the Danube basin', in Teichova, A., Lévy-Leboyer, M. and Nussbaum, H. (eds), *Multinational enterprise in historical perspective*, Cambridge, pp. 185–99.

März, E. (1968), *Österreichische Industrie- und Bankpolitik der Zeit Franz Josephs I. Am Beispiel der k.k. priv. österreichischen Credit-Anstalt für Handel und Gewerbe*, Vienna.

März, E. (1981), *Österreichische Bankpolitik in der Zeit der großen Wende 1913–1923*, Vienna, trans. by Charles Kessler (1984), as *Austrian Banking and Financial Policy Creditanstalt at a Turning Point 1913–1923*, London.

März, E. and Weber, F. (1983), 'The antecedents of the Austrian financial crash 1931', *Zeitschrift für Wirtschafts- und Sozialwissenschaften*, pp. 103–5, 497–519.

Matis, H. and Weber, F. (1992), 'Economic *Anschluß* and German *Großmachtpolitik*: the takeover of the Austrian Credit-Anstalt 1938', in *European Industry and Banking*, pp. 109–26.

Mosser, A. and Teichova, A. (1991), 'Investment behaviour of industrial joint-stock companies and industrial shareholding by the österreichische Credit-Anstalt: inducement or obstacle to renewal and change in interwar Austria', in James, H., Lindgren, H. and Teichova, A., *The role of banks in the interwar economy*, Cambridge and Paris, pp. 122–57.

Preßburger, S. (1959–76), *Das Oesterreichische Noteninstitut 1816–1966*, 7 vols, Vienna.

Reik, W. (1932), *Die Beziehungen der österrichischen Großbanken zur Industrie*, Vienna.

Rudolph, R. (1976), *Banking and industrialization in Austria-Hungary*, Cambridge.

Stiefel, D. (1983), 'The reconstruction of the Credit-Anstalt', in Teichova, A. and Cottrell, P.L. (eds), *International business and Central Europe 1918–1939*, Leicester and New York, pp. 415–30.

Stiefel, D. (1989), *Finanzdiplomatie und Weltwirtschaftskrise. Die Krise der Credit-Anstalt für Handel und Gewerbe 1931*, Franfurt am Main.

Teichova, A. (1974), *An economic background to Munich. International business and Czechoslovakia 1918–1938*, Cambridge.

Teichova, A. (1979), 'Versailles and the expansion of the Bank of England into Central Europe', in Horn, J. and Kocka, J. (eds), *Recht und Entwicklung der Großunternehmen im 19. und frühen 20. Jahrhundert*, Göttingen, pp. 366–87.

Teichova, A. (1992), 'Rivals and Partners. Banking and Industry in

Europe, 1900–1939', in Cottrell, P.L., Lindgren, H. and Teichova, A. (eds), *European Industry and Banking*, pp. 17–29.

Weber, F. (1985), 'Die österreichischen Großbanken in der Zwischen-kriegszeit', *Christliche Demokratie*, p. 4.

Czechoslovakia

Čechoslovakische Nationalbank (ed.) (1937), *Zehn Jahre čechoslo-vakische Nationalbank*, Prague.

Hájek, J. (1986), *Rozvoj národně českých bank od konce 19. století do roku 1914* (The development of the national Czech banks from the end of the nineteenth century to 1914) and *Česká státní spořitelna* (The Czech State Savings Bank), Prague.

Horejsek, J. (1971), 'Kapitalová expanze Živnostenské banky do jihovýchodní Evropy v letech 1907–1918', (The capital expansion of the Živnostenská bank into southeast Europe 1907–1918, in *Sborník prací historických. Acta universitatis Palackiense Olomucensis, Historika XV*, Prague.

Jindra, Z. (1957), 'K rozvoji českého bankovního kapitálu pred první světovou válkou' (The development of Czech banking capital before the First World War), *Československý časopis historický*, pp. 506–26.

Lacina, V. (1983), 'Živnobanka a její koncern v letech velké hospodářské krize 1929 az 1934' (The Živnobank and its concern in the years of the world economic crisis 1929–1934), *Československý časopis historický*, pp. 350–77.

Lacina, V. (1990), 'Živnostenská banka pred a během první světové války (1907–1919)' (The Živnostenská bank before and during the First World War 1907–1918), *Československý časopis historický* (3), pp. 276–303.

Nečas, C. (1980), 'K počátkum české kapitálové expanze do jihovýchodní Evropy' (The beginnings of the expansion of Czech capital into southeast Europe), in *Sborník prací filozofické fakulty Brnenské univerzity*, C 27, Brno.

Nečas, C. (1987), *Na prahu české kapitálové expanze* (At the threshold of Czech capital expansion), Brno.

Pimper, A. (1929), *Ceské obchodní banky za války a po válce* (The Czech commercial banks during and before the War), Prague.

Hungary (also see Chapter 20, References)

Ránki, G. (1983), 'The Hungarian General Credit Bank in the 1920s', in Teichova, A. and Cottrell, P.L. (eds), *International Business*, pp. 355–73.

CHAPTER NINETEEN

Central European Banking between 1850 and 1950

Fritz Weber

In the history of Austrian banking different phases can be distinguished: the formative years of modern banking (1855–85), the years of glory and power (1885–1914/18), the period of crisis (1918–38), the German interlude (1938–45), and the period of nationalized banking after 1945. The following comment centres on the interwar years, i.e. on the causes and consequences of the 1931 crisis, and on what it means for the historian writing the history of these difficult days in the life of a renowned bank.

Were the banks promoters of industrialization?

The question as to whether the central European Crédit Mobilier banks have really performed what Alice Teichova calls a 'missionary role' in developing the industrial system in a backward area of the continent has caused a long and controversial debate between economic historians.

Alice Teichova, too, doubts the Alexander Gerschenkron argument that the new banking type was able to assist industry in the most crucial stages of its making. In my opinion she is right.

In its early days, the first Austrian Crédit Mobilier bank, the Creditanstalt für Handel und Gewerbe in Vienna, was moving on unsafe ground and therefore had to follow the sometimes painful trail of learning by doing. The real history of banking had little to do with the ideal scheme of the French Péreire brothers. Founded in 1855, the Creditanstalt almost immediately was shaken by the repercussions of a severe stock exchange crash in 1857, which for decades cut the newly established ties with industries related to the railway sector. After 1857 the Creditanstalt was still in the railway business, but only as a pure financier, who refrained from being directly engaged in constructing the lines.

I would disagree, however, with Alice Teichova's explicitly negative judgement concerning the role of private banks in Austria prior to the 1850s. That banks should be the promoters of (proto)-industry was an idea already formed by the early Austrian mercantilist Wilhelm von

Schroeder; there were various examples of bank–(proto)-industry relations in the late eighteenth century, and even the Austrian Rothschilds
were less conservative than is commonly alleged. They introduced the
steam railway system in the Habsburg Monarchy; the Kaiser Ferdinand-
Nordbahn, opened in 1837, was their foundation, and the iron works of
Witkowitz were developed as the most advanced establishment of that
kind in central Europe under the aegis of two private Viennese banking
houses: S.M. v. Rothschild and Gebrüder Gutmann.

From 1857 onwards, the Creditanstalt acted cautiously, recovered
from the crash of 1873 (which made it even more guarded) and only
rediscovered its industrial mission in the 1890s, then turned into a
Universalbank, which combined short-term business and long-term
financing of investments with permanent ownership in industrial shares
in order to gain control over the management of industrial firms, to an
extent which let Hilferding speak of a veritable 'fusion' of industrial and
banking capital. Even if Hilferding did mainly refer to the German case,
the reality reflected by his *Finanzkapital* has to be sought in the Habsburg
Monarchy, where the predominance of the banking system over industry
was even more marked than in Germany.

The symbiosis between banking and big industry was due to the under-
developed capital market in Austria-Hungary; bank credit undoubtedly
enabled a faster industrial growth in a country where investment capital
could only be raised by self-financing. The rise of firms like the Skoda
works was linked to the access to credit facilities of their patronizing
banks. In this respect Schumpeter was right to link industrial growth to
bank credit; he failed, however, supposing that banks helped to create
'new productive combinations' in the emphatic sense of the word: the
Austrian banks were never the vanguard of industrial development; they
preferred financing well-respected, prosperous, medium-sized enterprises
instead of channelling money into entrepreneurial new ground.

On the eve of the First World War the Austrian banks were, although
showing some signs of potential immobilization, at the height of their
power and influence. But this power was related to the stability of the
political environment, the Danube Monarchy, too. The Viennese banks
had hardly ever followed imperialistic tendencies *vis-à-vis* the Balkans
prior to 1914; they could only be accused of *Binnenimperialismus*,
inland imperialistic aspirations within the multinational empire, and of
favouring cartelization and monopolization in a protected market by
their client firms.

When the Habsburg Monarchy fell apart in 1918, the empire of the
Viennese banks was doomed to failure, too. It was political as well as
economic nationalism which brought to an end the historical predominance of the Austrian banks in the Danube basin. And the greatest

Viennese bank, the Creditanstalt, was the first to sell, in immense haste, its biggest and most important (and now foreign) branches to 'national' capital groups in Upper Italy, Slovenia and Czechoslovakia.

This spirit of panic, however, did not last for a long time. Soon the management of the Creditanstalt (and of other Viennese banks) discovered the saving way out: the asking in of western banks. By the year 1920 the foundations were laid for a development which started with the banks as prisoners of their own multinational history and soon ended up with them as prisoners of the once chosen postwar strategy of multinationalization.

In order to be prepared for a new offensive business policy *vis-à-vis* the successor states of the Habsburg Monarchy, the Viennese banks were forced to maintain a huge, expensive and unproductive apparatus. In reality, however, they only had to bear the costs for hoarding the labour force in vain, because they never succeeded in regaining influential footholds abroad, except in a limited sense in Poland and Yugoslavia.

Far greater losses approached, however, not from transnational adventures, but from inland business. A disastrous stock exchange crash in Vienna in spring 1924 forced the banks to intervene on behalf of their combines (and of course of their own interests as shareholders in those firms), and it ruined the Austrian capital market for the rest of the interwar years. From 1924 onwards the banks were condemned to financing industry on a greater scale then ever before. Austrian industry had a great capital demand for investments necessary to increase the competitiveness on the (now) foreign eastern European markets. And since the banks were the main shareholders of industry, those credits also served as a means of keeping the value of shares intact, which were stored in the strong-rooms of the banks.

In a certain sense the banks behaved as if they wanted to confirm Ludwig von Mises's theory of the business cycle: according to Mises the business cycle is the consequence of credit inflation caused by the banking system. By creating credit industrial projects are undertaken, which under 'natural' conditions would be left undone as unprofitable. However, the big difference from Mises's theory lay in the abnormally high interest rates in Austria as a result of both hyperinflation and monopolistic credit markets controlled by the banks.

The Austrian banks followed a dangerous strategy: financing an upswing in advance by granting credits to debtors who, under normal circumstances and applying strict criteria, would hardly have been rated as sound and creditworthy. By way of contrast, the Czech banks had chosen a far more cautious policy, and claimed interest rates lower than in Austria. The Czech banks had more room for manoeuvre from the beginning of the interwar period. However, even if we attribute a good deal of the difficulties of the Austrian banks to the consequences of hyperinflation, there is enough space left for thinking of problems as 'home-made' in the management floors of Vienna.

Going east or the joint venture of foreign capital and Viennese banks in the interwar years

Alice Teichova clearly shows the eminent role of foreign capital in the interwar banking system of central Europe. In my opinion, however, she is wrong in believing that foreign capital still played a vital role in the Austrian banking sector immediately before the Second World War. To be sure, the Länderbank, formerly an Austrian institution, had been transformed into a branch of the Banque des Pays de l'Europe Centrale in autumn 1921, and the Mercurbank, the only remaining middle-sized bank, was entirely controlled by the Dresdner Bank in 1937. However, the majority of the shares of the Österreichische Creditanstalt-Wiener Bankverein, which comprised two-thirds of the country's banking business, were owned by the Austrian State, the central bank and the pensions funds of the bank itself. The foreign share, which had been about 30 per cent before the 1931 crisis, amounted to about 25 per cent.

Being the holder of one-quarter of the capital of the Creditanstalt, however, did not mean being interested in the future of the bank. The 25 per cent represented the remainder of former vital interests, a historical burden, adhered to involuntarily, and ready to be given up on the first possible opportunity. It seems important to stress the fact that the Deutsche Bank, which became the main shareholder of the Creditanstalt after 1938, could dispose of only 695 preferred shares (of a total of 334,000 ordinary and preferred shares) prior to the Anschluß.

Percentages hardly ever tell the true story of dependence and influence. True, in 1930 about 30 per cent of the shares of the Creditanstalt were owned by foreign shareholders. These shareholders, however, had not taken any decisive interest in the everyday conduct of business for years. Only after the collapse of the Boden-Credit-Anstalt in 1929 and its merger with the Creditanstalt, had the Bank of England, as one of the main shareholders, delegated one of its confidants in the board of managers of the bank: in time, only to witness the last stage of a development, which culminated in the banking crisis of 1931; too late, however, to take the helm.

Until 1929 the managers of the Viennese banks acted independently of the foreign shareholders. I wonder what the case in other regions of central or eastern Europe was. Were there managerial interventions of western banks or did they acquire the shares as portfolio rather than as direct investment?

To me it seems that the real power of foreign capital did not depend on shareholding, but on the position as creditor. The collapse of the Creditanstalt and the story of its reconstruction by the Austrian State, jealously guarded and fussily controlled by the Creditanstalt International Committee in London, clearly show the validity of this argument.

As Alice Teichova correctly states, the prerequisite of the multinational orientation of the Viennese banks in the 1920s was foreign financial backing; and the Austrian banks would not have dared to ogle at the Danube basin without western short-term credits. On the other hand, one also has to consider these funds as an important contribution to easing the burden of dear investment credits for Austrian firms. Western credits were not a mere transitory item in the transnational books of the Viennese banks.

In my opinion, Alice Teichova is also wrong in believing that the Austrian savings banks sector 'hardly provided domestic resources for the commercial banks'. The savings banks were passing on funds but, due to the fierce competition for deposits, on conditions quite unfavourable to the banks – another reason for them to prefer the much cheaper western loans.

The politics of window dressing

In her paper Alice Teichova lays strong emphasis on the argument that the Austrian bankers acted negligently in comparison to their Czech colleagues. But the permanent crisis of the Viennese banking community cannot only be regarded as a mere consequence of mismanagement. There were also difficulties of an 'objective' kind, like the different performance of the two economies (see Table 19.1). Moreover, Austria suffered from severe hyperinflation in 1921–22, whereas Czechoslovakia succeeded in stabilizing the currency soon after the First World War.

Evidently, hyperinflation must have affected institutions, which by definition deal with money, and as any other economic subject of the time, the Austrian banks desperately tried to avoid the adverse effects of inflation. One of the methods chosen was transforming industrial credits into shares by issuing new capital: at the end of the inflationary period the banks possessed abnormally huge equity stocks, which they could sell only temporarily during the stock exchange boom in 1923, but which they had to repurchase after the crash in spring 1924.

After 1924 the Viennese banks proved unable to get rid of those shares because of the poor performance of the Austrian economy. Nobody was willing to buy non-paying equities, and the growing indebtedness of the firms (regardless of whether they might have resulted from losses

Table 19.1   Average compound growth rates of GNP, 1913–38, (%) in different successor states of the Habsburg Monarchy

	Austria	CSR	Average of Austria, CSR, Hungary, Yugoslavia
1913–29	0.3	2.7	1.6
1929–38	−1.8*	−0.2*	0.4

* 1927–37

Source: Maddison, A., 'Economic Policy and Performance in Europe' in Cipolla, C.M. (ed.), *The Fontana Economic History of Europe*, vol. 5, part 2, p. 453.

covered by bank loans or from investments for the future) made things even worse for the banks. The marasmus of the Viennese stock exchange forced them to grant new credits to their clientele without being able to transform those advances into shares to be sold to the market as had been the case prior to 1914.

Sooner or later (and with time, to an ever greater extent) the bank managers had recourse to questionable methods of window dressing to hide imminent or actual sources of losses to the public. Credits were granted to industrial companies with the sole purpose of enabling the distribution of dividends, even if no profit could be drawn upon. The ulterior motive of such practices was the dubious hope that the shares of client firms could be sold to the public more easily, when the desperately longed-for economic upswing would occur.

Sometimes firms were even compelled to pay dividends by their patron banks: according to the minutes of the board of directors of the Boden-Credit-Anstalt, the Mautner works (one of the greatest central European textile firms) had announced their intention to reduce the dividend rate in 1925. The BCA, however, insisted on the continuation of high dividends. In June 1926, on the occasion of preparing the Goldbilanz (which served to draw a final stroke to inflation), on the advice of the Boden-Credit-Anstalt, the Danube Navigation Company had to raise the dividend rate by one-third and reassess various assets, in order to adjust the capital of the firm upwards.

By such dubious tactics the Viennese banks succeeded in hiding their great difficulties and in presenting to the public quite optimistic balance sheets. Between 1923 (the first year after hyperinflation) and 1929 the Creditanstalt stated cumulated net profits of AS 58.4 million; in reality, however, there had only been two profitable years, if any: 1925 and 1923. 1923 was the year of the great stock exchange boom. However, when the statement for 1923 had to be prepared, the crash was already under way, and it has to be doubted whether it was very wise not to make provisions for measurable losses.

Austrian banking legislation, on the other hand, did almost nothing to force the banks to lay their cards on the table, and left them huge room for manoeuvre. Thus the banks were inventing ever new instruments for hiding or (as they saw it themselves) putting off losses. Not only were they systematically over-revaluing the so-called secret reserves allegedly resting in the equity portfolios, but they also created new categories of assets like Besserungsscheine ('bills of betterment') and bedingte Nachlässe ('conditional reductions' of paying interest on loans), which both served to excuse the banks from confessing losses already made or to postpone imminent losses into the far future, when economic prosperity was expected to have eradicated them. Then, following the arguments of the bankers, the industrial firms would honour the 'bills of betterment' and redeem the loans received in bad times.

The same over-optimistic spirit fired the imagination of the bankers in constructing profits. Only by tapping hidden reserves were they able to pay handsome dividends. The 'Stern expertise' of 1932, which was based on the true figures of the Creditanstalt, showed the extent to which the bank had taken recourse to assessments in order to pay dividends (see Table 19.2).

Table 19.2   Internal reassessments of the Creditanstalt, 1926–29

	1926	1927	1928	1929
Reassessments (ASm.)	4.2	12.5	10.1	16.5
As a % of annual shown profits	53.5	120.0	96.0	180.0

Source: Stern expertise, 1932.

The times of radical economic recovery never came, but the world depression of the 1930s did. After 1929 the manipulations of the late twenties – a time of relatively bright economic performance – called forth their fatal consequences. The accumulated secret losses of many years had to be avowed; only this explains the huge loss of AS 140 million declared by the Creditanstalt in May 1931, far more than the bank had been able to show as total profits between 1923 and 1929, which could never have occurred within one single year only.

I do not have the space here to refer to other examples of balance-sheet facelifting of other Austrian banks like the Boden-Credit-Anstalt (which had to be amalgamated with the Creditanstalt in autumn 1929) or the Niederösterreichische Escompte-Gesellschaft which was practically liquidated as a commercial bank in 1934, when the Creditanstalt took over its current business and the NEG itself was renamed Österreichische Industriekredit AG, an institution which conducted the industrial combine of the former bank and settled the long-term liabilities of the firms *vis-à-vis* the NEG. Nor is it possible to give prominence to the conservative and correct behaviour of the management of the Wiener Bankverein, which refrained from questionable methods of window dressing.

What has to be stressed, however, is the surprising fact that in Austria, in contrast to other countries like Czechoslovakia or Germany, no new banking law was introduced after the crisis of 1931. The Austrian government had been forced to prepare a law by the financial committee of the League of Nations in 1931. But the bill produced in 1932 was too radical for the liberal experts of the international organization. The bill then disappeared to be revised, and was never mentioned again.

After the Anschluß of 1938, the German bank regulations were adopted and, although there were several attempts to introduce a new and improved law after 1945, the governments of the Second Austrian Republic failed to break the delaying actions of the banks (the biggest of them nationalized since 1946). Only the Kreditwesengesetz of 1979 and further measures undertaken in the 1980s in view of Austria's intended joining the EC have led to legislative innovation, almost forty years after the dramatic crisis of the Creditanstalt.

The role of personality in banking

Since banking is done by human beings, the question of the role of personality in the history of banking is quite a reasonable one. Changes in the pattern of commercial behaviour should also be attributed to generation changes in the management of firms, related to alterations in the overall economic climate.

The interwar years provide a good example of how the selection and the behaviour of bank managers influenced business strategies, not only in Austria. Whoever carefully studies German banking history will find similar proof of bank failures caused by bad decisions of expansionary-minded managers like Mr Goldschmied of the Darmstädter Bank.

What we encounter in the first floors of the Austrian banks in the 1920s, is a mélange of two different main attitudes: pre-1914 banking, and a mentality which I would call inflationary banking. We see a generation of managers at work who had either made their decisive experience during the belle époque formative years of the *Finanzkapital*, when expansion seemed nearly unlimited within the overheated economic climate of the Second Gründerzeit (E. März), or had entered the banking business during the years of inflation when every business was mixed up with speculation. The more cautious and conservat ive type of bankers, who also had the Great Depression of the 1870s and 1880s in mind, had already been replaced before or during the war.

The bankers of the interwar period were, with a few exceptions, expansionary-minded in business matters and conservative in politics. They cooperated with right-wing parties, and it is well known that the Austrian Bankenverband (association of banks and bankers) supported the anti-democratic Heimwehren. On the other hand they favoured economic liberalism and non-interventionism, an attitude which clearly expressed itself in opposing an efficacious banking law. The counterfactual question must be allowed: what would have happened in Austria with bankers more conservative in business and more liberal, or at least less narrow-minded, in political matters?

The close connection with the political élite may, as the liberal Walther Federn had already presumed in 1931, have favoured a certain carelessness – the Creditanstalt had got the government out of a scrape by agreeing to the fusion with the Boden-Credit-Anstalt in 1929, and the bankers seem to have been sure that one good turn would deserve another, should anything go wrong with the bank in the future. Although Federn's hypothesis cannot be proved, what happened in May 1931 seems to have been nothing other than the gigantic enlargement of practices already carried through during the mid-1920s, when a whole series of provincial banks (usually connected with the leading Austrian party, the conservative Christlichsoziale Partei), had been subsidized by the state. A touch of this narrow provincial spirit in dealing with banking matters can also be felt everywhere in the events of 1931.

In the end a new generation of bankers took over the leadership in Austrian banking. The new managers of the Creditanstalt recruited from the provinces, like Josef Joham, were experts coming from the industry like Erich Heller, or foreigners like Adrianus van Hengel. They introduced and carried through the policy of Austrification of the Viennese banking system in the 1930s: the limiting of the radius of action within the confines of Austria and the disposal of the foreign assets of the Creditanstalt. The most radical idea, however, the transformation of universal banking into deposit banking of the western type, was buried with Van Hengel, who died in an accident in 1936. His successor Joham slightly but steadily turned the rudder again in traditional waters.

How to write and what to have in mind when writing the history of a bank

So finally, how should a historian write the history of a bank? He should have general history in mind (for instance, the impact of the nationality conflict in Austria-Hungary prior to 1914) and, of course, general economic history. In particular, the history of a universal bank cannot be separated from the overall economic fate of a country or a region. And the historian should also take into account individual history: the social environment, and the professional training of bank managers.

Above all, however, working as a banking historian requires the abilities of a detective. Under normal circumstances he never finds what he is looking for in bank archives. He is therefore compelled to use his imagination in order to find the missing links and to advance wise hypotheses. (Except if there is a banking crisis, which usually leads to public investigations revealing the inner secrets of the banks concerned.)

There will always be a field of tension left between the expectations of the bank commissioning the writing of a historical book, and the high demands of the historian, who wants to find out the truth and nothing else but the very historical truth, even if it should be painful for the patron.

The banks have to learn that banking history does not mean writing the sunny success story of a bank by eliminating the dark days of the past. Almost everybody, for instance, has a rudimentary knowledge about the crisis of the Creditanstalt in 1931. And very often historical prejudice does supply the 'man in the street' with half-truths and arguments far worse than any true history of the crisis could tell him. Isn't it, in the end, better to have a historian at hand, even if his conclusions seem to be inconvenient at first sight?

Corporate identity, in the true sense of the word, should also include the knowledge of sad events in the life of an enterprise. What else is history useful for, if not for learning from past failures? At least it is far less costly than learning by doing, without knowing the consequences of bad decisions long ago.

CHAPTER TWENTY

Hungarian Banking – Research and History

Agnes Pogány

Before 1945, monetary and banking history in Hungary was dominated by the anniversary volumes commissioned by the banks to celebrate jubilees. They are of lesser value for contemporary research because they are mostly descriptive and narrow-minded. Although there was some work of lasting value (Sándor Jirkovsky's (1944) and István Varga's (1964) essays on Hungarian monetary and banking history), all in all, banking history was only of partial importance between the wars.

After 1947, with the socialization of the Hungarian banking sector, interest in monetary history declined further. No monograph about banking history was written in these decades and the topic was hardly touched by the comprehensive works about Hungarian economic history prepared then. In the fifties, sixties and even in the seventies banking history was identical to the problem of the 'Finanzkapital', that is, how banks depleted the industrial enterprises belonging to their sphere of influence.

In the 1970s, a new evaluation of the economic history of the Austro-Hungarian Monarchy evolved in Hungary. The new approach shook and drastically changed the treatment of the banks' role, which until then had been characteristically hostile and negative. In the volumes written jointly by Iván Berend and the late György Ránki, adapting the hypothesis of Alexander Gerschenkron, the authors attributed a positive role to the banks in the process of Hungarian modernization and, in contradiction to Gerschenkron, showed that the development of the Hungarian banking system followed the Austro-German pattern and not the Russian one as Gerschenkron assumed.

The real breakthrough, however, took place as late as the 1980s. The essays written by György Kövér (1982, 1986) depicted the banks not as power-drunk monsters but as complex phenomena and as active and important participants in the economy. In the second half of the eighties social history researchers made studies on business élites, in which 'haute' finance occupied a leading position. György Lengyel's book (1989) *Entrepreneurs, Bankers and Merchants* shows the results of this research group.

From 1986 on, Hungarian scholars took part in the project 'Bank–

Industry Relations in Interwar Europe: Austria, Czechoslovakia, Hungary and Sweden' under the direction of Professor Alice Teichova. The last workshop of the research team was held in Budapest in September 1992. It dealt with international comparison of universal banking in several European countries. The conference, which attracted more than 40 historians and bankers from 13 countries, was of enormous importance for the strengthening of Hungarian banking history.

Banking history does not exist without an existing banking sector. This commonplace has been evidenced by the events in Hungary since the late 1980s, as the interest in banking history was vehemently increased by the abolition of the state-owned one-bank system and by the formation of the new commercial banks in 1987. In the same year, the Hungarian National Bank decided to start and finance a research project on the history of Hungarian central banking.

This project is still in progress, the first volume (from 1816 – the foundation of the Austrian National Bank – to 1924 – the establishment of the autonomous Hungarian National Bank) was published in 1993. The second and third volumes dealing with the interwar years and the period from 1949 to 1987 respectively, will be written by a group of scholars in the years to come. A shortened German and English version is planned by the publisher.

In 1991, a new project was started on the history of Hungarian money institutions, which is sponsored by the Hungarian Banking Association, the Hungarian National Bank, the International Educational Centre for Bankers and by other financial institutions. Research is focused on four topics:

- A structural analysis of Hungarian money institutions in selected benchmark years (1912–13, 1937–38 and 1946–47, before its nationalization).
- Relations between the banks: rivalry and competition.
- Relations between the banks and their clients; the sphere of interest of the Budapest big banks.
- Relations between state and banks, legislation, effects of the monetary and financial policy on the banks; the role of the banks in obtaining foreign resources for the government, etc.

Apart from these bigger research programmes mentioned, there have been several individual attempts. The newly established Hungarian commercial banks are eager to choose a predecessor for themselves from the last century. The eagerness was evident as early as the moment when they gave names to themselves. By choosing names slightly resembling those of the former big Budapest banks, the new ones tried to demonstrate a historic continuity and the acceptance of the traditions. In Hungary, the legitimacy of the existing institutions is supposed to rest on historical foundations. No wonder that the new banks, in seeking their ancestors and historical legitimacy, have published several works on banking history. In these works, as a critical review has shown recently, professional competence and deepest research are lacking. They mostly revitalize the uncritical attitude of the anniversary works of the pre-Second World War period.

Hungarian banking history is now forming. It would like to create its own educational forms, organization and periodical. This academic meeting in Amsterdam will surely be a great stimulus for that.

References

Alföldi, Antal (1928), *A budapesti pénzintézetek története napjainkig*, Budapest.

Berend, T. Iván and Ránki, György (1966), *Magyarország gazdasága az elsö világháború után 1919–1929*, Akadémiai Kiadó.

Berend, T. Iváv and Ránki, György (1972), *A magyar gazdaság 100 éve*, Budapest, Kossuth és KJK.

Boross, Elisabeth A. (1984), 'The Role of the State Issuing Bank in the Course of Inflation in Hungary between 1914–1924', in Feldman, G.D, Holtfrerich, C.L., Ritter, G.A. and Witt, P.-C. (eds), *Die Erfahrungen der Inflation im Internationalen Zusammenhang und Vergleich*, Berlin and New York, Walter de Gruyter.

Jirkovszky, Sándor (1944), *Az Osztrák-Magyar Monarchia jegybankjának tötténete*, Budapest, Athenaeum.

Jirkovszky, Sándor (1945), *A magyarországi pénzintézetek története az elsö világháború végéig*, Budapest.

Kelemen, József (1938), *A magyar hitelügy töténete legújabb idokig*, Budapest.

Kövér, György (1982), *Iparosodás agrárországban*, Budapest, Gondolat.

Kover, György (1986), *1873. Egy Krach anatómiája*, Budapest, Kozmosz Könyvek.

Kövér, György (1991), 'The Austro-Hungarian Banking System: International banking 1870–1914', in Cameron, R. and Bovikin, V.I. (eds), *International Banking 1870–1914*, Oxford University Press, pp. 319–45.

Lengyel, György (1989), *Vállalkozók, bankárok, kereskedók. A magyar gazdasági elit a 19. században és a 20. század elso felében*, Budapest, Magvetó Kiadó.

Péteri, György (1985), *Montagu Norman és a magyar 'szanálási mu'*,

Századok, 1.

Pogány, Ágnes (1989), 'From the Cradle to the Grave? Banking and Industry in Budapest in the 1910s and 1920s', *The Journal of European Economic History*, vol. 18, no. 3.

Pogány, Ágnes (1992), 'Bankers and Families. The Case of the Hungarian Sugar Industry', in Teichova, Alice and Cottrell, Philip (eds), *European Industry and Banking 1920–1939: Review of Bank–Industry Relations*, Leicester University Press.

Ránki, György (1983), 'The Hungarian General Credit Bank in the 1920s', in Teichova, A. and Cottrell, P.L. (eds), *International Business and Central Europe, 1918–1939*, Leicester University Press.

Varga, István (1929), 'A magyar Nemzeti Bank és az Osztrák-Magyar Bank bankjegyforgalma, váltótárca és érckészlet adatainak magyarázata', A Magyar Gazdaságkutató Intézet 2. számú külön kiadványa, Budapest.

Varga, István (1964), *Az újabb magyar pénztörténet egyes elméleti tanulságai*, Budapest.

CHAPTER TWENTY-ONE

Comment Ecrire l'Histoire d'une Banque d'Epargne?

Leen van Molle

De toutes les manières de pratiquer la prévoyance, l'épargne est la simple, la plus commode, mais aussi la plus rudimentaire et la moins efficace pour prévenir les misères de l'existence – Louis Varlez, promoteur du syndicalisme socialiste à Gand, 1901.

Les banques d'épargne interviennent avec une grande efficacité dans le processus par lequel les fonds apportés par les prêteurs sont mis à la disposition des emprunteurs;. . . A ce titre, elles jouent un rôle important au sein de l'économie nationale. . . – Jean Godeaux, gouverneur de la Banque Nationale de Belgique, 1986.

Réflexions préliminaires

Parmi les chercheurs qui écrivent l'histoire des institutions financières, plutôt rares sont ceux qui se livrent à l'étude des caisses d'épargne. C'est un thème historiographique manifestement moins populaire. Ceci ressort également de la place qu'occupent les caisses d'épargne et les caisses coopératives de crédit dans les ouvrages de synthèse (tel par exemple Born, 1977; Kindleberger, 1984; ou, sous la direction de Van der Wee, 1991). Dans ces ouvrages de synthèse, l'histoire des caisses d'épargne et des caisses de crédit mutuel n'est traitée qu'en quelques pages, ou qu'en quelques lignes, sous un titre peu attrayant tel que: 'Les autres institutions financières' ou 'Other Banks'.

Est-ce à tort? Pas tout à fait. Kindleberger affirme à juste titre que ce n'étaient pas les caisses d'épargne, mais bien les grandes banques commerciales qui étaient les 'decision makers' et jouaient un rôle-clé dans la croissance économique.

L'importance des caisses d'épargne ne doit pourtant pas être sous-estimée. Un premier exemple est celui des caisses d'épargne et de crédit mutuel autrichiennes qui géraient à elles seules en 1908 la somme de 8.5 milliards de dépôts (en couronne), alors que les banques par actions autrichiennes ne recueillaient que 4.7 millions. En Allemagne, les dépôts dans les 3,133 caisses d'épargne en 1913 totalisaient la somme de 19.7 milliards de marks, tandis que les huit grandes banques commerciales allemandes totalisaient au même moment 5.5 milliards de DM de dépôts.

Les banques d'épargne belges privées (la Caisse générale d'Epargne et de Retraite non-incluse) ont aujourd'hui une part dans le marché belge des placements de presque 20 pour-cent et de 15 pour-cent dans le marché du crédit.

Ces quelques chiffres montrent suffisamment que les caisses d'épargne ont joué un certain rôle dans le monde des finances et dans l'économie en général. Mais la question est de savoir lequel, et comment et dans quelle mesure ce rôle a évolué. L'état actuel de la recherche révèle que la réponse à ces questions varie selon la période et le pays en question. L'origine des banques d'épargne se résume à des initiatives très disparates. Leur évolution varie d'un pays à l'autre, contrairement aux banques qui, dans l'ensemble, se développèrent d'une manière assez similaire. L'histoire des caisses d'épargne n'est donc pas chose facile à rédiger.

Toutes les caisses d'épargne se concentrèrent certes sur la collecte des économies du public, économies qu'elles placèrent ensuite à leur tour. Dans certains pays, c'était l'initiative des pouvoirs publics qui primait, comme en Grande-Bretagne apres la fondation du Post Office Savings Bank; dans d'autres pays, l'initiative privée prédominait. Une distinction doit être faite entre les caisses d'épargne sociales anglo-saxonnes et la combinaison que l'on trouve entre l'épargne et le crédit sur le continent.

Les caisses d'épargne les plus anciennes furent fondées dans un but purement philanthropique libéral ou caritatif religieux. Les sociétés hypothécaires par contre, qui attiraient des épargnes pour augmenter leurs moyens financiers, assumèrent entièrement leur mission commerciale dès leur constitution. Dans les caisses d'épargne publiques, le motif social allait souvent de pair avec des considérations financières et économiques d'un tout autre genre: les épargens devaient en effet contribuer à l'élargissement des moyens financiers des Etats et de l'industrie.

Il y avait des caisses d'épargne qui servirent des intérêts politiques ou idéologiques. C'est ainsi que l'on discerne des caisses d'épargne au profil chrétien, libéral et socialiste, tout comme naquirent des caisses d'épargne au profil socio-professionnel, qui trouvèrent leur clientèle parmi les ouvriers, les agriculteurs, la petite ou la haute bourgeoisie. Des institutions spécialisées furent fondées pour le crédit foncier, le crédit agricole et le crédit hypothécaire. Des associations coopératives de crédit se spécialisèrent dans les besoins de crédit spécifiques du petit artisan, du détaillant et du petit paysan.

A l'origine, la plupart des caisses d'épargne furent uniquement actives au niveau local ou régional, certaines avaient un rayon d'action national ou évoluaient dans ce sens. Leurs relations avec les banques commerciales pouvaient varier d'une collaboration très franche à une forme importante de réserve, voire d'hostilité.

Les premières caisses d'épargne doivent être situées quelque part dans le dernier quart du XVIIIe siècle et le début du XIXe siècle. De nombreuses caisses d'épargne virent le jour sous l'impulsion des mouvements de réforme sociale de la fin du XIXe siècle et du premier quart du XXe siècle. A l'heure actuelle, de nouvelles banques d'épargne sont encore fondées.

Partout, certes, on enregistre actuellement une évolution vers une uniformisation des banques d'épargne, tout comme une remarquable 'déspécialisation' entre banques d'épargne et banques commerciales. Mais l'historie continue néanmoins de marquer de son empreinte le monde des banques d'épargne, tant pour ce qui est de la philosophie de base et du statut juridique que des activités quotidiennes. L'historiographie des caisses d'épargne, établie sur une base scientifique, est donc un moyen tout indiqué de comprendre le présent en examinant le passé.

Cet article est en grande partie fondé sur l'historiographie belge. Le développement des caisses d'épargne en Belgique n'est pas entièrement représentatif pour le reste de l'Europe. Sous certains aspects, la Belgique a même connu une évolution particulière (voir chapitre 3). Mais les caisses d'épargne y sont très développées, elles ont subi de nombreuses influences de l'étranger et comptent à peu près tous les types importants de caisses d'épargne. L'historiographie belge en la matière a connu en outre un remarquable envol depuis les années quatre-vingts (chapitre 2), de sorte qu'elle constitue un bon point de départ pour une discussion historiographique et méthodologique plus large sur les possibilités et les problèmes de la recherche (chapitres 4 et 5).

L'historiographie: état de la question

A la demande des caisses d'épargne

Une grande partie des publications relatives à l'épargne ou à des caisses d'épargne individuelles furent réalisées à la demande même de ces caisses d'épargne ou des associations nationales de caisses d'épargne. Ceci explique pourquoi de nombreuses caisses d'épargne ont édité des albums commémoratifs, bien souvent rédigés par un membre du personnel, et qu'il faille déplorer un manque réel d'études objectives et impartiales.

Ces dernières années cependant, on note un changement dans ce domaine. Les histoires d'entreprises sont à la mode. Les historiens se consacrent à nouveau plus à l'étude des niveaux méso- et microéconomiques. Les études sectorielles et les histoires d'entreprises sont à nouveau remises en valeur parce qu'elles dégagent les fondements microéconomiques de la macro-histoire et parce que'elles révèlent les déterminants du comportement individuel. Les entreprises, quant à elles, considèrent que le fait de 'faire écrire' leur histoire constitue une forme de culture d'entreprise et une dépense justifiée dans le cadre de leurs relations publiques. On ne peut dès lors que se réjouir de voir, depuis peu seulement, les institutions financières s'adresser aux universités pour prendre en charge la rédaction de leur histoire.

L'interaction entre la demande des institutions financières d'une part et l'intérêt des historiens d'autre part aboutit cependant à des résultats très divergents. Le Deutscher Sparkassenverlag par exemple publia un bel ouvrage intitulé *Histoire de l'épargne de l'antiquité à nos jours* (Thurn, 1982), comptant 57 pages seulement de textes, 76 pages de photos en couleur de tirelires, de caisses de collecte et de cassettes à argent de tous les temps et des quatre coins du monde. En 1986, le Groupement Belge des Banques d'Epargne publia juste l'inverse: un volume de 857 pages contenant des articles rigoureusement scientifiques sur *Les Banques d'épargne belges. Histoire, Droit, Fonction économique et Institutions* (Van Put, 1986).

Le Groupement Belge des Banques d'Epargne choisit à dessein une approche purement scientifique. Elle mit au travail non moins de 19 scientifiques de plusieurs universités belges. Parmi eux, il y avait, outre des économistes et des sociologues, cinq historiens, un juriste, un psychologue et un philosophe. Cette manière de travailler se justifiait pleinement: comme il n'existait à l'époque guère de littérature historique et scientifique sur les banques d'épargne en Belgique, une publication vulgarisée aurait été un investissement inutile. La recherche scientifique doit en effet constituer la base de travaux de vulgarisation, et non l'inverse.

Le choix de l'approche scientifique n'est toutefois pas sans conséquences. La recherche prend du temps et est donc coûteuse; il est illusoire d'explorer un terrain vierge en relativement peu de temps. L'expérience faite par le Groupement Belge des Banques d'Epargne est révélatrice à ce propos:

> Lorsque, en 1981, le Groupement des Banques d'Epargne décida de publier, pour son 25e anniversaire, un ouvrage de référence sur le développement des banques d'épargne belges au cours du 19e et 20e siècle, on était convaincu qu'il serait possible de présenter, aujourd'hui, une étude de synthèse. La participation de nos universités devait permettre un travail interdisciplinaire d'historiens, d'économistes et de juristes. Malgré les efforts consentis, le résultat de cinq années d'études et de collaboration fait apparaître que notre but n'est que partiellement atteint. Trop de domaines sont encore à explorer, nombre de documents et de données statistiques sont encore à dépouiller. Il est prématuré de faire une véritable synthèse. (Van Put, 1986, p. 13)

Une bonne recherche engendre une fonction motrice. L'ouvrage de base de 1986, qui fit une approche globale des caisses d'épargne, a manifestement stimulé la recherche en Belgique. Depuis lors, la banque d'épargne socialiste Codep a fait rédiger une monographie scientifique de son histoire (Witte et De Preter, 1989), tandis que l'Association Belge du Crédit Immobilier et la banque d'épargne du mouvement ouvrier chrétien ont mis en place une équipe de recherche afin de faire écrire leur histoire (*Le crédit hypothécaire, 1992; Projet COB*). Par ailleurs, le Groupement Belge des Banques d'Epargne s'est engagé à tenir a jour les données statistiques qu'il rassembla pour sa publication de 1986, ce qui permet l'actualisation permanente des points de vue.

Quatre types de publication

En bref, on peut distinguer en ce moment quatre types de publications dans l'historiographie tant belge qu'étrangère:

1. Les albums de commémoration traditionnels constituent le premier type, surtout jadis très répandus. Ils furent généralement réalisés à l'occasion de jubilés. La mesure dans laquelle, faute de mieux, on y fait encore souvent référence, explique pourquoi certains mythes persistent. Ainsi, les caisses d'épargne soulignèrent volontiers la dimension sociale dans leur histoire, tandis qu'elles minimalisèrent leurs intentions commerciales ou politiques. Dans l'histoire de la Caisse Générale d'Epargne et de Retraite de Belgique (CGER), l'accent est mis sur la lutte contre la pauvreté comme motif de la création de la caisse d'épargne publique (*Mémorial 1865–1965*, 1965), alors qu'une récente recherche a permis d'établir que son fondateur, le ministre des Finances libéral Walthère Frère-Orban, poursuivit des objectifs financiers et économiques, à savoir l'élargissement du capital au profit de la bourgeoisie (Parmentier, 1986). Il est d'ailleurs frappant de constater que les caisses d'épargne avec des origines dans le discours philanthropique et social du siècle passé, ont fait l'objet d'un plus grand nombre d'études que p.e. les sociétés hypothécaires dont le discours a toujours été purement commercial.

2. Un deuxième type sont les monographies scientifiques. Au cours des années écoulées, certaines banques d'épargne belges se sont montrées disposées à ouvrir intégralement leurs archives à la recherche, et ce dans un esprit de liberté académique complète (par exemple Codep et COB). Elles ne se sont cependant pas encore résolues à mettre leurs archives en dépôt dans une institution scientifique d'archives. Certes, les grandes banques d'épargne ont ce qu'elles appellent un service 'archives'. Les vieux documents y sont généralement bien conservés, parfois même dans les coffres de la banque,

mais la plupart du temps, il faut déplorer l'absence d'un classement justifié et d'une politique active de collection d'archives.

3. Le souci des institutions commerciales d'entretenir leurs relations avec le grand public a permis récemment le développement d'un troisième type d'historiographie: des publications vulgarisées, basées sur de la recherche scientifique et joliment illustrées. A première vue, elles semblent le compromis idéal entre la demande formulée par ces institutions d'obtenir un livre agréable à lire d'une part, et l'exigence des historiens de ne pas renier leur scientificité d'autre part. Mais il s'agit d'un genre délicat, souffrant du manque de temps pour la réalisation de cette 'recherche contractuelle', du nombre limité de pages auquel doivent s'astreindre le plus souvent les auteurs – les photos y occupent généralement plus de place que le texte – au point que la qualité du résultat final en pâtit. Il en découle qu'après coup le besoin d'une recherche plus approfondie se fait quand même sentir.

4. Du quatrième type, seul un exemple m'est connu à ce jour, à savoir une banque d'épargne qui charge une équipe d'historiens et d'économistes d'effectuer une étude à double finalité: la publication d'une monographie scientifique et d'un document de formation à l'usage des cadres (*Projet COB*). Ce document renferme trois composantes: une histoire succincte de la banque d'épargne susceptible d'être présentée en un cycle de cinq cours, une anthologie de textes historiques qui incite à la réflexion et à la discussion, et enfin la présentation des chiffres marquants de la banque d'épargne. Dans ce cas, il est évident que la banque vise 'l'utilisation' de l'histoire à des fins éducatives, à savoir la formation du personnel dans un esprit conforme à celui que connaît l'entreprise depuis plusieurs générations.

L'historiographie belge

L'historiographique belge sur les banques d'épargne est relativement bien développée. Le récent ouvrage de synthèse examine les banques d'épargne sous trois aspects: leur histoire (de 1825 à 1975), leur statut juridique et leur fonction économique (surtout de 1970 à 1985) (Van Put, 1986). Il existe deux brèves monographies sur la création et le fonctionnement du Groupement Belge des Banques d'Epargne privées (*Vakgroep*, 1966; Raport dans Van Put, 1986). Il y a une publication commémorative sur l'Office central de la petite Epargne (*Office central*, 1959) qui assura le contrôle officiel des caisses d'épargne de 1934 à 1975. Il faut citer également deux monographies sur des banques d'épargne distinctes, à savoir l'une sur la caisse d'épargne publique CGER (*Mémorial 1865–1965*, 1965) et l'autre sur une banque d'épargne moyennement importante de tendance socialiste, c'est-à-dire Codep

(Witte et De Preter, 1989). La plus grande banque d'épargne privée belge actuelle, CERA, modelée selon le type Raiffeisen et liée au Boerenbond Belge, une organisation agricole catholique, a été étudiée surtout pour la période de l'entre-deux-guerres (Van der Wee et Verbreyt, 1985; Van Molle, 1990). Une étude approfondie de la deuxième banque d'épargne privée en ordre de grandeur, à savoir celle du mouvement ouvrier chrétien, la COB, est attendue pour l'année prochaine, ainsi qu'une publication sur le secteur du crédit hypothécaire.

Une analyse critique de cette littérature s'avère cependant nécessaire. Il est frappant de noter que pour les développements du XIXe siècle, elle est très tributaire du premier ouvrage de synthèse publié sur le phénomène des caisses d'épargne en Belgique, à savoir les trois volumes de Hamande et Burny en 1902. Il est également frappant de constater que la caisse d'épargne publique, avec ses origines typiquement libérales, et les caisses d'épargne cadrant dans les mouvements chrétiens et socialistes, ont fait l'objet d'un plus grand nombre d'études que les autres. Il y a donc des lacunes. La recherche a prêté peu d'attention aux quelques caisses d'épargne communales, les caisses d'épargne de grandes entreprises industrielles, les caisses d'épargne attachées à quelques grandes banques et les vieilles caisses hypothécaires qui, actuellement, occupent par ordre d'importance de la troisième à la septième place dans la hiérarchie des banques d'épargne belges.

Le besoin d'une recherche en profondeur reste en outre nécessaire, afin d'accentuer et de nuancer les perceptions. Le livre sur la CGER (*Mémorial 1865–1965*), certes méritoire mais vieilli et cherchant par trop la glorification de soi, doit être revu. A ce propos, nous renvoyons à nouveau à l'article de Sabine Parmentier (1986). Après une analyse approfondie des débats parlementaires, elle aboutit à la constatation que l'aile conservatrice et doctrinaire du libéralisme belge donna le ton à l'occasion de la création de la CGER, et non son aile réformatrice, progressiste et sociale. La fondation de la caisse d'épargne coïncidait totalement avec le concept du 'self-help', le salut par soi-même que prônait la variante libérale à la charité catholique. La caisse d'épargne a été conçue pardessus tout afin de stimuler l'octroi de crédits grâce à l'accumulation du capital dormant des moins nantis, et donc d'augmenter la masse totale d'argent en circulation. Elle contribuerait de cette manière à l'essor du capitalisme industriel et bourgeois. L'esprit d'économie des pauvres, c'est-à-dire le principe du 'self-help' propagé par les libéraux, devait en outre comprimer le budget de l'Etat destiné à la charité publique.

Le livre sur la CGER se termine sur l'année 1964 et conclut sur un ton d'autosatisfaction: 'L'histoire centenaire de la Caisse d'Epargne est caractérisée par d'importants succès: l'augmentation du nombre de livrets d'épargne et de comptes depuis un siècle; l'évolution de l'avoir total en fait foi'. Les chiffres étaient en effet impressionnants. Jusque dans les années soixante par exemple, le nombre de livrets d'épargne ne cessa d'augmenter, tant en chiffres absolus que relatifs (Tableau 21.1).

Tableau 21.1   Nombre de livrets d'épargne à la CGER par 1000 habitants

1870	10	1920	473
1880	36	1930	613
1890	120	1940	714
1900	256	1950	745
1910	377	1960	776

Source: Mémorial 1865–1965.

Mais la concurrence se faisait de plus en plus vive entre-temps. La CGER perdait du terrian par rapport aux caisses d'épargne privées (Tableau 21.2), une évolution dont elle ne souffle mot cependant dans son *Mémorial*.

Tableau 21.2   Total des livrets d'épargne et de dépôt (en milliards de FB)

Année	Caisses d'épargne privées	CGER	Banques	Crédit Communal	Total	% des banques d'épargne privées
1955	13.8	52.4	10.3	1.3	77.8	17.7
1956	15.7	56.1	10.7	1.6	84.1	18.7
1957	17.6	60.1	10.5	1.8	90.0	19.5
1958	20.2	66.7	11.4	2.2	100.5	20.1
1959	23.5	74.4	13.7	2.9	114.5	20.5
1960	25.8	78.9	14.1	3.2	122.0	21.1
1961	29.5	84.6	14.6	3.8	132.5	22.3
1962	34.8	92.7	17.9	4.9	150.3	23.2
1963	41.3	98.0	27.4	6.4	173.1	23.9
1964	46.7	102.4	33.7	7.0	189.8	24.6
1965	54.5	112.2	40.2	8.0	214.9	25.4

Source: Vakgroep, 1966, tableau VII.

Dans le cas de la CGER, le *Mémorial* a donc mis en vedette les côtés positifs de l'histoire, tout en omettant les aspects moins reluisants. L'historiographie scientifique par contre, a souvent un effet de démystification. Un effet auquel les caisses d'épargne semblent particulièrement sensibles. Tenant en haute estime leur fonction sociale et attachant énormément d'importance à leur image de fiabilité, elles ressentent avec d'autant plus d'acuité la divulgation d'erreurs commises par la direction ou dans la gestion. Ce motif mit d'ailleurs régulièrement un frein à la volonté des caisses d'épargne de rendre leurs archives disponibles. Il faut reconnaître que les caisses d'épargne belges connurent des problèmes dans le passé. La crise des années trente eut des effets dévastateurs, en sonnant le glas notamment de la banque d'épargne socialiste (précurseur de Codep) et de la Middenkredietkas ou Caisse Centrale de Crédit (précurseur de CERA). Ces deux banques d'épargne ont entre-temps autorisé l'étude de cet épisode de leur histoire. Les banques d'épargne doivent comprendre qu'une narration objective des événements est le seul moyen de couper court définitivement aux propos insinuants sur le passé.

L'histoire de l'épargne et des Banques d'Epargne à vol d'oiseau

La légitimation idéologique de l'épargne

L'organisation naissante de l'épargne, à la fin du XVIIIe siècle, doit être située dans le contexte des Lumières. La prise de conscience grandissante des responsabilités de l'Etat à l'égard de la société incita des bourgeois éclairés à lutter contre la pauvreté et à rechercher une augmentation générale du bien-être de la population. L'essor du capitalisme industriel et l'appauvrissement de la population dans les villes industrielles constituèrent le bouillon de culture de leur action.

L'enseignement, la prévoyance sociale et l'épargne furent les trois piliers sur lesquels s'appuya la politique sociale bourgeoise. L'épargne individuelle, et donc le salut par soi-même, fut considérée comme étant la clef de succès de l'ascension sociale individuelle et, à terme, la solution à l'ensemble du problème social. Cette vision libérale de l'épargne coïncidait en outre, dans ses grandes lignes, avec la doctrine chrétienne qui édifia l'esprit d'économie en vertu. Le 'self-help' libéral et la charité chrétienne ne modifièrent en fait aucunement le libéralisme économique. Tant les philanthropes libéraux que les travailleurs sociaux-chrétiens organisèrent l'épargne dans une approche paternaliste.

La justification bourgeoise et chrétienne de l'épargne fut cherchée dans l'inégalité naturelle entre les hommes. Côté chrétien, on la qualifia d'inégalité voulue par Dieu, étant entendu que les biens matériels étaient un don de Dieu dont pouvait disposer librement l'humanité. La propriété était un droit naturel. Le libéralisme économique, qui prévalut au XIXe siècle, et la néo-scolastique catholique accentuèrent la notion de propriété individuelle. La propriété fut considérée comme un droit démocratique, une nécessité pour le maintien et l'épanouissement de chaque être humain. On en déduisit la recherche naturelle de l'amélioration matérielle du sort de tout un chacun, mais tout autant le devoir chrétien d'amour du prochain. La doctrine sociale de l'Eglise mit l'accent sur le fait que la propriété privée et le lucre devaient toujours être subordonnés à l'intérêt général. La propriété devait être bénéfique à la société. Cette même attitude altruiste régnait également dans les milieux sociaux libéraux. D'un point de vue purement économique, il fut en outre souligné que la propriété privée ne pouvait rester improductive; les réserves d'épargne devaient être rentables par conséquent pour l'ensemble de la société, grâce à d'intéressants placements.

Au niveau de la société, l'épargne se vit constamment recevoir les valeurs bourgeoises suivantes: primo, l'accumulation des épargnes fut considérée commme étant la base de l'augmentation du niveau de bienêtre et du progrès de la civilisation. Secundo, une dimension sociale prononcée fut liée à ce raisonnement économique, à savoir la lutte contre le paupérisme et donc 'l'édification générale de la population'. Tertio, l'accent fut mis sur l'effet patriotique: quiconque épargnait, et avait dès lors des propriétés à défendre, avait tout intérêt à ce que l'ordre et la paix sociale règnent dans l'Etat. Dans les milieux bourgeois, l'épargne devint par conséquent une arme contre le socialisme collectiviste, considéré comme une menace pour la sécurité de l'Etat. Quarto, l'épargne se vit aussi attribuer une valeur importante dans la formation sociale: le fait d'inciter la population à l'épargne équivalait tout autant à l'éduquer dans le sens d'une prise de conscience sociale et à faire preuve de civisme, éléments qui correspondaient à l'obligation chrétienne d'amour du prochain.

La même échelle de valeurs bourgeoises fut appliquée au niveau de l'individu. L'épargne se traduisait par une amélioration du sort matériel, l'épanouissement par l'effort personnel. L'épargne voulait dire en outre prévoir, et était donc une forme de prévoyance sociale. Celui qui épargnait avec discernement, était en mesure de passer du prolétariat à la propriété, de la condition d'ouvrier à celle de patron: tel était le message qu'on adressait au XIXe siècle à la classe ouvrière.

Cette légitimation idéologique de l'épargne resta valable pendant tout le XIXe siècle. On la retrouve d'ailleurs dans une grande mesure au XXe siècle. Le développement concret des caisses d'épargne n'est cependant pas une reproduction parfaite de ce discours. Nous concrétisons l'évolution des choses à partir de l'exemple de la Belgique.

L'histoire des banques d'épargne, spécialement en Belgique

La Grande-Bretagne prit les devants dans l'organisation de l'épargne. Il est vrai que l'industrialisation précoce y avait aussi hâté le processus d'appauvrissement. Les caisses d'épargne y furent fondées en tant qu'institutions philanthropiques en faveur des classes sociales les plus basses. La Ruthwell Savings Bank, fondée en 1810 à Edimbourg par E.H. Henry Duncan, est généralement considérée comme étant la plus ancienne. Huit ans plus tard, on dénombrait déjà 465 caisses d'épargne dans les 'parish communities' britanniques. En 1861, le réseau britannique de caisses d'épargne privées fut complété par des caisses d'épargne publique de la poste.

Mais la philanthrophie n'explique pas tout, ni en Grande-Bretagne et ni ailleurs. La fondation de caisses d'épargne postales dans plusieurs pays se faisait pour des motifs sociaux, mais également dans l'espoir de voir diminuer le budget des pouvoirs publics dans le domaine de l'assistance publique. Les caisses d'épargne privées de la Grande-Bretagne, de la France et de l'Allemagne furent en outre obligées de placer une grande partie de leurs moyens financiers en rentes d'Etat ou bons du Trésor, a fin de fournir de l'argent aux pouvoirs publics.

Les Pays-Bas protestants et un certain nombre d'Etats allemands sont comptés parmi les premiers imitateurs du modèle britannique. La France, l'Autriche et la Suisse ne suivirent que plus tard. En 1909 déjà, les caisses d'épargne allemandes reçurent l'autorisation d'effectuer des paiements par chèque.

La première caisse d'épargne sur le territoire belge date de 1825. Il s'agissait de la caisse d'épargne communale de Tournai, une des deux banques d'épargne communales que compte encore la Belgique à l'heure actuelle. Vient ensuite, pendant le reste du XIXe siècle jusqu'à la Première Guerre mondiale, une longue période d'incubation au cours de laquelle quantité de formes de caisses d'épargne furent lancées, dont quelques-unes seulement subsistèrent.

Les Pays-Bas méridionaux et septentrionaux formèrent un royaume uni de 1815 à 1830. Il est clair que la politique philanthropique du souverain de l'époque, Guillaume Ier, fut déterminante dans le lancement du système des caisses d'épargne. Il inspira une décision gouvernementale qui obligea les communes à créer des caisses d'épargne. Cette décision fut bien respectée dans le Nord protestant; en 1828, on y signala 66 caisses d'épargne. Dans le Sud, à prédominance catholique, on n'en signala que 14, dont sept à peine fonctionnaient véritablement. A la suite de la révolution belge de 1830, trois durent cesser leurs paiements; toutes trois furent reprises par le secteur privé. La loi communale belge de 1836 prévit certes encore la création de caisses d'épargne dans les villes industrielles, mais ce fut en vain. Entre-temps, les banques commerciales avaient pris la relève.

L'industrialisation rapide de la Belgique fut pour une bonne part financée par trois banques, à savoir la Société Générale, la Banque de Belgique et la Banque liégeoise, lesquelles se livrèrent une concurrence sans répit, également sur le plan de la conquête des épargnes. Leurs activités dans le domaine de l'épargne n'avait rien à voir avec la philanthropie ou la charité. Elles fondèrent des caisses d'épargne afin de drainer les moyens financiers de la bourgeoisie fortunée vers l'industrie, et ce par l'octroi de crédits. Ces banques-caisses d'épargne, soutenues par l'establishment politique, connurent momentanément un gros succès. Leur gestion s'avéra toutefois compliquée et coûteuse et certainement pas en rapport avec les moyens financiers recueillis. Elles se montrèrent en outre très vulnérables eu égard à la faible marge de liquidités qu'elles observèrent. Les événements de 1848 leur donnèrent le coup de grâce. Celles qui ne furent pas totalement supprimées, ont après coup fortement réduit leurs activités.

La suprématie remarquable de la 'haute finance', durant la phase initiale du développement des caisses d'épargne, eut cependant des conséquences graves. Après 1848, la Belgique devint une terre inexploitée en matière d'épargne. En 1860, la Grande-Bretagne comptait un épargnant par 15 habitants. An Autriche et en Prusse, cette proportion était de un sur 34, en France un sur 36 et en Belgique un à peine sur 137! Les quelques caisses d'épargne créées par de grandes entreprises industrielles, ne furent pas en mesure de renverser la vapeur: elles ne touchèrent qu'une élite, les ouvriers se méfiant de l'initiative patronale et n'étant souvent même pas capables de faire la moindre économie sur leur maigre salaire.

Le vide fut comblé en 1865 par la création de la Caisse Générale d'Epargne et de Retraite (CGER), une caisse d'épargne du secteur public avec garantie de l'Etat et soumise à des dispositions strictes en matière de placements afin de protéger les épargnants. Du fait qu'elle opérait depuis les filiales de la Banque Nationale de Belgique et, à partir de 1870, par le biais des bureaux de poste, elle put toucher rapidement un très vaste public. En 1890, elle totalisa 90.7 pour-cent du volume belge des dépôts d'épargne, contre 5.4 pour-cent seulement pour les banques-caisses d'épargne et 2.5 pour-cent pour les dernières caisses d'épargne communales. Le résultat des caisses d'épargne liées à des entreprises fut insignifiant. Le nombre d'épargnants était entre-temps passé de un sur 137 en 1860 à un sur huit en 1890. Un examen détaillé démontre cependant que la CGER trouvait surtout sa clientèle parmi le personnel domestique et les classes moyennes.

C'était surtout les caisses d'épargne postales et les caisses d'épargne et de crédit, système Schulze-Delitzsch, Raiffeisen, Durand, Haas et autres, qui, en Belgique et ailleurs, ont contribué, durant la seconde moitié du XIXe siècle, à la démocratisation de l'épargne et du crédit. Ces caisses ont introduit une forme de capitalisme parmi de larges couches de la population. Elles constituaient en outre un vrai mouvement de masse avec lequel il fallait compter, mais elles n'ont certainement pas réussi à atteindre le but qu'on leur réservait dans le discours: faire fonction d'assurance sociale individuelle.

Il est arbitraire évidemment de souligner, outre les brillants résultats de la CGER, le succès croissant des caisses d'épargne privées durant la période de 1890 à 1914. On dénote cependant une modeste tendance à la privatisation du système belge de l'épargne. Les classes moyennes et la haute bourgeoisie constituèrent l'épine dorsale des nombreuses sociétés hypothécaires qui virent le jour à partir de la fin du XIXe siècle. Elles s'efforcèrent de satisfaire la demande croissante de crédit hypothécaire en attirant les épargnes courantes, à côté de l'émission d'obligations. A côté de celles-ci naquirent toute une série de petites caisses d'épargne dans la zone d'influence catholique, libérale et socialiste. On peut donc franchement parler d'une 'pilarisation' naissante de l'épargne. Tous les mouvements sociaux eurent recours aux caisses d'épargne pour promouvoir l'émancipation de 'leurs' membres, et dès lors comme levier du mouvement lui-même. Les banques coopératives populaires d'après le modèle allemand de Schulze-Delitzsch qui, à l'exception d'une seule, furent soutenues par les milieux libéraux, ne rencontrèrent guère de succès en Belgique. Le résultat le plus éclatant fut enregistré par les caisses Raiffeisen qui, lancées en 1892, devinrent très vite l'assise financière du mouvement agricole catholique. A la veille de la Première Guerre mondiale, la CGER comptait une filiale pour deux communes; à l'époque, les caisses Raiffeisen étaient déjà présentes dans une commune sur quatre. En 1913, un Belge sur 2.4 possédait un livret d'épargne à la CGER.

L'expansion économique et l'amélioration du niveau de vie durant les années vingt ont fortement accéléré l'expansion des caisses d'épargne privées belges. Leur développement portait tant sur l'accroissement des dépôts d'épargne que sur la diversification des placements et l'octroi de crédits. Le morcellement du système des caisses d'épargne eut en outre tendance à s'amplifier. Le manque de distinction entre banques et caisses d'épargne ne fut pas de nature à rendre le paysage financier plus transparent. Eu égard à la dépréciation des valeurs des fonds d'Etat, toutes les institutions financières se tournèrent de plus en plus vers les participations financières et industrielles et octroyèrent des crédits à long terme à toutes sortes d'entreprises. L'optimisme régnant sur les marchés financiers et la concurrence mutuelle les poussèrent en outre vers des placements téméraires. Quand les autorités belges pressentirent le danger, au moment des premières faillites en 1930, elles chargèrent une commission d'enquête de mettre au point un système de contrôle de l'Etat sur les caisses d'épargne privées.

Le résultat se fit attendre, à fortiori parce que les caisses d'épargne elles-mêmes s'efforcèrent d'échapper au contrôle de l'Etat. Durant la dépression économique des années suivantes, un nombre de plus en plus grand d'institutions financières fut confronté à des problèmes de liquidités, une trentaine d'entre elles firent faillite. En 1934, tant la Banque du Travail socialiste que la Middenkredietkas catholique, c'est-à-dire la Caisse Centrale de Crédit chapeautant la majeure partie des caisses Raiffeisen, furent contraintes de fermer leurs portes. Les mesures que prirent ensuite les pouvoirs publics, à savoir la législation des 7 et 15 décembre 1934 et du 10 avril 1935, s'attachèrent surtout à protéger l'épargnant. La liberté quasi totale avec laquelle les caisses d'épargne avaient pu se développer dut céder la place à la réglementation et au contrôle de l'Etat. Le système bancaire mixte, qui plaça des dépôts d'épargne immédiatement exigibles dans des participations industrielles de longue durée, fut complètement démantelé en Belgique. Les caisses d'épargne privées furent dorénavant soumises aux consignes sévères en matière de placements.

Une première conséquence de ce changement fut une nouvelle configuration du paysage embrouillé des caisses d'épargne, polarisée autour de quelques grandes caisses d'épargne mieux structurées: c'est ici qu'il convient de situer la création de Codep et de la COB. Une seconde conséquence fut que dans ces caisses d'épargne plus grandes, l'inspiration sociale et émancipatrice dut céder quelque peu la place au professionnalisme et au sens de la réalité économico-financière.

Le rétablissement de la confiance se traduisit par un essor constant. Après la Deuxième Guerre mondiale, les banques d'épargne privées belges connurent à nouveau une expansion remarquable. Elle s'exprima à sept niveaux:

1. L'accroissement fulgurant des dépôts d'épargne; en termes réels, l'augmentation spectaculaire du volume d'épargne pendant la période de 1960 à 1974 ne s'avéra pourtant pas supérieur à celle des années 1944 à 1959.
2. La fondation de nouvelles banques d'épargne, surtout pendant les 'golden sixties'.
3. La décentralisation très poussée des opérations par l'ouverture de centaines de nouvelles filiales: à elles seules, les caisses d'épargne privées disposaient en 1974 de 22,000 points de contact.
4. La 'déspécialisation', d'abord au niveau des activités d'épargne et ensuite celui de l'octroi de crédit; elle commença à la suite de l'assou

plissement du statut des caisses d'épargne privées paru dans l'AR du 18 avril 1967 et dans la loi du 30 juin 1975.
5.   Le professionnalisme plus grand de la direction.
6.   L'introduction de techniques électroniques et de l'ordinateur.
7.   L'ouverture vers les marchés financiers internationaux, du moins dans les grandes banques d'épargne.

Cette évolution n'est certainement pas terminée. Il s'agit d'un processus radical, qui touche aussi l'ensemble du paysage financier. Il est clair tout d'abord que, depuis les années soixante, le secteur public perd progressivement de son importance au profit du secteur privé combatif, et ce tant sur le plan des placements que celui de l'octroi de crédits (Tableaux 21.3 et 21.4).

Tableau 21.3   Parts dans l'ensemble du marché des placements

	Banques d'épargne	Banques	Secteur public
1953	7.2	39.4	53.4
1962	11.4	33.0	55.6
1969	14.3	38.9	46.8
1970	14.6	39.1	46.3
1971	15.0	39.4	45.6
1972	15.5	40.4	44.1
1973	15.8	41.1	43.1
1974	16.0	40.6	43.4
1975	16.4	40.3	42.3
1976	16.6	40.9	42.5
1977	16.4	40.5	43.1
1978	16.7	40.3	43.0
1979	16.9	40.2	42.9
1980	16.8	40.0	43.2
1981	16.9	40.5	42.6
1982	16.7	40.6	42.7
1983	16.8	41.1	42.1
1984	17.8	40.2	42.0

Source: Van Put (1986, p. 484, tableau B.18).

Tablau 21.4   Parts dans l'ensemble du marché du crédit (en%)

	Banques d'épargne	Banques	Secteur public
1969	12.8	42.4	44.8
1970	13.1	43.0	43.9
1971	13.5	42.8	43.7
1972	14.0	44.2	41.8
1973	14.1	45.4	40.5
1974	14.0	45.3	40.7
1975	14.5	45.4	40.1
1976	14.9	45.5	39.6
1977	14.5	44.8	40.7
1978	14.9	44.7	40.4
1979	14.7	45.6	39.7
1980	14.3	47.1	38.6
1981	14.4	47.8	37.8
1982	14.5	47.4	38.1
1983	15.1	48.7	36.2
1984	15.4	47.6	37.0

Source: Van Put (1986, p. 480, tableau B.10).

Depuis les années soixante, les banques et banques d'épargne se font une véritable concurrence. La pression constante des innovations technologiques à introduire en est une expression, l'élargissement permanent de l'offre de services en est une autre. Le rapprochement du statut des banques d'épargne de celui des banques à part entière n'est pas encore terminé. A l'heure actuelle, la situation est même très ambigüe. D'une part, les banques d'épargne se fondent toujours sur le principe de la spécialisation, à savoir l'organisation de l'épargne conformément à leur origine historique. D'autre part, elles évoluent – poussées en cela par leur dynamique interne, la concurrence et les aspirations de la clientèle – dans le sens d'un service bancaire à part entière. D'ailleurs, le vieux livret d'épargne a quelque peu perdu sa fonction initiale. Depuis l'organisation de la sécurité sociale obligatoire en Belgique en 1944, l'épargne individuelle sert moins à remplir la fonction de prévoyance sociale qu'à assouvir les besoins de consommation. Le rôle du livret d'épargne lui-même a entre-temps été ramené à celui d'un 'pseudo-compte à vue', tandis que l'épargant s'est de plus en plus tourné vers les formes de placement plus rentables. Ce phénomène se traduit en outre par une fidélité décroissante de l'épargnant et donc sans doute aussi par la 'dépilarisation' progressive de l'épargne.

Les thèmes de la recherche

Les connaissances historiques existantes permettent de déterminer les thèmes que l'on peut aborder dans l'historiographie des banques d'é-pargne. En d'autres mots, nous nous efforçons de dresser une liste mod-èle des thèmes de la recherche. Nonobstant l'hétérogénéité historique des caisses d'épargne, trois approches s'imposent pour leur étude histori-ographique.

La recherche de la fonction économico-financière des caisses d'épargne, la question ultime étant celle de leur part dans l'amélioration du bien-être

L'amélioration du niveau de vie depuis la révolution industrielle est étroitement liée à la situation sur les marchés financiers et monétaires. Les banques d'épargne jouèrent un rôle dans les économies modernes, en même temps que les banques centrales et les banques commerciales. Quelle était l'importance de leur influence et quelle était sa spécificité? Il s'agit d'une problématique macro-économique qui, vu la complexité de l'évolution économico-financière, s'avère aussi difficile dans la réponse à y donner.

La problématique peut être spécifiée comme suit:

- Qu'est-ce qui explique la création et la continuité des banques d'é-pargne, à côté des différents autres types d'institutions financières? Quelle était leur spécificité? Quelle place leur était réservée sur le marché au moment de leur fondation et quelle place ont-elles pro-gressivement conquise?
- Quelle était la part des caisses d'épargne dans l'accumulation des moyens financiers? Les éléments de la recherche peuvent être les suiv-ants (que ce soit au niveau de chaque caisse d'épargne ou de l'ensem-ble des caisses d'épargne):
    le nombre de points de contact avec les clients;
    le nombre de filiales en rapport avec le nombre de communes;
    leur nombre en rapport avec la densité de la population;
    la répartition géographique des caisses d'épargne;
    la répartition géographique des livrets d'épargne et des dépôts, en
        relation également avec l'importance de la population;
    l'évolution des dépôts;

l'évolution du nombre de livrets;

l'évolution du montant moyen par livret;

la répartition des dépôts d'épargne: livrets d'épargne ordinaires, dépôts à terme, bons de caisse et obligations;

la répartition des dépôts selon le type de banque d'épargne: sociétés hypothécaires, caisses de crédit agricole, banques populaires urbaines, caisses d'épargne communales, etc.

le taux d'intérêt sur les épargnes; la part sur le marché des placements: par rapport à d'autres caisses d'épargne et aux banques commerciales; le rapport entre le secteur privé et le secteur public.

- Quelle fut la part des caisses d'épargne dans l'allocation des moyens financiers?

le taux d'intérêt sur les prêts;

la répartition des placements: moyens liquides (en caisse, traites, etc.), fonds de l'Etat, prêts hypothécaires, divers;

les conditions posées en cas d'octroi de crédit: échéance, garantie;

la part sur le marché du crédit: par rapport à d'autres caisses d'épargne et aux banques commerciales; le rapport entre le secteur privé et le secteur public.

- Quelle était la structure financière et administrative des banques d'épargne?

le capital social:

l'importance du capital social;

la composition du groupe des actionnaires;

la structure administrative:

l'organigramme;

la composition du groupe des fondateurs et administrateurs;

l'analyse des bilans et le compte des pertes et profits, surtout au niveau des liquidités, de la solvabilité et de la rentabilité;

le rapport entre les dépôts d'épargne et l'octroi de crédits.

La recherche relative à la fonction sociale des caisses d'épargne, c'est-à-dire leur contribution dans la répartition du bien-être

La répartition du bien-être entre les diverses couches de la société fut notamment la conséquence d'importants mouvements sociaux. Les premières banques d'épargne naquirent d'un souci de charité chrétienne ou de philanthropie libérale; de nouvelles banques d'épargne ancrées dans les mouvements socio-catholiques et socialistes virent le jour à la fin du XIXe siècle. Dans ces cas, l'étude des banques d'épargne doit tenir compte de leurs rapports avec les mouvements sociaux correspondants. Les approches spécifiques peuvent être:

- Le fondement social et la légitimation sociale de l'épargne; le discours théorique et propagandiste
- Sur le plan de l'accumulation de moyens:
    la répartition socio-professionnelle des épargnes: agriculteurs, ouvriers, petite bourgeoisie, etc.; le rapport entre sexes; l'épargne scolaire;
    l'importance des montants épargnés par groupe socio-professionel; leur évolution peut ensuite être comparée à l'évolution du pouvoir d'achat;
    dans le cas de banques d'épargne liées à des mouvements sociaux: l'origine des dépôts, à savoir la quantité provenant d'organisations du mouvement, de membres du mouvement et de non-membres
- Sur le plan de l'allocation de moyens:
    l'importance des prêts accordés et leur but: pour l'achat par exemple de charbon en prévision de l'hiver, pour l'achat de bétail, pour la rénovation d'une habitation, etc.
    la présence de contrôle social en cas d'octroi de crédit: il semble que dans les petites caisses d'épargne, les notables du village aient souvent eu une voix décisive dans l'attribution des prêts;
    dans le cas de banques d'épargne liées à un mouvement social: l'octroi de crédit au mouvement lui-même, aux membres et aux non-membres
- Sur le plan de la direction:
    quelle est l'origine socio-professionnelle de la direction et des actionnaires?
    quels sont les liens personnels et financiers entre les banques d'épargne et les mouvements sociaux?
    dans quelle mesure les bénéfices des banques d'épargne sont-ils transférés dans les mouvements sociaux?

L'approche institutionnelle

- L'étude du cadre légal dans lequel fonctionnent les banques d'épargne et types de banques d'épargne distincts. Le statut des banques d'épargne est fondé, dans son essence, sur la liberté de commerce et d'industrie. Cette liberté fut restreinte dans une mesure plus ou moins grande par un vaste assortiment de règlements et de mécanismes de contrôle afin de:
    protéger les épargnants;
    déterminer clairement la relation entre caisse d'épargne publique et caisses d'épargne privées;
    spécifier la relation entre banques et caisses d'épargne.

Une partie des banques d'épargne possèdent le statut de sociétés anonymes, d'autres celui de sociétés coopératives: quelle est la motivation qui fut à la base du choix de l'un ou l'autre type de société et quelles furent les implications futures de ce choix?

• L'étude du cadre fiscal.
  De par leur fonction sociale, les caisses d'épargne bénéficièrent régulièrement d'un régime fiscal avantageux. Il est bien connu que dans certains cas, des caisses d'épargne ont obtenu des subventions de l'Etat.
• L'étude des associations nationales et internationales de banques d'épargne qui toutes deux font figure d'organes de concertation mutuelle et de groupes de pression à l'égard des autorités, tels par exemple:
  'l'Institut International des Banques d'Epargne', fondé en 1924;
  'l'Association des Banques d'Epargne de la Communauté Economique Européenne', active depuis 1963.
• L'étude des institutions publiques chargées du contrôle de l'épargne.
  A ce propos, il convient de souligner la relation subtile entre les institutions contrôlées et l'autorité de contrôle.

Considerations méthodologiques

La problématique des sources

Pour de nombreuses grandes banques d'épargne, les sources disponibles relatives au XIXe siècle, voire souvent même une partie du XXe siècle, sont limitées. Il n'en existe même plus pour la plupart des petites caisses d'épargne locales, sans reconnaissance légale. L'expérience nous apprend que les archives de banques d'épargne liées à de grands mouvements sociaux sont mieux conservées que celles de banques d'épargne 'neutres' sentimentalement moins attachées à leur passé.

La majeure partie des sources conservées est de nature officielle et normative: textes légaux, règlements, statistiques officielles, actes de constitution de sociétés anonymes et coopératives, rapports annuels publiant les bilans et comptes annuels. Assez régulièrement, ces sources renferment, du moins en Belgique, des données précises sur la répartition socio-professionnelle des épargnants et emprunteurs (par exemple, Tableau 21.5).

S'ils ont été conservés, les rapports manuscrits des Assemblées Générales et surtout des Conseils d'Administration contiennent souvent plus d'informations internes nécessaires à une historiographie 'vivante'.

Tableau 21.5   Caisses Raiffeisen, dépôts (en FB)

	Solde dépôts	Epargne moyen./ livret	Epargne moyen./ paysan	Epargne moyen./ non-paysan	%Dépôts non-paysans	% Emprunté
1895	260,303	224	185	438	30.2	42.2
1896	459,848	161	132	293	32.6	61.4
1897	1,302,545	229	214	286	26.6	35.8
1898	2,065,547	264	242	357	26.4	35.8
1899	2,249,787	235	218	308	24.3	46.8
1900	2,930,287	251	221	405	26.0	52.7

Source: *Exposé statistique de la situation des associations d'intérêt agricole, 1895–1900.*

La prospection créative peut apporter quantité d'informations complémentaires. Pour ce qui est du secteur public par exemple, l'étude des débats parlementaires, des procès-verbaux de conseils communaux et de la presse peut compléter avantageusement les données officielles. Pour ce qui est des caisses d'épargne privées, il s'avère que certaines filiales possèdent encore de vieux registres très détaillés sur l'octroi de crédits, des informations qui permettent même d'identifier les emprunteurs et d'évaluer leur pouvoir d'achat et leur situation sociale (Tableau 21.6).

Pour ce qui est enfin du récent passé, nous voulons mettre explicitement l'accent sur l'importance des sources orales. A cet égard, nous ne pensons pas seulement aux interviews de membres du personnel de la banque d'épargne faisant l'objet d'une recherche, mais aussi, là où c'est possible, de personnes appartenant à d'autres institutions financières (concurrentes).

Le problème de la définition

Qu'est-ce que l'épargne? Qu'est-ce qu'une caisse d'épargne? Succinctement, on pourrait définir 'l'épargne' comme étant tout simplement la 'non-consommation'. Mais cette définition prend une connotation différente selon l'approche adoptée.

• La vision sociale pessimiste conçoit l'épargne comme étant une stratégie de survie d'une société prolétarisée; c'est la remise à plus tard d'une consommation, par crainte de voir qu'à l'avenir les temps seront plus durs.

Tableau 21.6   Caisse Raiffeisen de Bertem, registre des prêts, 1897

	Somme prêtée (FB)	Terme (ans)	Profession emprunteur	Destination
4 juil.	900	9	marchand de bétail	extension commerce
4	200	6	menuisier	achat parcelle de terre
4	1000	20	ouvrier	achat de maison
11	100	2	menuisier	supplément achat maison
13	150	1	cultivateur	paiement de dettes
4 août	75	3	ouvrier	meubles mariages
8	200	8	pauvre cultivateur	achat d'un boeuf
10	1400	14	marchand de bétail	achat d'une maison
13	1200	13	ouvrier	achat d'une maison
13	467	1	ouvrier	meubles, habill. mariage
6 sept.	100	2.5	petit cultivateur	achat d'un chariot
20	400	10	maçon	supplément achat maison
11 oct.	300	3	plafonneur	achat d'une vache
17	200	4	petit cultivateur	supplément achat vache
24	1000	16	ouvrier	achat maison et jardin
25	250	6	ouvrier	achat d'une vache
1er nov.	300	1	petit cultivateur	achat d'une vache
18	200	4	ouvrier	achat d'une vache
27 déc.	100	4	ouvrier	achat de porcs

- La théorie économique classique (A. Smith) souligne les implications favorables à long terme de l'épargne: l'épargne est en effet le report de la consommation en prévision d'une croissance économique future.
- Keynes met l'accent sur les effects défavorables à court terme de l'épargne, à savoir le retrait de pouvoir d'achat potentiel du marché; l'épargne s'avère alors un frein à la croissance économique.
- Marx considérait l'épargne comme une forme de concentration de capital aux effets aliénants et comme une dose soporifique dans la lutte sociale; dans l'optique marxiste, la problématique sociale ne devait pas être résolue par l'esprit d'économie de l'individu, mais par une refonte totale des rapports socio-économiques.

Ces conceptions divergentes se retrouvent dans les sources auxquelles l'historien est confronté. Elles peuvent aussi influencer l'interprétation historique elle-même. Ainsi, par exemple, où faut-il commencer l'histoire d'une banque d'épargne socialiste? Le socialisme du XIXe siècle était opposé à l'épargne individuelle, au système d'épargne bourgeois. Il eut certes recours à plusieurs formes d'épargne collective ou solidaire, par exemple pour le financement de manifestations, d'actions de propagande ou de grèves. Les caisses de résistance et associations syndicales social-istes sont-elles une forme précoce de caisses d'épargne socialistes? Où faut-il placer les mutualités où l'on 'épargnait' à titre de prévoyance sociale contre la maladie, le chômage ou le décès? Où place-t-on les coopératives de consommation qui permirent aux membres affiliés de réaliser des 'économies' sur les dépenses ménagères de tous les jours?

Des problèmes de définition peuvent également surgir sur le plan technico-financier. En Belgique, le statut légal de la 'caisse d'épargne' ne date que de 1935. Avant cela prédominait le système bancaire mixte avec une intrication poussée entre banques, caisses d'épargne et holdings. Dans pareil cas, l'histoire de l'épargne ne peut être scindée impunément de celle du système bancaire et financier dans son ensemble.

Références selectives

Europe

Born, K.E. (1977), *Geld und Banken im 19. und 20. Jahrhundert*, Stuttgart.
Cassis, Y. (1992) éd., *Finance and Financers in European History 1880–1940*, Cambridge.
Kindleberger, C.P. (1984), *A Financial History of Western Europe*, Londres.
Thurn, H.P. (1984), *L'histoire de l'épargne de l'antiquité à nos jours*, Paris (1e éd. Stuttgart, Deutscher Sparkassenverlag, 1982).
Van der Wee, H. (1991), éd., *La Banque en occident*, Anvers.
Vogler, B. (1991), *L'histoire des caisses d'épargne européennes*, 1, *Les origines des caisses d'épargne 1815–1848*, Paris.

Belgique

Banques et institutions financières en général
Dombrecht, M. et Plasschaert, S. (1992²), *Het financiewezen in België: instrumenten, instellingen en markten*, Deurne.
Durviaux, R. (1947), *La banque mixte, origine et soutien de l'expansion économique de la Belgique*, Bruxelles.

Timmermans, A.P. (1969), *Les banques en Belgique, 1946–1968*, Courtrai.

Van der Wee, H. et Tavernier, K. (1975), *La Banque Nationale de Belgique et l'histoire monétaire entre les deux guerres mondiales*, Bruxelles.

Van der Wee, H. et Verbreyt, M. (1985), *Mensen maken geschiedenis. De Kredietbank en de economische opgang van Vlaanderen 1935–1985*, Bruxelles.

Vandeputte, R. Abraham, J.P. et Lempereur, C. (1982–83), *Les institutions financières belges*, 2 vol., Namur.

Caisses d'épargne et banques d'épargne

Le credit hypothécaire de l'independence de la Belgique à la Communanté Européenne (1992), Bruxelles.

De Fiscale geschiedenis van het spaarboekje (1986), Aspecten en Documenten 52, Bruxelles.

Hamande, L. et Burny, F. (1902), *Histoire, exposé des opérations et statistiques des caisses d'épargne en Belgique considérées principalement au point de vue des classes ouvrières*, 3 vol., Louvain.

Kwanten, G. (1991), 'De christelijke coöperatieve bedrijven', dans Gerard, E. (éd.) *De christelijke arbeidersbeweging in België 1891–1991*, KADOC-Studies 11, vol. 2. Louvain, pp. 273–315.

Mahillon, L. (1890), *Rapport sur les caisses d'épargne belges, de 1830 à 1880, présenté à l'Exposition de Paris de 1889*, Bruxelles.

Mémorial 1865–1965 de la Caisse générale d'Epargne et de Retraite de Belgique (1965), Bruxelles.

Mouling, R. (1955), *L'épargne privée de 1935 à 1954*, Bruxelles.

De nieuwe beschermingsregeling voor deposito's (1985), Aspeten en Documenten 37, Bruxelles.

L'Office central de la petite Epargne, 1935–1959 (1960), Bruxelles.

Parmentier, S. (1986), 'Het liberaal staatsinterventionisme in de 19de eeuw. Een concreet geval: de oprichting van de ASLK', *Revue belge d'histoire contemporaine*, XVII, pp. 379–420.

Pasleau, S. (1988), 'La politique de placement de la Caisse d'Epargne et de Retraite (1955–1984)', *Revue belge d'histoire contemporaine*, XIX, pp. 499–541.

Projet COB (textes préparatoires): Vormingsdocument opgesteld in opdracht van de BAC Spaarbank CV. Louvain, (1990); Documentatiedossier over het christelijk arbeiderssparen. Louvain, (1990).

Raport, A. (1978), 'De privé-spaarkassen in België. Evolutie van hun wettelijk statuut (1934–1975)' dans Lindemans, J., Tommissen, P. et Baeyen, R. (éds), *Liber amicorum aangeboden aan Raf Hulpiau: ter gelegenheid van zijn zestigste verjaardag*, Gand, pp. 241–62.

Vakgroep Private Spaarkassen (1966), Bruxelles.

Van Molle, L. (1990), *Chacun pour tous. Le Boerenbond belge 1890–1990*, KADOC-Studies 9, Louvain.

Van Put, A. (1986), e.a., (éds), *Les banques d'épargne belges. Histoire, Droit, Fonction économique et Institutions*, Tielt.

Witte, E. et De Preter, R. (1989) (éds) *Histoire de l'épargne sociale à travers l'évolution de la banque d'épargne Codep et de ses prédécesseurs*, Bruxelles.

Autres pays

Pays-Bas

Buning, R.J.A. (n.d.), *De Nederlandse Spaarbankbond 1907–1957*.

De Vries, J. (1973), *De coöperatieve Raiffeisen- en Boerenleenbanken in Nederland 1948–1973. Van exponent tot component*.

Eizenga, W. (1985), *De ontwikkeling van de spaarbanken na de Tweede Wereldoorlog*, Serie Bank- en Effectenbedrijf 22, Deventer.

Ribbe, D.A. (1890), *Het spaarbankwezen in Nederland*, Haarlem.

Grande-Bretagne

Johnson, P. (1956), 'Credit and Thrift and the British Working Class, 1870–1939' dans Winter, J. (éd.) *The Working Class in Modern British History*, Cambridge, pp. 147–70.

France

Gueslin, A. (1978), *Les origines du Crédit Agricole (1840–1914)*, Nancy.

Priouret, R. (1966), *La Caisse des Dépôts. 150 ans d'histoire financière*. Paris.

Allemagne

Biehal, M. (1982), *Der Württembergische Sparkassenverbund 1916–1982*, Berlin.

Conze, W. et Engelhardt, U. (éds) (1981) *Arbeiterexistenz im 19. Jahrhundert. Lebensstandard und Lebensgestaltung deutscher Arbeiter und Handwerker*, Stuttgart.

Deutsche Bankgeschichte (1982–83), 3 vols, Francfort.

Ditt, K. (1981), 'Soziale Frage, Sparkassen und Sparverhalten der Bevölkerung im Raum Bielefeld um die Mitte des 19. Jahrhunderts' dans Conze et Engelhardt (1981), pp. 516–38.

Kiesewetter, H. (1981), 'Zur Entwicklung sächsicher Sparkassen, zum Sparverhalten und zum Lebenshaltung sächsischer Arbeiter im 19. Jahrhundert (1819–1914)', dans Conze et Engelhardt (1981), pp. 446–86.

Trende, A. (1957), *Geschichte der deutschen Sparkassen bis zum Anfang des 20. Jahrhunderts*, Stuttgart.

Autriche

150 Jahre Sparkassen in Österreich (1972), 2 vols, Vienne.

Michel, B. (1976), *Banques & banquiers en Autriche au début du XXe siècle*, Paris.

CHAPTER TWENTY-TWO

Comments

Helge W. Nordvik

My comments will fall into two sections. First, I shall make some remarks based on my reading of the excellent paper by Dr van Molle on the problems and possibilities of the history of savings banks with special reference to Belgium. This will be followed by some remarks based on my own research experience in connection with the writing of savings banks history.

Let me start by complimenting Dr van Molle on her succinct and wide-ranging survey of both the historiography and the research agendas of savings bank history. As you no doubt noted, she made a strong plea for the 'professional' approach to banking history – a sentiment that is no doubt shared by all of us present here today. I was particularly interested to hear in detail about the existence of a leading work of synthesis on Belgian savings banks.[1] The advantages of such a volume are obvious: it provides a yardstick and a frame of reference for serious scholarly work in savings bank history.

Banking history is perhaps more than any other branch of business history characterized by the fact that the institutions themselves constitute not only an important point of departure for the writing of banking history, but are in the market, so to speak, for historical studies on their own development. This presents the historian with both opportunities and problems: on the one hand the historian is in demand as a writer of commissioned history, on the other hand the very fact that this demand exists represents a potential bias inasmuch as certain subject matters will quite naturally receive more attention than others. As Dr van Molle points out the bulk of historical writing on savings banks comes in the form of commemorative volumes of varying scope and perspective. Her general comments on and classification of different types of publications could no doubt be replicated for most of the countries represented at this conference.

From the point of view of both general economic history as well as from a business history standpoint, I would hazard the guess that the writing of savings bank history is one of the less developed fields of professional historical enquiry. This is no doubt partly due to the fact that the financing for modern industrial development in both the nineteenth and twentieth centuries has to a large extent been associated with the development of joint-stock commercial banking. You will certainly recall the many studies inspired by Professor Rondo Cameron and his associates, all of them fundamentally concerned with the relationship between commercial banking and industrial development. The savings banks seem to have played a non-existent or at best wholly subordinate role in national industrial development. Not surprisingly, when Dr van Molle discusses the historiography of Belgian savings bank history, she puts great emphasis on the ideological and social history aspects of savings banks – not their role in financing economic growth. I would surmise that the social history aspects of savings banks have tended to dominate historiography in most countries. In other words, emphasis has been on savings more than on banking. Both approaches are in my view legitimate as well as necessary – and Dr van Molle's paper quite properly stresses the need for a multifaceted approach to research topics in savings bank history.

Let me, however, end my comments on the research agenda for savings bank history based on Dr van Molle's paper by making a plea for the study of savings banks and their history from the perspective of banking and economic development rather than from the savings perspective. This is not because the former is intrinsically more valuable or interesting than the other, but because it seems to me that we need to understand in what sense savings banks are unique institutions or whether they are simply a special type of bank. An added justification for such an approach is precisely the point made by Dr van Molle when she commented on the tendency of savings banks and commercial banks to become more and more alike.

Savings banks in Scandinavia

I now pass on to the second part of my commentary: some remarks on the writing of savings bank history from a Scandinavian, and more particularly a Norwegian perspective.

This history of modern banking in the nineteenth-century Norwegian economy is very much the history of the rapid growth of savings banks and the slow growth of the commercial banking sector. For the whole of the nineteenth century after the first Norwegian savings bank was established in 1822 in Christiania (now Oslo), total assets of the savings bank sector surpassed the assets of the commercial banking system. It was only in the first two decades of the twentieth century that strong asset growth in the commercial banking sector definitely allowed the commercial banks to take the lead in Norwegian banking.

After the initial wave of savings banks established in the main towns in the 1820s and 1830s, rural savings banks were established in practically every local town and district. By 1914 there were over 500 local savings banks in Norway, compared to around 100 commercial banks. The number of savings banks continued to grow in the interwar period, and reached around 600 by 1939. A severe crisis in the commercial banking sector during the 1920s led to a shift back to the situation as it had been for much of the second half of the nineteenth century, with savings banks once again playing a leading role in the financing of local and rural industries.

By the 1970s, the savings bank system had started a process of amalgamation, which by the late 1980s had led to the system changing from essentially local savings banks to regional savings bank groups. Nevertheless, one of the most noteworthy features of the Norwegian savings bank system, as opposed to the two other Scandinavian countries, is the absence of national or nationwide savings banks. The closest approximation of this model has been the government-owned Postal Savings Bank, with a branch network of all post offices.

The fact that savings banks as a general rule were to be found in both towns and rural areas before the establishment of a commercial banking system during the second half of the nineteenth century gave them an important 'first mover advantage'. In fact, the slow development of joint-stock commercial banking in Norway can partly be explained by the rapid development of the savings bank system. Not only were the Norwegian savings banks more important than the joint-stock commercial banks in monetizing the economy during the nineteenth century, but they were also quite important in financing economic development in the period up to the First World War. Both the Danish and Swedish savings banks likewise played an important role in the economic growth process before 1914.[2]

Thus, when two colleagues and I were approached by a regional savings bank in western Norway, a result of merger between more than 20 individual savings banks in 1976, and asked to write a book to commemorate the 150th anniversary of the first savings bank taking part in that merger, I suggested that we use this opportunity to research the role of savings banks in stimulating regional economic development.[3] By combining the records of individual savings banks with local and central government records we were able to document and analyse the role of savings banks in the economic growth process over a long time period.

Specifically, we concluded that savings banks played a leading role in financing investments in and modernization of agriculture, that they played a crucial role in the first phase of the electrification process in the first decades of the twentieth century, and even more surprisingly, that they were important in mobilizing regional savings for development of rural industrial development, such as textile firms, agricultural implements and machinery as well as the dairy industry in the period from the 1880s to the 1930s. Some of the larger town savings banks also made a significant contribution to maritime industries from the 1890s to around 1920, specifically steam shipping and the fishing industry.

There are of course a number of possible approaches one can take when researching and writing savings bank history. In view of the fact that so much interest has been directed towards the role of joint-stock commercial banks as financial intermediaries and sources of capital both directly and indirectly in the industrial development of European countries in the nineteenth century up to the First World War, my plea is simply for studying the 'small steps' in this process.

Railway building and large industrial projects were of course of vital importance to modern economic growth during the first and second industrial revolutions, but we should not forget that a lot is going on below the very visible 'tree-tops' of economic change. Certainly, in the Scandinavian countries, the dense undergrowth of local and regional savings banks played an important role in the economic development of the large regions outside the main cities. In my view, these aspects of savings bank history deserve more attention than they have hitherto received. In particular, I want to stress the role played by savings banks in the economic growth process in the Scandinavian countries up to the interwar period. After the Second World War, the savings banks in all three Scandinavian countries have continued to play a leading role in mobilizing personal savings, although their role as sources of finance for local industries has declined in relative importance. To compensate for this, they has taken an active role in financing infrastructure investments, both in terms of housing and local government initiated projects, as well as continuing to play a leading role in providing credit to consumers.

Notes

1. Van Put, A. et al. (1986), *Les Banques d'Epargne Belges. Histoire. Droit. Fonction Economique et Institutions,* Groupement Belge des Banques d'Epargne.
2. More information on banking and economic development in the Scandinavian countries in the nineteenth century up to the First World War can be found in the following three articles, all published in the *Journal of European Economic History:* Hansen, S.A. (1982), 'The Transformation of Bank Structures in the Industrial Period. The Case of Denmark' (3), pp. 575–603; Nygren, I. (1983), 'Transformation of Bank Structures in the Industrial Period. The Case of Sweden 1820–1913' (1), pp.29–68; Egge, Å. (1983), 'Transformation of Bank Structures in the Industrial Period: The Case of Norway 1830–1914' (2), pp. 271–94. See my own recent contribution: Nordvik, H.W. (1993), 'Banking, Industrialisation and Economic

Growth in Norway, 1850–1914', *Scandinavian Economic History Review* (3), pp. 52–72.

3.   Nordvik, Helge W., Nerheim, Gunnar and Brandal, Trygve (1989), *Penger spart, penger tjent. Sparebanker og okonomisk utvikling på Sor-Vestlandet fra 1839 til 1989*, SR-Bank Stavanger.

Index